LAROUSSE

PATISSERIE
& BAKING

LAROUSSE

PATISSERIE
& BAKING

**THE ULTIMATE EXPERT GUIDE, WITH MORE THAN
200 RECIPES AND STEP-BY-STEP TECHNIQUES**

Contents

EQUIPMENT

Make sure you have the right tools before diving into the creation of a dessert. Pastry making requires basic kitchen tools as well as specific utensils and appliances.

Basic Tools

MIXING BOWL: It should be wide and deep enough to let you beat with an electric beater, knead dough, or protect the dough while it rises.

STAINLESS STEEL BOWL: This metal bowl is available in many different formats and is especially well suited to whipping egg whites and heating chocolate, eggs, and sauces over a bain-marie (*see* page 494).

WOODEN SPOON AND SPATULA: One to stir and mix, the other to scrape out or remove a dessert from its pan.

RUBBER SPATULA: This is used to even out, stir, or scoop out batter.

METAL SPATULA: A flat and flexible metal knife used to decorate and ice desserts.

WHISK: They come in many sizes and are used to whip cream or beat eggs.

CONICAL STRAINER: Cone-shaped strainer that catches the impurities of sauces, coulis, and syrups.

SIFTER OR SIEVE: Used to sift flour and remove lumps.

FOOD MILL: This tool is equipped with a series of perforated disks and is used to make marmalades, fruit purees, and compotes. It's also used to remove the skin and seeds of certain fruit.

PITTER: This is a kind of pincer used to remove the pit of cherries, plums, and other stone fruit.

APPLE CORER: A short cylindrical tool with a sharp edge that lets you remove apple cores while leaving the outer fruit intact.

ZESTER: Bladed tool used to grate citrus zest finely.

Pastry-making Tools

ROLLING PIN: Used to roll out dough. Opt for a wooden (beech wood) model without handles so you can apply a more uniform pressure with your hands.

PASTRY CUTTER OR CARVING TOOL: These come in stainless steel or plastic and in a wide range of shapes and sizes. They let you cut out dough for shaping cookies or to decorate tarts. Sharp-edge cutters are best, because they do not flatten the dough.

BAKING SHEET: This sheet goes in the oven. Opt for a nonstick version, which is easier to clean.

WIRE RACK: It helps cakes to cool down without becoming soggy after they've been removed from their pans. Racks with feet facilitate the cooling process.

CERAMIC OR METAL PIE WEIGHTS: These are used to blind bake pastry shells. You can also use dried beans.

PASTRY BAGS AND TIPS: These are essential for stuffing choux buns, decorating cakes, and piping batters onto a baking sheet. Made of plastic or stainless steel, the tips come in many sizes and shapes, allowing for a variety of decorations.

PASTRY PINCHER: It can provide an attractive finish to the edge of the dough.

PASTRY CRIMPER: This gives the edges of the dough a serrated look.

BASTING BRUSH: Used to grease pans, apply egg wash to pastry shells, and seal turnovers.

Baking Papers and Food Wraps

NONSTICK PARCHMENT PAPER: Sometimes referred to as baking paper, it is treated to resist heat (up to 425°F) and is microwavable. It is used to line baking pans (instead of greasing them) or to line baking sheets before piping out pastries, which keeps the batter from sticking to the metal.

ALUMINUM FOIL: Used to wrap foods during the cooking process (the shiny side should face the food). It keeps food warm.

PLASTIC WRAP: This ultrathin material preserves the flavor of refrigerated foods and keeps raw dough from drying out. Thicker plastic wrap is available for using in microwave ovens.

SILICONE-COATED PAN LINER: This nonstick paper can handle temperatures of up to 500°F. As with nonstick parchment paper, it's used to line baking sheets, but it can be reused indefinitely. It is highly pliant and can be cut to the size of your pan, if necessary. It doesn't need to be greased and can be washed with a quick pass of a damp sponge.

Measuring Tools

MEASURING CUPS AND SPOONS: These come in various sizes to measure ingredients by volume. A standard set of kitchen measuring cups comes in increments of ¼ cup, ⅓ cup, ½ cup, and 1 cup. A set of standard measuring spoons includes ¼ teaspoon, ½ teaspoon, 1 teaspoon, and 1 tablespoon. Unless otherwise directed, level off the ingredients with the straight edge of a knife.

LIQUID MEASURING CUP: Whether plastic, glass, or stainless steel, opt for a model with a handle and a spout. When measuring, check the liquid against the marks at eye level.

THERMOMETER: Pastry making requires specific types of thermometers. An instant-read probe thermometer is made to measure temperatures up to about 220°F. In pastry, for example, you would use it to check the temperature of a bain-marie while cooking crème anglaise. A candy thermometer measures higher temperatures between 175 and 400°F. It lets you test the cooking stage of preserves or syrups.

TIMER: It will help you to keep track of cooking or resting times throughout the preparation of a dessert.

Electric Tools

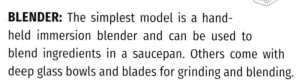

ELECTRIC HANDHELD MIXER: This tool comes with multipurpose beaters. It's much easier to beat egg whites or whip cream with an electric mixer than by hand. Some models come with dough hooks.

BLENDER: The simplest model is a hand-held immersion blender and can be used to blend ingredients in a saucepan. Others come with deep glass bowls and blades for grinding and blending.

FOOD PROCESSOR: It's usually made up of a bowl attached to a pedestal. In addition to the three basic accessories it comes with (emulsifying disk, dough hook, and whisk), additional options are available (meat grinder, knife blade, or food strainer).

ICE CREAM AND SORBET MAKERS: These appliances prepare mixtures while keeping them at suitably cold temperatures. Electrical ice cream makers come with a motor-run mixer and a removable tank that keeps the ice cream cold. The tank should be placed in the freezer at least 12 hours before use. The more expensive automatic ice cream maker is similar to those that professionals use but has a lower capacity. It can make ice cream in 30 minutes.

JUICERS: These extract fruit juice for gelatins without having to use filters or strainers.

MICROWAVE OVENS: They can be useful for defrosting frozen food quickly, heating milk without letting it overflow or sticking to the bottom of a container, softening butter straight out of the refrigerator, and melting butter or chocolate without a bain-marie (as long as you use it in short, successive bursts).

Warning: Be sure to use "transparent" containers in this type of oven. Containers should let the waves pass through them without being reflected or absorbed.

Traditional Pans

BRIOCHE MOLD: This is made of metal and comes in a nonstick version. Its sides can be fluted and funneled, round or rectangular. It's often used to make brioches or some desserts.

RECTANGULAR CAKE PAN: It can have straight sides or be slightly wider at the top. It comes in many sizes. It's best to choose a nonstick version.

CHARLOTTE MOLD: This metal pan has smooth sides, comes with little handles (to help turn it over when removing a dessert), and always comes in the shape of a small bucket. It can also be used to make flans and baked desserts.

CAKE PAN: This metal pan can be ribbed or smooth, round or square. It can be used to make Genoise or sponge cakes, tarts, and mini tarts.

TUBE PAN OR SAVARIN PAN: It is often made of metal and is distinguished by the hole in the center, which gives cakes the shape of a crown.

SOUFFLÉ PAN: This round pan is often made of ovenproof white porcelain and comes with high, straight, pleated sides. They also come in glass.

SILICONE PANS: These pans combine flexibility with nonstick qualities, ease of removal, and easy cleaning. They don't require greasing. They come in the same shapes as all the traditional models (tart pans, springform pans, and so on).

Their weakness: Too much flexibility makes it hard to carry them when filled with a liquid mixture (you have to place the pan on a rack or baking sheet before lining it or filling it). Silicone pans should not be used in temperatures above 475° F.

PIE PAN OR TART PAN: These metal or silicone pans come with smooth or fluted sides. Sizes vary from 6 to 12 inches in diameter. Round tart pans with removable bottoms are recommended for fruit tarts, because they facilitate the removal of the tart from the pan.

Individual Pans

PETIT FOUR PANS: These miniature individual metal or silicone molds come in a wide range of shapes. They're also used to make candies.

MULTI-CUP PANS: These pans—both the rigid nonstick and the flexible silicone versions—have small compartments in the shape of mini tarts, barquettes, small cakes, or madeleines, allowing for you to bake up to 24 cakes at a time.

MINI TART AND BARQUETTE MOLDS: The first are round, while the second are oval. They come in various sizes and are often made of stainless steel.

RAMEKINS: These are small soufflé dishes used to cook crème caramels. Usually made of ovenproof porcelain, they can easily travel from oven to refrigerator to table.

Special Pans

BAKING SHEET: These are rectangular and used to cook batter for layer cakes or roulades.

SPRINGFORM PAN: This deep, round metal pan has a locking system that causes the sides to come away and open up the bottom, making it easier to remove desserts (such as cheesecakes, custards, and cakes) from the pan.

KUGELHOPF PAN: A crown-shaped pan with diagonal ribbing. It's usually made of glazed terra-cotta. However, it is best to opt for a nonstick version, which facilitates the removal of the kugelhopf.

PIE PLATE: This glass or ceramic mold flares out toward the top. Its wide rim lets you connect and seal two pastry disks or fasten a dough lid onto a pie.

TARTE TATIN DISH: A thick pan for making tarte tatins. It can be placed directly on a source of heat to facilitate caramelization of butter and sugar. Opt for a nonstick version.

CAKE RINGS AND SQUARE DESSERT RINGS: These are bottomless shapes in stainless steel. They're either placed on silicone-coated parchment paper or on a sheet of nonstick parchment paper lining a baking sheet. There is no need to worry about removing the dessert from the pan. You can find these tools in the shape of individual circles, double rolled tart rings, or as cake rings (with higher sides).

GENOISE MOLD: This metal rectangular pan has high sides that are either straight or flared at the top. It's used to make Genoise sponge, custard flans, and more.

BUCHE CAKE OR LOG MOLD: Used for Christmas yule logs.

WAFFLE IRON: This two-plate mold is connected by hinges and is usually in cast iron. It's used to make waffles and wafers. There are two types: one goes over a hotplate or stove, the other is electric.

BASIC
ingredients

Good-quality ingredients are the key to making
successful cakes and delicious desserts.

Flour

Pastry making usually requires wheat flour. When other flours
are used—chestnut or buckwheat, for example—they're mixed
in with wheat flour, because they're not suitable for baking on
their own. The various types of wheat flour are
classified by use. All-purpose flour or
cake flour (or pastry flour) are best for
making cakes. They are low in volume,
white and refined, and rich in gluten.
We recommend sifting flour before
adding it to a mixture.

Starch

This powder is derived from grains (rice or corn) or roots
(potatoes or cassava). Cornstarch is most commonly used
in pastries. It's used to thicken creams, reduce liquids, and
prepare cakes. It must be added cold or after being diluted in
a cold liquid.

Butter

We can't imagine making pastries without butter. It's used to
make all doughs (except bread dough), creams, confectionary,
chocolate frosting, and more. Good butter should not be brittle
or lumpy at room temperature. Buy it as fresh as possible.

And beware: Butter easily takes on odors that can impregnate
it. This is why it should be kept in a sealed container. If you
have to work butter into a cream (making it creamy), first let it
warm up to room temperature for at least 30 minutes. Unless
otherwise specified, these recipes use unsalted butter.

Sugar

We can't talk about cakes without talking about sugar. It brings
sweetness and crunchiness to desserts and gives baked goods
a nice color.

White superfine sugar is the most commonly used type of
sugar in pastry making. Its small grains melt quickly.

Confectioners' sugar is finely ground and contains a small
amount of starch (3 percent) to prevent it from clumping. It is
used for sprinkling, decorating, or for making royal icing.

**Unrefined sugars (piloncillo, muscovado, raw, brown, and
so on)** have a defined flavor (such as liquorice or caramel) and
fine, dark brown grains. They're used in cakes with pronounced
flavors (banana bread, pain d'épice, chocolate cake). But beware:
These sugars turn light-colored desserts, such as vanilla creams
or cheesecakes, an unsightly beige.

Vanilla sugar is superfine sugar that is combined with at least
10 percent natural vanilla extract. It is used to flavor cake batter
or creams. Avoid vanilla sugar that uses artificial vanilla.

11

Eggs

Opt for cage-free, pasture-raised eggs, if possible. Keep them refrigerated in their original container, pointed side up. Remove them from the refrigerator ahead of time so that they are at room temperature before use. For recipes that don't require cooking, such as mousses, make sure the eggs are extra fresh. Eggs with broken or cracked shells should be thrown out.

A large egg weighs about 2 ounces:

Egg white: 1 oz/2 tbsp
Egg yolk: ½ oz/1 tbsp

CLASSIFICATION
of eggs

There are different hen-housing methods:

Organic Eggs are produced from free-range hens that feed on an organic diet and are raised on organic land.

Pasture-raised Hens have access to the outdoors and feed on grass and bugs; there are no specific guidelines.

Free-range Hens have some access to the outdoors; there are no specific guidelines.

Cage-free Hens can roam vertically or horizontally in indoor houses so hens can exhibit natural behavior.

Leaveners

These important ingredients bring volume and lightness to cakes and breads.

Baking powder is a white powder used to prepare cakes, cookies, and so on. It shouldn't be added to the dough too soon or it will lose some of its leavening power.

Yeast is a natural product (a fungus) that makes brioches, breads, croissants, and other baked goods rise. Fresh yeast comes in beige, easily crumbled cakes. It can be found at bakeries, including in some large grocery stores, or online. It lasts for a maximum of two weeks when refrigerated or it can be frozen. Dry yeast comes in the form of small granules or flakes and keeps for several months. Yeast needs time to become active. It expands the dough by producing carbon dioxide when it comes into contact with sugar.

Cream

Heavy cream brings sweetness and creaminess to desserts. It can be used in cold or hot preparations. It can also be used to make whipped cream or—by adding sugar—Chantilly cream. For it to whip nicely, it should have a high fat content of about 30 percent and be cold.

Crème fraîche brings flavor and creaminess. It can be used as an accompaniment (for example, for crisps or cakes), but it doesn't lend itself well to recipes that require cooking.

Cocoa Powder

Always opt for the sugar-free type. Powders used to make hot chocolate have no place in cake making.

Chocolate

Chocolate is made by mixing cocoa paste, sucrose, and, if desired, cocoa butter. It can be bitter, semisweet, or white, depending on the recipe. For recipes requiring bittersweet chocolate, opt for chocolate bars containing at least 50 percent cocoa solids. For frostings, confectionary, or Easter eggs, it's best to use **couverture chocolate**; it contains more cocoa butter than the others, which lets the chocolate melt more easily. But beware: You have to melt the chocolate over medium heat in a bain-marie (*see* page 494) or in the microwave (in which case, stop the cooking every minute and stir) and never on direct heat or it will become grainy. Ideally, you should melt the chocolate according to the tempering technique (*see* page 487) to create a shiny and smooth look.

Chocolate chips are easy to use and perfect for making cookies, muffins, cakes, and so on. You can make your own by coarsely chopping a bar of chocolate.

Salt

A number of recipes call for a pinch of salt, because it acts as a flavor enhancer by bringing out the flavor of the other ingredients. Certain recipes call for *fleur de sel*; its saltiness is not as strong and it adds a nice crunch.

Gelatin

This setting agent comes in either translucent sheets or in powder form. It's used to make mousses, charlottes, Bavarian creams, gelatins, and so on. The gelatin sheets must be soaked in cold water and drained before use. They are then mixed into hot ingredients. Gelatin powder must be combined with a liquid, then heated and melted before being mixed in with other ingredients.

Store-bought dough

If you don't have enough time to make a homemade dough for a tart or quiche, you can use store-bought dough. There are different types of easy-to-use doughs, including pie dough crust and puff pastry. They are usually sold already rolled, either rolled up or in flat layers, or sometimes as a cookie crust pressed into a disposable pan. Opt for those labeled "all-butter," if available, which are tastier. It might also be possible to buy puff pastry at a bakery.

Vanilla

Vanilla comes in bean form, as a powder (ground beans), or as a liquid extract. It is the most commonly used spice in pastry and cake making. A good vanilla bean should be soft, flexible, and thick; when dried, it loses much of its flavor. Before adding it to a batter or dough, the bean should be halved and its grains scraped out with a small knife. Instead of throwing out a bean after a single use, rinse and dry it, then store it in a container filled with sugar. Once you've collected a number of beans, blend them with the sugar and sift the powder through a sieve to make your own homemade vanilla sugar.

Extracts (butter almond, vanilla, coffee)

These are made by distilling a product that has been dissolved in water or alcohol by various means (infusion, maceration, distillation, or percolation). They perfume and flavor creams, cookies, ganaches, petit fours, and more. You only need a small amount to flavor a mixture.

Distilled water (orange blossom, rose)

These are made with water—sometimes with small amounts of alcohol—and the desired flavoring. They add flavor to brioches, doughnuts, petit fours, creams, coulis, and so on. You only need a small amount to flavor a mixture.

Cakes
& gâteaux

YOGURT
cake

Serves 4–6 | **Preparation time: 15 minutes** | **Cooking time: 35 minutes**

INGREDIENTS

1¾ tablespoons unsalted
butter, for greasing

1⅔ cups all-purpose flour

2½ teaspoons baking powder

1 unwaxed orange
(or 1 unwaxed lemon)

3 eggs

1 cup superfine sugar

A pinch of salt

¾ cup sunflower oil

½ cup plain yogurt

FOR THE SYRUP

1 cup water

¾ cup superfine sugar

1 Preheat the oven to 350°F. Grease a 9½-inch round cake pan. Sift the flour and baking powder into a bowl. Grate the zest of the orange (or lemon) and squeeze its juice, setting aside the juice for the syrup.

2 In a large bowl, combine the eggs with the superfine sugar and salt, beating until the mixture becomes pale and frothy. Add the oil, orange (or lemon) zest, and yogurt, then mix again. Add the sifted flour and baking powder and mix the batter until it is evenly combined.

3 Pour the batter into the cake pan and bake for about 30 minutes.

4 For the syrup, pour the measured water into a saucepan, then add the freshly squeezed juice and superfine sugar. Bring to a boil and cook for about 5 minutes. Let cool before pouring it over the cake.

TIP

This foolproof cake is ideal for teaching children to bake. We also recommend adding pieces of fruit.

VARIATION

For a lighter cake, separate the egg whites from the yolks, beat
until stiff, then combine both with the sugar and salt.

POUND
cake

Serves 6–8

Preparation time: 15 minutes

Cooking time: 40 minutes

INGREDIENTS

3 large eggs

1⅓ cups all-purpose flour,
plus extra for dusting

¾ cup + 1 tablespoon
superfine sugar

1½ sticks (6 oz) unsalted butter,
plus extra for greasing

A pinch of salt

1 Preheat the oven to 400°F. Grease and flour an 8¾-inch round cake pan. Sift the flour. Separate the egg whites from the yolks.

2 In a large bowl, beat the egg yolks, superfine sugar, and butter until the mixture is pale. Add the flour and mix until the batter is evenly combined. In a clean, dry bowl, beat the egg whites into stiff peaks along with a pinch of salt, then use a spatula to fold them carefully into the batter.

3 Pour the batter into the cake pan and bake for 15 minutes. Reduce the temperature to 350°F and continue baking for 25 minutes. Wait for the cake to cool before removing it from the pan. Serve as an afternoon snack with homemade preserves.

VARIATION

Replace the butter with lightly salted butter.

VANILLA SPONGE
cake

Serves 8 | Preparation time: 15 minutes | Cooking time: 35 minutes

INGREDIENTS

Unsalted butter, for greasing

½ cup cornstarch, plus
2½ tablespoons for dusting

4 eggs

⅓ cup + 1 tablespoon
all-purpose flour

½ cup superfine sugar

1½ teaspoons vanilla
sugar (*see* page 13)

A pinch of salt

1 Preheat the oven to 325°F. Grease a 10¼–11-inch round cake pan and dust it with cornstarch. Separate the egg whites from the yolks. Sift together the flour and cornstarch into a bowl.

2 In a large bowl, beat the sugars and egg yolks together until the mixture is smooth and pale.

3 Beat the egg whites and salt into stiff peaks and, using a spatula, carefully fold them into the egg yolk-and-sugar mixture, alternating with the sifted flour mixture.

4 Pour the batter into the cake pan and bake for 35 minutes. To make sure the cake is cooked, insert the blade of a knife into it; the blade should come out clean. Remove the cake from the pan as soon as it is baked. Serve cold.

MARBLE
cake

Serves 6–8 | **Preparation time: 15 minutes** | **Cooking time: 40 minutes**

INGREDIENTS

1½ sticks (6 oz) unsalted butter,
plus extra for greasing

3 eggs

1⅓ cups + 1 tablespoon
all-purpose flour

1 teaspoon baking powder

1 cup superfine sugar

¼ cup unsweetened cocoa powder

3 tablespoons milk

A pinch of salt

1 Preheat the oven to 350°F. Grease a 9 × 5-inch loaf pan. Separate the egg whites from the yolks. Melt the butter in a saucepan. Sift together the flour and baking powder into a bowl.

2 Whisk the melted butter together with the superfine sugar, add the egg yolks while continuing to mix, then gradually add the sifted flour and baking powder to the mixture.

3 Mix the cocoa powder into the milk. Separate the batter into 2 equal parts and stir the cocoa powder mixture into one part.

4 Whisk the egg whites into stiff peaks with the salt, then use a spatula to carefully fold half the mixture into each of the batters.

5 Pour an initial layer of cocoa batter into the loaf pan, followed by a layer of the plain batter. Alternate layers until the cake pan is full.

6 Bake for 40 minutes. To make sure the cake is cooked, insert the blade of a knife into it; the blade should come out clean.

NOISETTINE

Serves 6

Preparation time: 20 minutes

Cooking time: 45 minutes

INGREDIENTS

7 tablespoons unsalted butter, plus extra for greasing

¼ cup coarsely chopped hazelnuts

6 egg whites

¾ cup superfine sugar

1¼ cups ground hazelnuts

⅓ cup all-purpose flour

1 Preheat the oven to 300°F. Grease an 8¾-inch round cake pan or two 5½-inch loaf pans. Place the chopped hazelnuts on a baking sheet and roast them for 15 minutes or until golden.

2 In a large bowl, combine the egg whites and superfine sugar. Add the ground hazelnuts, sift in the flour, and stir.

3 Melt the butter, add it to the hazelnut mixture, and stir until the butter is completely absorbed. Increase the oven temperature to 400°F. Pour the batter into the cake pan(s) and bake for 25–35 minutes, depending on the size of pan you use.

4 Remove the cake(s) from the oven, let cool, remove from the pan(s), and decorate with the toasted hazelnuts.

WALNUT
delight

Serves 6

Preparation time: 20 minutes

Cooking time: 50 minutes

INGREDIENTS

1¾ tablespoons unsalted
butter, for greasing

1½ cups shelled walnuts

4 eggs

¾ cup + 2 tablespoons
superfine sugar

¾ cup + 1 tablespoon cornstarch

FOR THE ICING

1 cup confectioners' sugar

2 tablespoons water

1 tablespoon instant coffee

1 Preheat the oven to 375°F. Generously grease an 8¾-inch round cake pan. Set aside ¼ cup of the walnuts for the decoration and coarsely chop the rest using a food processor. Separate the egg whites from the yolks.

2 Whisk together the egg yolks and superfine sugar in a bowl until the mixture is pale. Add the cornstarch and chopped nuts, then mix well with a wooden spoon.

3 Whisk the egg whites into stiff peaks. Remove 2 tablespoons of the egg whites and quickly mix them into the walnut mix to lighten it. Then, carefully fold in the remaining egg whites, scooping in all of the mixture to avoid deflating it.

4 Pour the batter into the cake pan and place it on the middle rack of the oven. Bake for 50 minutes. To make sure the cake is cooked, insert the blade of a knife into it; the blade should come out clean. Remove the cake from the oven, let it rest for 10 minutes, then remove it from the pan and let cool on a wire rack.

5 For the icing, dissolve the confectioners' sugar in the measured water, add the instant coffee, and mix well until the paste is fairly thick but smooth. Spread it on top of the cake with a spatula. Decorate the cake with the extra walnuts, then serve.

The HISTORY of CAKES

the Pavlova

(*See* recipe, page 356)

This cake is made with meringue, whipped cream, and fresh fruit. Both Australia and New Zealand claim it as their national dessert. It was created by a New Zealand pastry chef in honor of **Anna Pavlova**—a prominent early twentieth-century Russian dancer—who was touring in the southern hemisphere. The dessert's "flouncy" shape is reminiscent of a **tutu.**

the Paris-Brest

(*See* recipe, page 300)

A crown of choux pastry filled with praline cream and slivered almond, the Paris-Brest is a baker's pride and joy. Its shape, which recalls a **bicycle wheel,** was created in 1910 by Louis Durand, a Maisons-Laffitte baker, as a tribute to the **bicycle race** between **Paris and Brest.**

the tarte tatin

(See recipe, page 104)

Created in Lamotte-Beuvron at the end of the nineteenth century, this caramelized apple tart, which is cooked under a layer of dough and turned over onto a serving dish, was discovered by accident. One of the **Tatin sisters** placed the fruit in the oven without the dough, so she added it later to stop the cooking. However, this is probably **a myth.** In reality, this tart is a regional speciality that the two sisters popularized largely thanks to the location of their small hotel—right in front of the train station.

financiers

(See recipe, page 382)

In the seventeenth century, the religious order of the Visitandines, near Nancy, made **visitandines,** small cakes with almonds, sugar, flour, and eggs. During the nineteenth century, a Parisian baker, Lasne, whose bakery was located near the stock market, gave these cakes the shape of a **small gold bar** and called them "financiers" to cater to his **client base of stockbrokers.**

rum babas

(See recipe, page 338)

We have Stanisław Leszczyński, the king of Poland and father-in-law to Louis XV, to thank for these. While exiled in Nantes, he found his **kugelhopf to be too dry** and so he asked his baker, Nicolas Stohrer, to change the recipe. Stohrer soaked the cake in an alcoholic syrup to soften it, then filled it with crème pâtissière and raisins. The **Stohrer Pâtisserie** still exists and is located on Rue Montorgueil, Paris. It's the oldest pâtisserie in the world. The savarin cake is an alcohol-free version of the same cake. After traveling to southern Italy, bakers also created versions soaked with Limoncello or Marsala. The "bouchon" shape was created in Italy, while France kept the kugelhopf's **traditional crown shape.**

the Charlotte

(See recipes, pages 324, 328, and 330)

This cake dates back to the start of the nineteenth century and was created as a tribute to **Princess Charlotte,** Queen Victoria's grandmother. This **English dessert** was originally made with a crown of sliced bread or buttered brioche and topped with fruit compote (apple or pear). It was cooked for a long time and served hot. It wasn't until 1900 that **Antonin Carême**, the famous French baker who was working in England at the time, altered the recipe by using ladyfingers and Bavarian cream and serving it cold.

CARROT
cake

Serves 8 | Preparation time: 20 minutes | Cooking time: 40–50 minutes

INGREDIENTS

1 stick + 1 tablespoon (4½ oz) unsalted butter, at room temperature, plus extra for greasing

2 cups canned pineapple slices

½ cup superfine sugar

⅔ cup packed brown sugar

3 eggs

3 cups shredded carrots

⅔ cup walnuts (or pecans)

1¾ cups all-purpose flour

1 tablespooon baking powder

1 teaspoon salt

1 teaspoon baking soda

1 teaspoon ground cinnamon (or allspice)

½ teaspoon ground ginger

FOR THE FROSTING

½ cup cream cheese

⅔ cup confectioners' sugar

4 tablespoons unsalted butter, at room temperature

1½ teaspoons vanilla sugar (*see page 13*)

2 tablespoons lemon juice

1 Preheat the oven to 350°F. Grease two 7–8-inch round cake pans. Use a food processor to chop the pineapple coarsely, then drain it thoroughly.

2 In a large bowl, whisk together the butter, superfine sugar, and brown sugar until creamy. Add the eggs and mix again. Add the carrots, pineapple, and nuts (reserving some for decoration) and stir.

3 Sift together the flour, baking powder, salt, and baking soda, then add them to the mixture along with the spices. Stir until the batter is evenly combined.

4 Divide the batter between the cake pans and bake for 40–50 minutes. To make sure the cakes are cooked, insert the blade of a knife into them; it should come out clean. Remove the cakes from their pans and let them cool on a wire rack.

5 For the frosting, whisk all the ingredients together until creamy. Spread half of it on the first cake, cover with the second cake, then use a spatula to spread the rest of the frosting on top. Decorate the cake with the reserved nuts.

TIP

Because of the carrots, this cake will be moist and dense, so it's absolutely necessary to separate the batter into two parts, because a thicker cake wouldn't cook in the middle.

KUGELHOPF

Makes 2 kugelhopf	Preparation time: 40 minutes	Proofing time: 4 hours
	Dough resting time: 2½ hours	Cooking time: 35–40 minutes

¼ cup confectioners' sugar, for dusting

1 large (2-oz) cake fresh yeast or 3½ tablespoons active dry yeast

⅓ cup milk

1 handful whole almonds

⅔ cup raisins

¼ cup rum

⅓ cup superfine sugar

4½ cups all-purpose flour, plus extra for dusting

2 egg yolks

1 stick (4 oz) unsalted butter, plus extra for greasing + a little extra, melted

INGREDIENTS

FOR THE DOUGH

⅔ cup raisins

¼ cup rum

3⅔ cups all-purpose flour, plus extra for dusting

3 pinches of salt

⅓ cup superfine sugar

2 egg yolks

1 stick (4 oz) unsalted butter, plus extra for greasing + a little extra, melted

1 handful whole almonds

¼ cup confectioners' sugar, for dusting

FOR THE LEAVENING

¾ cup + 2 tablespoons all-purpose flour

1 large (2-oz) cake fresh yeast or 3½ tablespoons active dry yeast

⅓ cup milk

1 Soak the raisins in the rum.

2 Prepare the leavening: Combine the flour, yeast, and milk in a bowl and mix well. Cover the bowl with a wet dish towel and place in the refrigerator for 4 hours.

3 After the resting time, prepare the dough: Combine the flour, salt, sugar, and egg yolks in the bowl of a food processor and mix with the hook attachment until the dough comes away from the edges of the bowl.

4 Add the butter and continue to work the dough until it comes away from the edges again.

5 Drain and add the steeped raisins. Mix them in, then cover the bowl with a cloth and let the dough sit for 1½ hours at room temperature, until it doubles in volume.

6 Grease 2 grooved Bundt pans. Place a whole almond at the bottom of each groove in the pans.

7 Turn the dough onto a lightly floured surface and separate it into 2 equal parts. Flatten each part with the palm of your hand to return it to its initial shape.

8 Create 2 balls of dough by folding the edges of each ball back toward the center. Roll each ball on the work surface by gripping it with the palms of your hands, in a circular motion.

9 Dust your fingers with flour, take each ball into your hand, push your thumb into the center of the ball, lightly stretch the dough into a crown, and place it in the pan. Cover it with a damp dish towel and let it rise again at room temperature for 1 hour.

10 Preheat the oven to 400°F. Bake the cakes for 35–40 minutes. Remove the kugelhopfs from the pans, place them on a wire rack, and drench them in the melted butter.

11 Let them cool, lightly dust with confectioners' sugar, and serve. To keep the cakes fresh, wrap them in plastic wrap.

BASQUE
cake

 Serves 6–8 | Preparation time: 30 minutes | Dough resting time: 1 hour | Cooking time: 45 minutes

INGREDIENTS

FOR THE CRÈME PÂTISSIÈRE

1 cup milk

½ vanilla bean

1 whole egg + 2 egg yolks

¼ cup superfine sugar

⅓ cup all-purpose flour

2 tablespoons orange
blossom water

FOR THE DOUGH

2⅓ cups + 1 tablespoon
all-purpose flour

¾ cup superfine sugar

A pinch of salt

1 teaspoon baking powder

1 whole egg + 2 egg yolks

1½ sticks + 1 tablespoon
(6½ oz) unsalted butter,
at room temperature, plus
extra for greasing

FOR THE GLAZE

1 egg yolk

1 tablespoon milk

1 Prepare the crème pâtissière: Bring the milk and vanilla to a boil. Whisk together the whole egg, egg yolks, and superfine sugar until creamy. Add the flour while continuing to whisk, then gradually add the boiling milk. Pour the cream into a saucepan and cook over medium heat while continuing to whisk until the first bubbles appear. Remove from the heat, add the orange blossom water, and let stand.

2 Prepare the dough: In a large bowl, combine the flour, superfine sugar, salt, and baking powder. Make a well in the center and add the egg, egg yolks, and softened butter. Using a wooden spoon, mix the ingredients starting from the center. Then knead the dough by hand until it is evenly combined. Shape it into a ball and let rest in a cool place for 1 hour.

3 Preheat the oven to 400°F. Grease a 9½-inch round cake pan. Separate the dough into 2 unequal portions (two-thirds and one-third). Stretch out the larger portion to cover the bottom of the cake pan, pulling the dough so that it reaches the edges.

4 Remove the vanilla bean, then pour the crème pâtissière over the dough. Place the second piece of dough on top to cover the crème, stretching it out to reach the edges of the pan. When in place, wet the edges and gently press them together to seal. Whisk together the egg yolk and milk for the glaze, and brush it over the top of the dough.

5 Bake for 20 minutes, then reduce the temperature to 350°F and bake for another 20 minutes. Remove the cake from the oven and let cool before removing it from the pan. Serve warm or cold.

VARIATION

You can also make Basque cake with black cherry
preserves instead of crème pâtissière.

FLOURLESS ORANGE
cake

Serves 4

Preparation time: 20 minutes

Cooking time: 55 minutes

INGREDIENTS

3 eggs

⅔ cup superfine sugar

2 teaspoons baking powder

1 unwaxed orange

A pinch of salt

1⅓ cups ground almonds

FOR THE DECORATION

A handful of almonds,
coarsely sliced

Confectioners' sugar, for dusting

Fruit coulis (optional)

1 Preheat the oven to 350° F. Line an 8-inch round cake pan with nonstick parchment paper. Beat the eggs and sugar until the mixture is pale. Add the baking powder, zest and juice of the orange, salt, and ground almonds. Mix well.

2 Pour the batter into the cake pan and bake for 55 minutes, until the cake is golden on top. To make sure the cake is cooked, insert the blade of a knife into it; the blade should come out clean.

3 Decorate the cake with sliced almonds and dust with confectioners' sugar, or top it with a fruit coulis, if using. Serve warm or cold.

PUMPKIN AND PECAN
cake

Serves 4–6

Preparation time: 30 minutes

Cooking time: 65 minutes

INGREDIENTS

5 tablespoons lightly salted butter, melted, plus extra for greasing

1¼ cups peeled and seeded 1-inch pumpkin pieces

2 tablespoons water

1⅓ cups light brown sugar

1⅔ cups all-purpose flour

2½ teaspoons baking powder

4 eggs

2 tablespoons orange blossom water

½ cup coarsely chopped pecans

Confectioners' sugar, for dusting

1 Preheat the oven to 350°F. Grease an 8 × 10-inch rectangular baking dish or pan. Cook the pumpkin in a casserole dish with the measured water for 20 minutes. Drain it and blend it in a food processor.

2 Add the melted butter, sugar, flour, and baking powder. Mix well. Add the eggs and orange blossom water and blend until the batter is evenly combined.

3 Add the pecans to the pumpkin batter. Pour the batter into the dish or pan and bake for 45 minutes, until the cake has risen and is golden on top. To make sure the cake is cooked, insert the blade of a knife into it; the blade should come out clean. Let the cake cool before dusting the top with confectioners' sugar and serving.

LEMON DRIZZLE
cake

Serves 6–8 | Preparation time: 30 minutes | Cooking time: 40–45 minutes

INGREDIENTS

¼ cup chopped candied
lemon peel, to decorate

FOR THE *MANQUÉ* BATTER

5 tablespoons unsalted butter,
plus extra for greasing

1 unwaxed lemon

4 eggs

¾ cup superfine sugar

¾ teaspoon vanilla sugar
(*see* page 13)

¾ cup + 1 tablespoon
all-purpose flour

½ cup chopped candied
lemon peel

½ teaspoon salt

FOR THE ROYAL ICING

¾ cup confectioners' sugar

1 egg white

Juice of ½ a lemon

1 Preheat the oven to 400°F. Grease an 8¾-inch round cake pan. Carefully remove the rind from the lemon using a sharp knife. Immerse the lemon rind in boiling water for 2 minutes, run it under cold water, dry it off, and cut into fine strips.

2 Prepare the *manqué* batter: Melt the butter in a small saucepan and let cool. Separate the egg whites from the yolks. In a large bowl, whisk together the yolks, superfine sugar, and vanilla sugar until frothy and pale. Sift in the flour and add the melted butter, candied lemon peel, and strips of fresh lemon rind. Mix well until the mixture is evenly combined. In a bowl, whisk the egg whites and salt into peaks, then carefully fold them into the mixture.

3 Pour the batter into the cake pan and bake for 15 minutes, then reduce the temperature to 350°F and cook for 25–30 minutes. To make sure the cake is cooked, insert the blade of a knife into it; the blade should come out clean. Wait for the cake to cool before removing it from the pan, then let cool completely.

4 Prepare the royal icing: In a large bowl, combine the confectioners' sugar, egg white, and lemon juice. Whisk until the mixture is smooth.

5 When the cake is cold, use a spatula to cover it with the icing. Decorate with the chopped candied lemon peel.

CRAMIQUE

Serves 6

Preparation time: 25 minutes

Dough resting time: 2 hours

Cooking time: 40 minutes

INGREDIENTS

1 cup freshly prepared black tea

⅔ cup raisins

3 eggs

A pinch of salt

4 cups all-purpose flour

1 tablespoon superfine sugar

7 tablespoons unsalted butter, cut into small pieces, plus extra for greasing

1 teaspoon pearl sugar, to decorate (optional)

FOR THE LEAVENING

¾ cup + 1½ tablespoons milk

1 small (⅔-oz) cake fresh yeast or 3½ teaspoons active dry yeast

⅓ cup + 1 tablespoon all-purpose flour

1 Soak the raisins in the freshly prepared hot tea. Beat 2 eggs with a pinch of salt.

2 Prepare the leavening: Warm the milk. Crumble the yeast into a large bowl, pour in a little of the warmed milk, and mix. Gradually add the flour by mixing with a wooden spoon to create a soft paste.

3 Place the flour on a flat surface and make a well in the center. Place the leavening in the hole. Add the beaten eggs, sugar, and the rest of the warmed milk. Let rise for 1 hour.

4 Grease an 11-inch-long rectangular cake pan. Work the dough by hand and knead it until it becomes elastic. Add the butter. Continue to knead. Drain the raisins and add them. Knead the dough a little more to mix them in.

5 Shape the dough into a log and place it in the cake pan. Beat the final egg and brush the egg wash over the dough. Let rise in the pan for 1 hour at room temperature.

6 Preheat the oven to 400°F. Sprinkle the pearl sugar on top of the cramique, if using, then bake for 10 minutes. Reduce the temperature to 350°F and bake for another 30 minutes. Remove from the pan and let cool.

Serving
suggestion

Serve this *cramique* with
fruit compote, chocolate
cream, or fruity ice cream.

LEMON POPPY SPONGE
cake

Serves 6–8

Preparation time: 25 minutes

Refrigeration time: 30 minutes

Cooking time: 50 minutes

INGREDIENTS

1 stick (4 oz) unsalted butter,
plus extra for greasing

½ cup + 1 tablespoon
packed brown sugar

3 eggs

1¼ cups all-purpose flour,
plus extra for dusting

2½ teaspoons baking powder

1 unwaxed lemon

2 tablespoons poppy seeds

FOR THE TOPPING

2 tablespoons superfine sugar

1 tablespoon water

Finely grated zest of
1 unwaxed lemon

A few poppy seeds

1 In a large bowl, beat the butter and sugar until the mixture is pale. Add the eggs, flour, and baking powder and stir until the batter is evenly combined.

2 Remove the zest from the lemon with a grater or zester and juice the lemon. Add the juice and zest to the batter along with the poppy seeds.

3 Grease and flour a 10-inch-long rectangular cake pan. Pour in the batter and refrigerate for 30 minutes.

4 Preheat the oven to 325°F. Bake the cake for 50 minutes, until well risen and the blade of a knife inserted into the cake comes out clean. Let the cake cool on a wire rack.

5 Make the topping: Melt the sugar in a saucepan with the measured water. Brush the top of the cake with the syrup. Sprinkle the lemon zest and poppy seeds on top.

FRUIT
cake

 Serves 6–8 | Preparation time: 20 minutes | Refrigeration time: 30 minutes | Cooking time: 50 minutes

INGREDIENTS

⅔ cup raisins

4 teaspoons sherry (or Kirsch)

1 stick + 1 tablespoon
(4½ oz) unsalted butter,
at room temperature, plus
extra for greasing

⅓ cup + 1 tablespoon
superfine sugar

3 eggs

1⅓ cups + 2 tablespoons
all-purpose flour

2½ teaspoons baking powder

½ cup finely chopped
candied fruit or peel

1 Soak the raisins in the alcohol. In a large bowl, beat the butter with the sugar until the mixture is pale. Add the eggs, one at a time, mixing well in between. Add the flour and baking powder.

2 Stir in the raisins, the alcohol they were soaking in, and the candied fruit. Mix well and put the bowl into the refrigerator for at least 30 minutes.

3 Preheat the oven to 400°F. Grease and line a 10-inch-long rectangular cake pan. Transfer the cold batter to the cake pan. Bake for 10 minutes, then reduce the temperature to 325°F and bake for another 40 minutes. The cake must be well risen and golden, and the blade of a knife inserted into the center should come out clean. Let the cake cool before removing it from the pan.

CAKE
decorations

An attractive edible decoration will do wonders to spruce up a simple cake. Decorations can be made with sugar, caramel, chocolate, marzipan, or whatever you want (*see* pages 52–53).

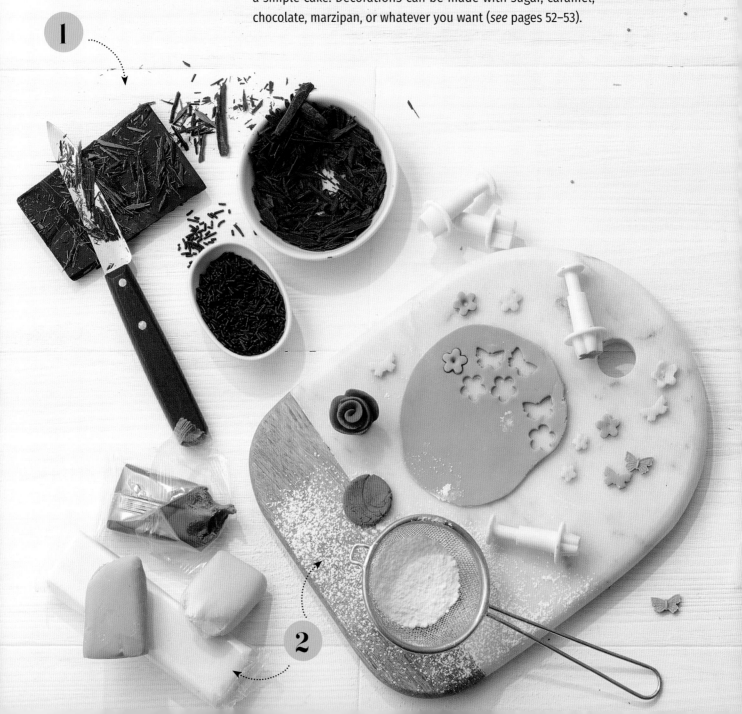

CAKE
decorations

Chocolate
decorations

1

Make chocolate flakes by scraping the back of a chocolate bar with a knife or vegetable peeler. The more adventurous baker can melt the chocolate, roll it out on a cold surface, such as a marble slab, let it set, and scrape it up with a spatula. A more advanced technique is to temper the chocolate (*see* page 487) and make large, soft, shiny, and crisp shavings, like at a pâtissérie. Tempering is also great for making chocolate eggs, chocolate white sardines, or simple chocolate shapes.

Decorations for the sides of cakes

When the cake is covered in chocolate frosting or buttercream, cover the sides with toasted slivered almonds (use ¾ cup for a cake). For a crunchier effect, combine the almonds with ¼ cup packed brown sugar before toasting them, then spread them over nonstick parchment paper and let cool. You can use the same technique with coconut shavings, chopped walnuts or hazelnuts, or muesli.

Marzipan
AND
fondant

2

You can easily find rolls of marzipan or ready-to-use fondant in grocery stores. Use a rolling pin to roll them onto a surface dusted with confectioners' sugar. Cut out shapes by hand or with small pastry cutters bought on the Internet or in speciality kitchen stores. You can also make cute shapes, such as flowers.

STORE-BOUGHT
sugar
decorations

3

Use the wide variety of store-bought decorations—such as multicolored pearls, colorful crystallized sugar, mimosa balls, stars, or flowers made of sugar or rice paper—as simple ways to decorate cakes for special occasions.

④ Caramel
decorations

Make a golden caramel by putting ¾ cup white superfine sugar (darker sugar is more difficult to caramelize) into a saucepan or nonstick skillet. Melt the sugar over medium heat while swirling the pan in a circular movement to stir its contents—never stir with a spatula, because this will cause the sugar to crystallize and the caramel to harden. When you've achieved the desired color, use a spoon to drip the caramel over a baking sheet lined with nonstick parchment paper to form small pearls, or use a fork to make strips.

> **Work fast,** because caramel sets quickly! Don't refrigerate it afterward, because doing so will make it sticky and soft.

⑤ Piping
decorations

Pastry bags are the quintessential baker's tool. They make it possible to fill choux pastries or verrines properly and to decorate desserts. They're made of plastic, silicone, or even silicone-coated fabric that can be washed and reused indefinitely. You can also find packages of disposable bags, which are useful if you don't use them very often. Pastry bags that are at least 12 inches long, or even 16 inches long, will give you the best performance, because you'll be able to put a large quantity of your mixture into them. The benefits? Reloading a dirty bag can be complicated.

> **Think outside the box:** If you don't have a pastry bag, you can use a freezer bag by filling it with your mixture and cutting out a small corner.

Piping tips

TYPES

FLUTED PIPING TIP
Makes cute roses or Chantilly stars.

SMOOTH PIPING TIP
For round and even macarons.

SAINT-HONORÉ PIPING TIP
For a nice shell shape.

RUSSIAN PIPING TIP
For more complicated shapes, such as buttercream flowers on cupcakes.

THIN AND SMOOTH PIPING TIP
To write messages on a cake in melted chocolate or to make the chestnut vermicelli for mont-blancs.

BANANA
bread

Serves 6

Preparation time: 10 minutes

Cooking time: 1 hour

INGREDIENTS

¼ cup canola oil,
plus extra for greasing

1 cup whole-grain spelt flour,
plus extra for dusting

4 ripe bananas

2 teaspoons baking powder

⅓ cup unrefined sugar

3 eggs

1⅓ cups rolled oats

2 teaspoons ground cinnamon

1 Preheat the oven to 350°F. Grease and flour an 8 × 4¾-inch rectangular cake pan and line the bottom with a sheet of nonstick parchment paper. Mash 3 bananas with a fork. Combine the flour and baking powder. Mix together the mashed bananas, sugar, eggs, and oil and add the rest of the ingredients except for the final banana.

2 Pour the batter into the cake pan. Slice the remaining banana lengthwise and place it on top.

3 Bake for 45 minutes. Cover with aluminum foil and continue to bake for another 15 minutes.

CARAMELIZED APPLE
cake

Serves 6 | Preparation time: 30 minutes | Cooking time: 40 minutes

INGREDIENTS

FOR THE BATTER

1 stick (4 oz) unsalted butter,
at room temperature, plus
extra for greasing

1½ cups + 1½ tablespoons
all-purpose flour, plus
extra for dusting

2 eggs + 2 egg whites

⅔ cup superfine sugar

2 tablespoons lemon juice

1 teaspoon baking powder

A pinch of salt

FOR THE FILLING

3 apples (about 1 lb),
halved and cored

⅓ cup superfine sugar

1 Preheat the oven to 350° F. Grease and flour a 9½-inch round cake pan.

2 Prepare the batter: Separate the egg whites from the yolks. Beat together the butter, superfine sugar, egg yolks, and lemon juice until creamy. Gradually sprinkle in the flour and baking powder. Whisk the egg whites into stiff peaks with the salt and fold them into the batter with a rubber spatula. Pour the batter into the cake pan.

3 Prepare the filling: Place the apple halves flat on a board and slice them without completely cutting through, so that the slices remain attached. Sprinkle them with superfine sugar and press them into the batter with the sugary part facing up. Bake for 40 minutes.

VARIATION

Replace the butter with slightly salted butter.

CHOCOLATE CAKE
with candied ginger

Serves 4–6　|　Preparation time: 20 minutes　|　Cooking time: 40 minutes

INGREDIENTS

1¼ sticks (5 oz) unsalted
butter, at room temperature,
plus extra for greasing

1¼ cups all-purpose flour,
plus extra for dusting

3½ oz semisweet chocolate,
broken into pieces

1 cup + 2 tablespoons
confectioners' sugar

3 eggs

2½ teaspoons baking powder

⅔ cup finely chopped
candied ginger

FOR THE GLAZE

3½ oz semisweet chocolate,
broken into pieces

3½ tablespoons light cream

1 teaspoon ground ginger

¼ cup finely chopped
candied ginger

1 Preheat the oven to 340°F. Grease and flour a 10-inch-long rectangular cake pan. Melt the chocolate over a bain-marie (*see* page 494). Beat the butter and confectioners' sugar until creamy. Add the eggs and whisk well. Add the melted chocolate. Carefully fold in the flour and baking powder. Add the ginger pieces to the batter.

2 Pour the batter into the cake pan and bake for 40 minutes. Let the cake cool completely before removing it from the pan.

3 Prepare the glaze: Melt the chocolate over a bain-marie with the cream and ground ginger. Slowly pour the glaze over the cooled cake. Sprinkle the top with candied ginger pieces and let cool.

VARIATION

Replace the candied ginger with candied orange peel.

FAR
Breton

 Serves 6–8 | Preparation time: 10 minutes | Cooking time: 40–50 minutes

INGREDIENTS

Butter, for greasing

4 eggs

2 cups all-purpose flour

A pinch of salt

½ cup superfine sugar

3 cups milk

1¾ cups soft, pitted prunes (dried plums)

⅓ cup raisins (optional)

Confectioners' sugar, for dusting (optional)

1 Preheat the oven to 400°F. Grease a 9½-inch round baking dish.

2 Thoroughly beat the eggs. Place the flour in a large bowl, add the salt and superfine sugar, and mix well. Add the eggs and milk. Whisk until the batter is evenly combined.

3 Sprinkle the prunes across the bottom of the baking dish (and raisins, if using) and pour the batter over the top. Bake for 40–50 minutes; the top should be golden. Dust with confectioners' sugar to serve, if you want.

FIADONE

Serves 4

Preparation time: 15 minutes

Cooking time: 30–40 minutes

INGREDIENTS

Butter, for greasing

2 unwaxed lemons
(or unwaxed clementines)

4 eggs

¾ cup superfine sugar

1 pound fresh brocciu
(Corsican goat or sheep
milk cheese) or ricotta

1 Preheat the oven to 350°F. Grease an 8-inch square cake pan.

2 Zest the lemons (or clementines). In a large bowl, beat the eggs with the superfine sugar until the mixture is frothy. Add the brocciu and lemon zest and mix well.

3 When the batter is combined, pour it into the cake pan. Bake for 30–40 minutes. After 15 minutes, reduce the temperature to 325°F. You can reduce the temperature even more if the top of the cake browns too quickly. Serve warm or cold.

VARIATION

Prepare a crust using dried, crushed cookies combined with butter,
like for a cheesecake, or pour the batter into a pie dough shell.

PECAN
brownies

Makes 30 brownies

Preparation time: 30 minutes

Cooking time: 15–20 minutes

INGREDIENTS

1½ sticks + 1 tablespoon
(6½ oz) unsalted butter,
plus extra for greasing

3½ oz semisweet chocolate,
broken into pieces

1 cup + 2 tablespoons
superfine sugar

3 eggs

¾ cup all-purpose flour

1¼ cups coarsely chopped pecans

1 Preheat the oven to 350°F. Grease a 10 × 14-inch rectangular cake pan.

2 Melt the chocolate with the butter and superfine sugar in a large bowl over a bain-marie (*see* page 494). The water should be barely simmering and should not touch the bottom of the bowl.

3 Whisk the mixture, then remove the bowl from the bain-marie. Add the eggs while whisking vigorously with a handheld mixer, then sift in the flour. Finally, stir in the pecans using a spatula.

4 Pour the batter into the cake pan, smooth the top with the spatula, and bake for 15–20 minutes. The batter should remain spongy; make sure the brownies are cooked through by piercing them with the tip of a knife. A little batter should stick to the knife as you remove it.

5 Let the brownie cool before removing it from the pan, turning it out of the pan and onto a dish. Let the brownie cool some more, then cut it into rows, cut the rows into 1½-inch squares, and place the brownies on a serving dish.

TIP

You can easily store these brownies for a few days in a sealed container.

KOUIGN-AMMAN

Serves 6

Preparation time: 40 minutes

Dough resting time: 1 hour

Cooking time: 30 minutes

INGREDIENTS

½ small (⅔-oz) cake fresh yeast
or 1¾ teaspoons active dry yeast

¾ cup + 1½ tablespoons
lukewarm water

2⅓ cups + 1 tablespoon
all-purpose flour

1¾ sticks (7 oz) lightly salted
butter, at room temperature,
plus 2 teaspoons melted
butter + extra for greasing

1 cup superfine sugar, plus
¼ cup for sprinkling

1 Dissolve the yeast in the measured water. In a large bowl, sift the flour into a mound. Place the dissolved yeast and melted butter in its center, then knead for about 10 minutes, until the dough is pliant and consistent. Cover it with a cloth and let rise in a warm place for about 1 hour, until double in volume.

2 Use a rolling pin to roll out the dough into a large pancake. Spread the soft butter over the pancake, leaving a ¾-inch margin around the edge, then cover with the superfine sugar. Fold the pancake twice to form a triangle.

3 Preheat the oven to 400°F. Generously grease an 8¾-inch round cake pan, then sprinkle it with superfine sugar. Spread the sugar evenly by tapping the pan as you turn it.

4 Let the dough rest for a few minutes, then roll it out again with a rolling pin. Fold it in four and roll it out again into a long rectangle. Roll the dough over on itself like a snail, then flatten it by hand, giving it a round shape with a diameter of about 8¾ inches. Place the dough in the cake pan.

5 Bake for 30 minutes, covering the dough in foil toward the end of cooking, if the top browns too quickly. Remove from the pan while still hot and serve warm.

PINEAPPLE
upside-down cake

Serves 4–6 | **Preparation time: 15 minutes** | **Cooking time: 35 minutes**

INGREDIENTS

1 cup drained, canned
pineapple slices
1¾ sticks (7 oz) unsalted butter
4 extra-large eggs
1 cup superfine sugar
1⅔ cups all-purpose flour
2 teaspoons baking powder

FOR THE CARAMEL
⅓ cup superfine sugar
3 tablespoons water

1 Preheat the oven to 400°F.

2 Prepare the caramel: Caramelize the superfine sugar with the measured water in a small saucepan over low heat (or in the bottom of a cake pan, if it is heatproof) until the caramel is golden and thick. Pour it into the bottom of an 8¾-inch round cake pan. Lay the pineapple slices on top of the caramel. Set aside.

3 Melt the butter in the microwave. Using an electric handheld mixer, combine the eggs and superfine sugar until the mixture is pale. Pour in the melted butter, stir, then sift in the flour and baking powder, stirring until the batter is smooth. Pour it on top of the pineapple and bake for 35 minutes.

4 Let the cake cool before removing it from the pan, then eat immediately.

TIP

If it's the right season, choose fresh pineapple instead of canned—the Queen Victoria variety is fragrant. If you have leftover pineapple (fresh or canned), cut it into cubes, skewer a toothpick into each cube, and eat them with the cake. You can also blend the rest of the pineapple into a puree and serve it with the cake.

STRAWBERRY AND LEMON
roulade

Serves 4-6

Preparation time: 30 minutes

Cooking time: 5-6 minutes

INGREDIENTS

3 eggs

½ cup superfine sugar

½ teaspoon vanilla extract

1 tablespoon milk

¾ cup + 1 tablespoon
all-purpose flour

1½ cups lemon curd

⅔ cup finely diced strawberries

FOR THE TOPPING

Confectioners' sugar

A few strawberries, halved

1 Preheat the oven to 400°F. Line a shallow rectangular baking sheet with nonstick parchment paper. Separate the egg yolks from the egg whites.

2 Using an electric handheld mixer, beat the egg yolks with the sugar and vanilla extract until the mixture is pale and doubles in volume. Add the milk, then sift in the flour and combine with a spatula. Whip the egg whites into soft peaks. Carefully fold them into the batter.

3 Spread the batter carefully over the baking sheet to a thickness of ¾ inch. Bake for 5-6 minutes. The cake should be lightly golden.

4 When out of the oven, turn out the cake onto a clean dish towel on a work surface and peel away the parchment paper. While it is still hot, start at one end and roll up the cake. Let it rest for 3 minutes, then unroll it.

5 Spread the lemon curd over the cake, then sprinkle the diced strawberries on top. Roll up the cake again and wrap it in nonstick parchment paper or in a dish towel until it has completely cooled.

6 Before serving, dust the cake with confectioners' sugar and top it with the strawberry halves.

TIP

You can prepare your own lemon curd (*see* page 490).

CHOCOLATE AND MIXED BERRY
roulade

Serves 8

Preparation time: 20 minutes

Cooking time: 20 minutes

Refrigeration time: 3 hours

INGREDIENTS

FOR THE CAKE
4 eggs
⅓ cup superfine sugar
⅔ cup all-purpose flour
¼ cup unsweetened cocoa powder

FOR THE FILLING
¾ cup + 1½ tablespoons
cold heavy cream
4 tablespoons fruit jelly or
mixed berry preserves
1⅓ cups mixed berries
of your choice
Unsweetened cocoa powder
(or confectioners' sugar)

1 Preheat the oven to 325°F. Line a shallow rectangular baking sheet with nonstick parchment paper Prepare the cake: Separate the egg yolks from the egg whites. Beat the egg yolks with half the sugar until the mixture is pale. Sift the flour with the cocoa powder.

2 Whip the egg whites into soft peaks, adding the remaining sugar halfway through. Carefully fold the egg whites into the egg yolk mixture, then mix in the sifted flour mixture. Spread the dough over the baking sheet. Bake for 20 minutes.

3 When out of the oven, turn out the cake onto a clean dish towel on a work surface and peel away the parchment paper. While still hot, start at one end and roll up the cake. Let it rest for 3 minutes, then unroll it.

4 Prepare the filling: Whip the cream. Add the jelly or preserves with a spatula, without stirring too much. Spread the filling over the cake, leaving a 1½-inch margin, then sprinkle the mixed berries on top (setting some aside for decoration). Roll the cake up again and refrigerate for 3 hours.

5 Dust the cake with cocoa powder and top with the remaining fruit. Serve cold.

APPLE
strudel

| Serves 6–8 | Preparation time: 50 minutes | Dough resting time: 2 hours | Cooking time: 40 minutes |

½ cup dry bread crumbs

1 egg yolk

3 tablespoons oil

1 teaspoon ground cinnamon,
plus extra for dusting

4 large apples
(about 2¾ lb)

¾ cup + 2 tablespoons
walnuts and ⅔ cup raisins

1¼ sticks (5 oz)
unsalted butter, pllus
extra for greasing

3¼ cups all-purpose
flour, plus extra
for dusting

¼ cup packed light
brown sugar

INGREDIENTS

Confectioners' sugar, for dusting

FOR THE DOUGH

7 tablespoons unsalted butter, plus extra for greasing

3¼ cups all-purpose flour, plus extra for dusting

1 teaspoon salt

1 egg yolk

3 tablespoons oil

FOR THE FILLING

4 large apples (about 2¾ lb), peeled, cored, and diced

3½ tablespoons unsalted butter

¾ cup walnuts

¼ cup packed light brown sugar

⅔ cup raisins

1 teaspoon ground cinnamon, plus extra for dusting

½ cup dry bread crumbs

1 Preheat the oven to 375°F. Grease a baking sheet. Prepare the dough: Sift the flour into a large bowl. Add the salt and egg yolk to a glass of warm water.

2 Pour the egg mixture and oil into the center of the flour and work rapidly to make a soft ball of dough.

3 Knead on a lightly floured surface until the dough is smooth and elastic. Cover it and let rest for 2 hours.

4 Prepare the filling: Brown the apples over high heat for about 5 minutes with the butter.

5 Chop the walnuts in a food processor and then toast them. Add the walnuts, sugar, raisins, cinnamon, and bread crumbs to the apples and let cool.

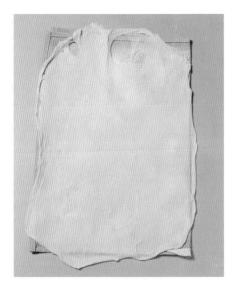

6 Place 2 clean dish towels on a flat surface to create a long rectangle measuring about 16 × 40 inches. Dust them with flour. Roll out the dough with a rolling pin, then stretch and press it with your fingers covered in flour, so that it is a thin layer.

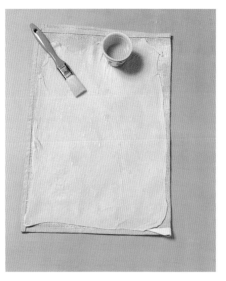

7 Cut the edges of the dough neatly to obtain a large rectangle. Melt the butter and spread some liberally over the dough using a brush.

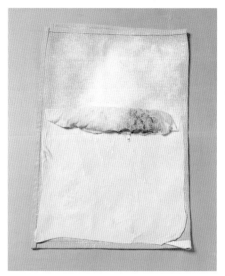

8 Spread the filling over the dough, leaving a 1¼-inch margin on each long edge, then roll the strudel toward you, using the dish towels as an aid.

9 Carefully place the strudel on the baking sheet, bending in both ends if it is long and placing the seam underneath.

10 Brush the top of the strudel with the rest of the melted butter, then bake for 35 minutes.

11 Use a tea strainer to sift some confectioners' sugar and cinnamon over it.

FRENCH SPICED
bread

Serves 6

Preparation time: 20 minutes

Cooking time: 1 hour

INGREDIENTS

1½ tablespoons unsalted butter, for greasing

⅓ cup + 1½ tablespoons milk

½ cup flavorful honey

⅓ cup superfine sugar

2 egg yolks

1 teaspoon baking soda

2⅓ cups + 1 tablespoon all-purpose flour

2 tablespoons lemon juice

½ cup coarsely chopped candied fruit

1 teaspoon ground cinnamon

Pearl sugar, to decorate

1 Preheat the oven to 350°F. Grease an 8¾-inch-long rectangular cake pan and line it with nonstick parchment paper.

2 In a small saucepan, bring the milk, honey, and superfine sugar to a boil over low heat, stirring continuously. Beat the egg yolks in a bowl and pour in half the milk-and-honey mixture. Add the baking soda and then the rest of the milk-and-honey mixture. Mix well.

3 Sift the flour into a large bowl. Gradually add the previous mixture, the lemon juice, candied fruit, and cinnamon, alternating the ingredients. Beat the batter for about 10 minutes.

4 Place the dough in the loaf pan, sprinkle with pearl sugar nibs, and bake in the oven for 1 hour.

5 Remove the bread from the pan and let cool on a wire rack. Wait at least 24 hours before serving.

TIP

This cake is best made in advance.

PINK PRALINE
brioche

Serves 4–6

Preparation time: 30 minutes

Dough resting time: 4 hours

Cooking time: 45 minutes

INGREDIENTS

⅔ cup pink pralines (*pralines roses*—almonds with a pink sugar coating)

FOR THE BRIOCHE DOUGH

1 teaspoon fresh yeast or
¾ teaspoon active dry yeast

1½ cups all-purpose flour

1½ tablespoons superfine sugar

½ teaspoon fine sea salt

3 eggs

1¼ sticks (5 oz) unsalted butter,
at room temperature,
cut into small pieces

1 Prepare the brioche dough: Crumble the yeast into a large bowl. Using a wooden spoon, mix it with the flour, superfine sugar, and salt. Add the eggs, one at a time, carefully stirring after each addition. Add the butter and mix well (the dough should come away from the sides of the bowl).

2 Coarsely chop ½ cup of the pink pralines and grind the remainder in a food processor; alternatively, fold them inside a clean dish towel and crush with a rolling pin. Add the chopped pink pralines to the brioche dough.

3 Cover the dough with a damp dish towel and let rest for 3 hours in a warm place, until doubled in volume.

4 Line a 4¾-inch cylindrical brioche pan with nonstick parchment paper. Quickly knead the ball of dough, put it onto the baking sheet or into the pan, and sprinkle the rest of the pink pralines on top. Let the dough rise for 1 hour.

5 Preheat the oven to 450°F. Bake the brioche for 15 minutes. Reduce the temperature to 350°F and bake for another 30 minutes. Serve the brioche warm.

CHOCO-PEAR
desserts

Serves 4

Preparation time: 25 minutes

Cooking time: 8–10 minutes

INGREDIENTS

5¾ tablespoons unsalted
butter, cut into small pieces,
plus extra for greasing

3½ tablespoons all-purpose
flour, for dusting

3 eggs

½ vanilla bean

4½ oz semisweet chocolate,
broken into pieces

A pinch of salt

3½ tablespoons superfine sugar

2½ tablespoons cornstarch

1 Bartlett pear, not too ripe,
peeled, cored, and diced

1 Preheat the oven to 340°F. Grease and flour 4 ramekins. Separate the egg whites from the yolks. Split open the vanilla bean and scrape out the seeds.

2 Melt the chocolate in a bowl over a bain-marie (*see* page 494). Remove from the heat and mix in the butter, then stir with a spatula until smooth. Add the vanilla seeds, salt, sugar, and egg yolks, then the cornstarch and diced pear. Mix well.

3 Beat the egg whites to stiff peaks. Fold them carefully into the mixture with a rubber spatula.

4 Divide the batter among the ramekins and bake at the bottom of the oven for 8–10 minutes. Let the desserts rest for 2 minutes (but not more) before removing them from the ramekins. Enjoy immediately.

VARIATION

Replace the pear with 1 cup raspberries.

VEGETABLE-BASED
desserts

We're all familiar with the famous carrot cake (*see* the recipe on page 30) and American pumpkin pie—which have elevated the carrot and pumpkin—but there are plenty of other possibilities to try.

AVOCADO CREAM
dessert

Brazilian cuisine often uses avocados to make desserts, including this quick and easy avocado cream.

> **Makes 6 servings • Preparation time: 10 minutes**

3 perfectly ripe avocados • 2 limes
2 tablespoons packed brown sugar • ¾ cup
unsweetened coconut cream

1 In a deep bowl, use a handheld immersion blender to blend the avocados, the juice of 1 lime, brown sugar, and coconut cream.

2 Pour the cream into 6 cups and decorate with lime slices.

CHOCOLATE ZUCCHINI
sponge cakes

As far as flavor goes, zucchini remains fairly inconspicuous here, but it does bring sponginess and moisture to the batter while letting you reduce the amount of butter required significantly. You can also make this recipe by substituting the zucchini with 1–1½ cups grated beets.

> Makes 6 small cakes • Preparation time: 15 minutes • Cooking time: 25 minutes

1 egg • ¼ cup packed brown sugar

3½ oz semisweet chocolate, broken into pieces

2 tablespoons unsweetened butter, cut into pieces

¾ cup + 1 tablespoon all-purpose flour

2 teaspoons baking powder • 1 zucchini

1 Preheat the oven to 350°F. Beat the egg and sugar until frothy. Melt the chocolate and butter in a saucepan. Add them to the previous mixture, then pour in the flour and baking powder.

2 Grate the zucchini and squeeze it between your hands to release a little of the water. Add 1½ cups of it to the batter. Mix well.

3 Divide the batter among 6 cups of a muffin pan that have been greased or lined with paper liners and bake for 25 minutes.

Which other vegetables can be used to make desserts?

• Consider adding mashed **sweet potatoes** to spiced orange muffins.

• Substitute some of the butter in brownies with **black bean puree**. It will add vegetable protein and allow for you to prepare a gluten-free version, because flour will no longer be necessary.

CHOCOLATE LAVA
cakes

Makes 4 cakes

Preparation time: 25 minutes

Refrigeration time: 2 hours

Cooking time: 12 minutes

INGREDIENTS

4 oz semisweet chocolate,
broken into pieces

1 stick (4 oz) unsalted butter,
pllus extra for greasing

3 eggs

¾ cup + 2½ tablespoons
superfine sugar

⅓ cup all-purpose flour,
plus extra for dusting

scoop of vanilla ice cream,
or vanilla or pistachio crème
anglaise, to serve (optional)

1 Melt the chocolate and butter over a bain-marie (*see* page 494) or in the microwave, mixing to obtain a smooth cream.

2 In a large bowl, beat the eggs with the sugar. Add the flour, mix well, then incorporate the melted chocolate and butter. Refrigerate for 2 hours.

3 Preheat the oven to 350°F. Grease and flour four 3¼-inch cake rings (or 4 large ramekins). Place the rings on a baking sheet lined with nonstick parchment paper. Fill the rings three-quarters full with the chocolate mixture. Bake for 12 minutes.

4 When out of the oven, let the cakes rest for 5 minutes, then use a knife to pry the rings off carefully.

5 Serve with a scoop of vanilla ice cream, or vanilla or pistachio crème anglaise, if using.

TIP

If using ramekins, we recommend leaving the cakes in them, otherwise they might collapse.

EXTRA-CHOCOLATY
chocolate cake

 Serves 8–10 | Preparation time: 10 minutes | Cooking time: 15–20 minutes

INGREDIENTS

2¼ sticks (9 oz) unsalted butter,
plus extra for greasing

½ cup all-purpose flour,
plus extra for dusting

9 oz semisweet chocolate,
broken into pieces

¾ cup + 2½ tablespoons
superfine sugar

¼ cup orange juice

Zest of ½ an orange

4 eggs

1 Preheat the oven to 300°F. Grease and flour a 9½–10¼-inch round cake pan (or a rectangular cake pan of an equivalent size).

2 In a small saucepan, melt the chocolate with the butter. Add the sugar, orange juice, orange zest, and eggs, one by one, while stirring continuously. Incorporate the flour. Pour the batter into the cake pan. Bake for 15–20 minutes.

3 Remove the cake from the oven. If it doesn't seem cooked in the middle, that's normal. Do not put it back in the oven. Ideally, serve the cake the following day.

 TIP

This cake is best made in advance. It is a rich cake and can be easily overwhelming, so it should be enjoyed in small servings. It keeps well in the refrigerator—if you don't finish it in one day.

QUEEN
of Sheba

Serves 8

Preparation time: 25 minutes

Cooking time: 35 minutes

INGREDIENTS

5 tablespoons unsalted butter, at room temperature, plus extra for greasing

3½ tablespoons all-purpose flour, for dusting

⅓ cup slivered almonds

4 oz bittersweet chocolate (at least 60 percent cocoa solids), broken into pieces

⅓ cup cornstarch

¼ cup unsweetened cocoa powder, plus extra to decorate

3 eggs

⅓ cup + 1 tablespoon superfine sugar

¾ cup ground almonds

A pinch of salt

1 Preheat the oven to 350°F. Generously butter an 8¾-inch round cake pan (or a 6¼-inch charlotte mold), then dust it with flour.

2 Lightly toast the almonds in a nonstick skillet. Let cool, then sprinkle them across the bottom of the cake pan. Refrigerate while you prepare the batter.

3 Melt the butter and chocolate in a small saucepan over low heat or over a bain-marie (*see* page 494), stirring gently until smooth. Sift the cornstarch with the cocoa powder.

4 Separate the egg whites from the yolks. Vigorously beat the yolks with the superfine sugar until the mixture is pale and frothy. While continuing to stir, add the chocolate cream, sifted cornstarch mixture, and ground almonds.

5 Beat the egg whites into stiff peaks with the salt. Quickly add 2 tablespoons of the egg whites to the chocolate mixture to lighten it, then carefully fold in the rest of the egg whites using a rubber spatula. Pour the batter into the cake pan and bake for 35 minutes.

6 Remove the cake from the oven. Remove it from the pan, turn it upside down, and place it on a wire rack to cool. Dust with cocoa powder before serving.

SOFT CHOCOLATE
sponge cake

Serves 8

Preparation time: 20 minutes

Cooking time: 25 minutes

INGREDIENTS

1 stick (4 oz) unsalted butter,
plus extra for greasing

9 oz semisweet chocolate,
broken into pieces

8 eggs

A pinch of salt

¾ cup superfine sugar

⅓ cup + 1 tablespoon
all-purpose flour

Confectioners' sugar, for dusting

1 Preheat the oven to 485°F. Grease an 8¾-inch round cake pan. Melt the butter and chocolate in a small saucepan over low heat or over a bain-marie (*see* page 494), gently stirring to obtain a smooth cream.

2 Separate the egg whites from the yolks. Beat the egg whites into a light mousse with the salt.

3 In a large bowl, beat the egg yolks with the sugar (by hand or using an electric handheld mixer) until the mixture is pale. Continue to beat as you add the egg whites, melted chocolate mixture, and, finally, the flour. The mixture should diminish slightly in volume.

4 Pour the batter into the cake pan and bake for 5 minutes, then reduce the temperature to 300°F and bake for another 20 minutes. Make sure the cake is cooked by inserting the blade of a knife into it; the blade should come out covered in a little chocolate.

5 Remove the cake from the pan and place onto a wire rack. Dust with confectioners' sugar and serve warm.

PAVÉ OF BITTER CHOCOLATE
with sweet spices

Serves 8–10 | Preparation time: 20 minutes | Cooking time: 1 hour

INGREDIENTS

2¼ sticks (9 oz) unsalted butter, cut into pieces, plus extra for greasing

¾ cup + 2½ tablespoons superfine sugar

⅓ cup + 1½ tablespoons water

9 oz bittersweet chocolate, broken into pieces

½ cup + 1½ tablespoons all-purpose flour

3 eggs

½ teaspoon vanilla powder

4 pinches of each of the following ground spices mixed together: cinnamon, green anise, and cardamom

FOR THE DECORATION (OPTIONAL)

1 tablespoon confectioners' sugar

½ teaspoon ground cinnamon

1 Preheat the oven to 340° F. Cover the bottom of an 8 × 8-inch square cake pan with nonstick parchment paper. Grease the paper. In a heavy saucepan, bring the sugar and measured water to a boil, then add the chocolate and butter. Reduce the heat and mix well, then remove from the heat.

2 Add the flour to a large bowl, beat in an egg, then add the remaining 2 eggs, one by one, mixing well. Add the vanilla and spices. Pour this mixture into the butter-and-chocolate mixture and stir vigorously.

3 Pour the batter into the cake pan. Place the pan into a larger baking pan filled halfway with hot water. Bake for 1 hour. Let the pavé cool, then remove it from the pan and dust with confectioners' sugar mixed with cinnamon, if using.

Tarts
& crisps

STRAWBERRY, MASCARPONE
and Chantilly tart

Serves 6 | **Preparation time: 25 minutes** | **Cooking time: 15–20 minutes**

INGREDIENTS

1 sheet of all-butter rolled
dough pie crust

1 tablespoon superfine sugar

1 lb strawberries, sliced

1¾ oz white chocolate

FOR THE CHANTILLY CREAM

1 cup cold heavy cream

½ mascarpone cheese

2 tablespoons confectioners'
sugar, plus extra for dusting

½ teaspoon vanilla extract

1 Preheat the oven to 350°F. Use the pie dough to line a 10-inch round tart pan, preferably one with a removable bottom. Sprinkle a layer of superfine sugar over the dough and blind bake it for 15–20 minutes. Let it cool completely.

2 Using an electric mixer, whip the cream with the mascarpone, confectioners' sugar, and vanilla extract to make a firm Chantilly cream Refrigerate the cream until needed.

3 Shortly before serving the tart, spread half the Chantilly cream over the bottom of the pastry shell and put the rest into a pastry bag with a fluted tip. Pipe Chantilly stars onto the tart and arrange the strawberries between them. Make white chocolate shavings using a vegetable peeler and sprinkle these on top of the tart, then dust with a little confectioners' sugar. Serve immediately to keep the tart from becoming soggy.

RHUBARB
mini tarts

Makes 4 mini tarts	Preparation time: 30 minutes	Macerating time: 8 hours	Dough resting time: 30 minutes	Draining time: 30 minutes	Cooking time: 30–35 minutes

INGREDIENTS

4-5 rhubarb stalks, cut into strips the same length as the cups in the mini tart pans

2½ tablespoons superfine sugar

Confectioners' sugar, for dusting

FOR THE SWEET FLAKY PASTRY DOUGH

1⅓ cups + 2 tablespoons all-purpose flour

6½ tablespoons cold, lightly salted butter, plus extra for greasing

2 tablespoons superfine sugar

¼ cup + 2 teaspoons cold water

FOR THE ALMOND CREAM

1 egg

⅓ cup superfine sugar

3 tablespoons milk

2 tablespoons light cream

¼ cup ground almonds

4 tablespoons cold unsalted butter

1 The night before you make the tarts, put the rhubarb strips into a large bowl and dust them with superfine sugar. Cover them and let macerate for at least 8 hours in the refrigerator.

2 The next day, prepare the sweet flaky pastry dough (*see* page 470). Roll it into a ball, wrap it in plastic wrap, and let rest for at least 30 minutes in the refrigerator.

3 Place the rhubarb in a strainer and drain for 30 minutes. Preheat the oven to 350°F. Grease 4 mini tart pans. Remove the pastry dough from the refrigerator and roll it out to a thickness of 1/16 inch. Line the mini tart pans with the dough and prick the bottoms with a fork. Cover the pans with nonstick parchment paper and fill with pie weights. Bake for 15 minutes.

4 Prepare the cream: Beat together the egg and superfine sugar in a bowl, then add the milk, cream, ground almonds, and butter. Mix well.

5 Remove the paper and weights from the mini tart shells. Arrange the rhubarb strips in them, then pour in the almond cream and bake for 15–20 minutes. Serve the mini tarts cold or barely warm, liberally dusted with confectioners' sugar.

Serving suggestion

Serve these mini tarts with a strawberry coulis or top them with Italian meringue (*see* page 484), then lightly brown them for 5 minutes under the broiler.

APPLE
pie

Serves 6–8

Preparation time: 30 minutes

Dough resting time: 30 minutes

Cooking time: 50 minutes

INGREDIENTS

7 apples (about 2¼ lb),
peeled, cored, and sliced

Juice of 1 lemon

1 egg

FOR THE FLAKY PASTRY DOUGH

1¼ sticks (5 oz) cold unsalted
butter, plus extra for greasing

2⅓ cups + 1 tablespoon
all-purpose flour

½ teaspoon salt

FOR THE FILLING

⅓ cup all-purpose flour

¼ cup packed light brown sugar

A pinch of vanilla powder

½ teaspoon ground cinnamon

A pinch of ground nutmeg

1 Grease an 8¾-inch round tart pan. Prepare the flaky pastry dough (*see* page 470); let it rest for at least 30 minutes in the refrigerator. Divide the dough into 2 balls, one three-fifths of the dough, the other two-fifths. Roll them out into ⅛-inch-thick circles and use the larger one to line the tart pan, letting it spill over the edges.

2 Prepare the filling: In a large bowl, combine the flour, brown sugar, vanilla, cinnamon, and nutmeg. Pour half of this mixture into the pan.

3 Preheat the oven to 400°F. Place the apples in the pan in the shape of a wheel, creating a small dome in the center. Drizzle the lemon juice on top, then sprinkle the rest of the flour-and-brown sugar mixture on top.

4 Cover the filling with the remaining dough circle. Beat the egg and brush it over the edges of the dough, then pinch the edges together. Make a small hole in the center of the pie with the tip of a knife, then brush it with the egg. Bake for 10 minutes. Remove from the oven, coat again with the beaten egg, and return to the oven for another 40 minutes.

Serving suggestion

Serve this pie still warm, with crème fraîche, a blackberry coulis, or a scoop of vanilla ice cream.

APPLE *tarte tatin*

Serves 6	Preparation time: 40 minutes	Dough resting time: 30 minutes	Cooking time: 40 minutes

1¾ sticks (6 oz) unsalted butter, plus extra for greasing

7 firm apples (about 2¼ lb)

⅔ cup crème fraîche or vanilla ice cream

1½ cups + 1½ tablespoons all-purpose flour

½ cup + 2 tablespoons superfine sugar

INGREDIENTS

FOR THE SWEET FLAKY PASTRY DOUGH

7 tablespoons unsalted butter

1½ cups + 1½ tablespoons all-purpose flour

A large pinch of salt

2 tablespoons superfine sugar

FOR THE FILLING

7 firm apples (about 2¼ lb), peeled, cored, and quartered

5 tablespoons unsalted butter, cut into pieces, plus extra for greasing

½ cup superfine sugar

⅔ cup crème fraîche or vanilla ice cream

1 Prepare the sweet flaky pastry dough (*see* page 470); let it rest for 30 minutes in the refrigerator.

2 Prepare the apples.

3 Grease a 10¼-inch round flameproof metal or cast iron pie pan. Sprinkle the bottom with the superfine sugar.

4 Arrange the apples in the pan and sprinkle the butter on top.

5 Place the pan on the stove and cook for 10 minutes over high heat until a caramel forms. It should be bubbling and golden brown.

6 Preheat the oven to 350°F. Use the palm of your hand to work the pie dough, then roll it out to a thickness of ⅛ inch.

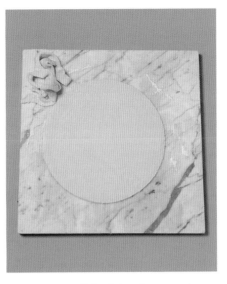

7 Cut out a disk of dough measuring 1½ inches greater than the diameter of the pan.

8 Cover the apples with the disk of dough and fold the edges of the dough toward the center of the pan to seal. Bake for 30 minutes.

9 If the apples release too much water, when you take the tart out of the oven, hold the pan with an oven mitt and gently tip it over a small saucepan to collect the juice. Bring the juice to a boil in a small saucepan until you get a thick caramel.

10 Place a plate over the pan and turn the whole thing upside down. Spread the caramel on top. It will soon turn to a gelatin.

11 Serve warm with crème fraîche or vanilla ice cream.

KIWI
tart

 Serves 6 | Preparation time: 20 minutes | Dough resting time: 30 minutes | Cooking time: 20 minutes

INGREDIENTS

7–8 kiwifruit, peeled and
sliced into thin slices

FOR THE SWEET
FLAKY PASTRY DOUGH

1½ cups plus 1½ tablespoons
all-purpose flour, plus
extra for dusting

A pinch of salt

2 tablespoons superfine sugar

7 tablespoons cold, unsalted
butter, cut into small pieces,
plus extra for greasing

5 tablespoons cold water

FOR THE CREAM

2 egg yolks

⅓ cup + 1 tablespoon
superfine sugar

1 teaspoon all-purpose flour

¾ cup + 1½ tablespoons milk

1 tablespoon red currant jelly

1 Prepare the sweet flaky pastry dough: Pour the flour into a large bowl and make a well in the center. Add the salt, superfine sugar, and butter. Rub the mixture with your fingertips until it resembles bread crumbs. Add the measured water to bring the ingredients together, then work the mixture until you have a pliable dough. Place the dough on a floured work surface and flatten it out, without kneading it too much. Shape the dough into a ball, then cover it with plastic wrap and let rest for at least 30 minutes in the refrigerator.

2 Preheat the oven to 400°F. Grease an 8–8¾-inch square tart pan. Roll the dough out to a thickness of ⅛ inch and use it to line the pan. Pierce the dough with a fork, cover it with nonstick parchment paper and pie weights, and bake for 20 minutes.

3 Meanwhile, prepare the cream: In a saucepan, whisk the egg yolks with the superfine sugar, flour, and milk. Cook over low heat, stirring, until the cream coats the back of a spoon. Remove from the heat and add the red currant jelly.

4 Remove the tart shell from the oven, let cool, remove the weights and paper, and pour the cream into it.

5 Place the kiwi slices on top of the cream so that they overlap slightly. Refrigerate until serving.

F LORAL TART

This is a traditional tart in terms of how it's made, but it requires more patience in its assembly. The aim is to create pretty petal arrangements that resemble flower buds.

the keys
TO SUCCESS

- Apples yield the best results. Opt for organic apples so you can keep the skin on and play on the contrast between the dark and light colors.

- Use a **sharp knife** or, better yet, a **mandoline,** to create perfect thin, even slices.

- For an even more sophisticated effect and a softer tart, spread a thin layer of **apple compote** over the bottom of the tart shell.

- You can **use other fruit,** such as pears, although they are more fragile, or mangoes, which roll up well once sliced and don't need to be precooked if they're ripe enough.

1 Wash the apples and core them with an apple corer. Cut them in half and slice them thinly, placing each slice in a large bowl with water and lemon juice as you work to keep them from turning brown. Microwave the bowl for 2 minutes on high. Stir carefully to make sure all the slices are submerged and microwave for another 2 minutes. Let the apples cool slightly in the water.

2 Place the apple slices on absorbant paper towels and line up 3 slices so that they overlap. Carefully roll them up to create a flower.

3 Place the flower vertically on the prepared tart dough, which should have been pricked with a fork and possibly precooked (*see* below). Continue to line up the flowers, placing them close together. Brush them with a slightly warm fruit jelly (quince or apple).

4 Dust the top of the tart with brown sugar and bake (*see* below).

FIRM OR
soft apples?

If you don't want to overcook your apples, blind bake the tart shell (*see* page 475) for 15 minutes at 350°F, without the filling, then bake again for 15 minutes with the apples.

If you like your apples softer, cook everything together in one baking for 25–30 minutes at 350°F.

APPLE

roses

Serves 6 | Preparation time: 20 minutes | Cooking time: 30 minutes

INGREDIENTS

1 sheet of ready-to-bake
all-butter puff pastry
3 apples
½ cup apple compote
1 teaspoon confectioners' sugar

1 Preheat the oven to 350°F. Roll out the dough and cut it into 1¼-inch-wide strips. Cut each strip in half widthwise.

2 Slice the apples with a mandoline to obtain strips about 1/16 inch thick. Soften them by cooking them for 10 minutes in a saucepan filled with boiling water.

3 Place some apple compote on the lower half of a strip of dough, then place 6 or 7 strips of apple on the upper half, letting them slightly overlap and poke out. Refold the strip of dough over the apples, then roll it up to form a rose. Repeat with the remaining strips.

4 Place the roses in muffin pans and bake for 20 minutes. Dust with confectioners' sugar before serving.

FRENCH PEAR
tart

Serves 6

Preparation time:
30 minutes

Dough resting time:
30 minutes

Cooking time:
30–40 minutes

INGREDIENTS

1 large jar of preserved pears (1 quart) or 8 homemade poached pear halves (see the recipe for Pear Charlotte, page 330)

FOR THE SWEET FLAKY PASTRY DOUGH

2 cups all-purpose flour

1 stick + 3 tablespoons (5½ oz) unsalted butter, at room temperature, cut into small pieces, plus extra for greasing

1 egg

⅓ cup superfine sugar

FOR THE FRANGIPANE CREAM

2 eggs

½ cup superfine sugar

1¼ cups ground almonds

1 stick (4 oz) unsalted butter, at room temperature

1 Prepare the sweet flaky pastry dough: Sift the flour onto a work surface. Add the butter and rub in with your fingertips until the mixture resembles fine bread crumbs. Make a well in the center of the mixture. Break the egg into it and pour in the superfine sugar. Use your fingertips to mix all the ingredients together. Knead the dough briefly to bring it together and smooth it out. Shape the dough into a ball and flatten it between your palms. Wrap it in plastic wrap and let it rest for at least 30 minutes in the refrigerator.

2 Preheat the oven to 375°F. Grease a 10¼-inch round fluted tart pan with a detachable bottom. Prepare the frangipane cream: In a large bowl, whisk the eggs with the superfine sugar, then add the ground almonds and butter. Mix well.

3 Roll the dough out to a thickness of 1/16 inch. Use the dough to line the pan. Spread the cream over the dough. Drain the pear halves, then cut them into slices on a cutting board. Use the palm of your hand to fan the pears out slightly, then use a spatula to lift them, one by one, and arrange them carefully on the cream in a rose pattern. Bake for 30–40 minutes.

4 Let the tart cool before removing from the pan. Serve cold.

TIP

The pastry is even better when the dough has rested for 24 hours in the refrigerator.

RASPBERRY
barquettes

 Makes 10–12 barquettes

 Preparation time:
15 minutes

 Dough resting time:
30 minutes

 Cooking time:
10–15 minutes

INGREDIENTS

1⅔ cups raspberries

5 tablespoons red currant
(or raspberry) jelly

FOR THE SWEET
FLAKY PASTRY DOUGH

1½ cups + 1½ tablespoons
all-purpose flour, plus
extra for dusting

A pinch of salt

2 tablespoons superfine sugar

7 tablespoons cold, unsalted
butter, cut into small pieces,
plus extra for greasing

5 tablespoons cold water

FOR THE CRÈME PÂTISSIÈRE

3 egg yolks

¼ cup superfine sugar

2 tablespoons + 2 teaspoons
all-purpose flour

1 cup milk

1 Prepare the sweet flaky pastry dough: Pour the flour into a large bowl and make a well in the center. Add the salt, sugar, and butter. Rub in with your fingertips until the mixture resembles fine bread crumbs. Add the measured water to bring the ingredients together, then work the mixture until you have a pliable dough. Place the dough on a floured work surface and flatten it out, without kneading it too much. Shape the dough into a ball, wrap it in plastic wrap, and let it rest for at least 30 minutes in the refrigerator.

2 Preheat the oven to 350°F. Grease 10–12 fluted barquettes. Remove the dough from the refrigerator and roll it out to a thickness of 1/16 inch. Using a pastry cutter or a small bowl, cut out disks from the dough and use them to line the barquettes. Prick the bottom of each pastry shell with a fork. Cut out some pieces of nonstick parchment paper and place them on top of each pastry shell, then fill with pie weights. Bake for 10–15 minutes.

3 Prepare the crème pâtissière: In a large bowl, vigorously whisk the egg yolks with the superfine sugar until the mixture is pale. Dust the top with flour, then quickly fold it in without working it too much. Meanwhile, bring the milk to a boil, then pour it, still boiling, over the mixture, stirring constantly with a wooden spoon to obtain a smooth cream. Pour the cream into a heavy saucepan. Cook over low heat until the cream thickens. Remove the saucepan from the heat as the first bubbles start to form and pour the cream into a large bowl to cool.

4 Fill the barquettes with the cooled pastry cream. Set aside the rest of the cream for later. Divide the raspberries between the barquettes. In a small saucepan, heat the jelly and, using a brush, carefully coat the raspberries with it. Serve cold.

TIP

Assemble the barquettes at the last minute; they do not last well in the refrigerator.

APRICOT AND ROSEMARY
brioche tart

Serves 6

Preparation time: 30 minutes

Dough resting time: 1½ hours

Cooking time: 25 minutes

INGREDIENTS

2¼ lb apricots, halved and pitted

FOR THE BRIOCHE DOUGH
⅓ small (⅔-oz) cake fresh yeast or
scant 1 teaspoon active dry yeast
2 tablespoons milk, warmed
1⅓ cups + 1 tablespoon
all-purpose flour
2 eggs
½ teaspoon salt
4 teaspoons superfine sugar
6½ tablespoons unsalted butter

FOR THE FILLING
1 egg
3½ tablespoons unsalted
butter, at room temperature
¼ cup superfine sugar
⅔ cup ground almonds
1 teaspoon chopped fresh
rosemary, plus extra
sprigs to decorate

1 Prepare the brioche dough: In a bowl, dissolve the yeast in the warm milk and let it rest for 10 minutes.

2 Pour the flour onto a work surface and make a well in the center. Add the dissolved yeast, eggs, salt, superfine sugar, and butter. Knead everything for at least 10 minutes, until the dough becomes smooth and elastic (you could knead the bread using a stand mixer with a hook attachment or in a bread maker).

3 Put the dough into a large bowl, cover it with a dish towel, and let rise in a warm place (close to a radiator in winter) for about 1½ hours, until doubled in volume.

4 Preheat the oven to 350°F. Line a baking sheet with nonstick parchment paper. Punch down the dough before transferring it to the baking sheet.

5 Prepare the filling: In a large bowl, whisk the egg with the butter and superfine sugar, then add the ground almonds and rosemary. Mix until smooth. Spread this cream over the dough. Place the apricots on top, cut side up, then bake the tart for 25 minutes. Serve warm, decorated with rosemary sprigs.

FINE FIG
mini tarts

Makes 6 mini tarts

Preparation time: 15 minutes

Cooking time: 35 minutes

INGREDIENTS

1 sheet of ready-to-bake all-butter puff pastry (about 8 oz)

FOR THE FILLING

1 tablespoon whole almonds (or whole hazelnuts)

1 tablespoon whole pistachios

3 tablespoons unsalted butter

6 fresh figs, each cut into 6

2–3 tablespoons honey

2 tablespoons fig vinegar (or balsamic vinegar)

1 tablespoon pine nuts

1 Preheat the oven to 350°F. Cut the dough into 6 disks, 3¼–4 inches in diameter. Place them on a baking sheet lined with nonstick parchment paper, cover with a second sheet of nonstick parchment paper, then with a second baking sheet. Bake for 10 minutes.

2 Prepare the filling: Coarsely chop the almonds and pistachios. In a skillet, melt the butter and add the fig slices. Pour in the honey and cook for 3 minutes over medium heat, carefully turning the figs over. Use a slotted spoon to remove them from the pan.

3 Reheat the fig cooking juice and add the vinegar. Bring to a boil, then remove from the heat.

4 Arrange 6 fig slices on top of each mini tart, sprinkle with the chopped nuts and whole pine nuts, then brush each mini tart with 1 tablespoon of the cooking juice. Bake for 20 minutes. Serve warm.

Serving
suggestion
──────
Serve with a scoop of caramel
or speculoos ice cream.

MINI MANGO AND COCONUT
tortes

Makes 6 tortes

Preparation time: 20 minutes

Dough resting time: 30 minutes

Cooking time: 40 minutes

INGREDIENTS

FOR THE FLAKY PASTRY DOUGH

2⅓ cups + 1 tablespoon
all-purpose flour, sifted,
plus extra for dusting

A pinch of salt

¼ cup superfine sugar (optional)

1¼ sticks (5 oz) cold unsalted
butter, cut into small pieces,
plus extra for greasing

½ cup cold water

FOR THE FILLING

2 tablespoons lightly salted butter

1½ teaspoons vanilla
sugar (*see page 13*)

¼ cup superfine sugar

2 mangoes, peeled,
pitted, and diced

6 tablespoons dry
unsweetened coconut

1 egg

1 Prepare the flaky pastry dough: Pour the flour into a large bowl and make a well in the center. Add the salt, superfine sugar (if using), and butter. Rub in with your fingertips until the mixture resembles fine bread crumbs. Add the measured water to bring the ingredients together, then work the mixture until you have a pliable dough. Place the dough on a floured work surface and flatten it out, without kneading it too much. Shape the dough into a ball, wrap it in plastic wrap, and let it rest for at least 30 minutes in the refrigerator.

2 Prepare the filling: In a skillet, melt the butter over low heat, then pour in the sugars and let them caramelize. Add the mango pieces and cook for about 5 minutes over medium heat.

3 Preheat the oven to 350°F. Grease 6 mini tart pans. Remove the dough from the refrigerator and roll it out to a thickness of ⅛ inch. Use a pastry cutter to cut 12 disks from the dough. Use 6 disks to line each of the 6 mini tart pans.

4 Divide 3 tablespoons of the dry coconut among the mini tarts, sprinkling it over the dough, then pour in the mango filling. Place the remaining dough disks on top and pinch the edges together tightly. Using a sharp knife, poke a small hole in the top of each mini tart and carve some geometric shapes into the dough. Beat the egg, then brush it onto the mini tortes. Bake for 35 minutes.

5 Remove the tortes from the oven, sprinkle with the remaining dry coconut, and serve warm.

VARIATION

Replace the fresh mango with frozen mango cubes.
Add a small amount of fresh grated ginger to the
mango as it cooks.

SALTED CARAMEL
mini tarts

 Makes 10–12 mini tarts

 Preparation time:
20 minutes

 Dough resting time:
30 minutes

 Cooking time:
25–30 minutes

 Refrigeration time:
2 hours

INGREDIENTS

FOR THE SWEET
FLAKY PASTRY DOUGH

½ vanilla bean (optional)

⅓ cup superfine sugar

2 cups all-purpose flour

1 stick + 3 tablespoons (5½ oz)
unsalted butter, at room
temperature, cut into small
pieces, plus extra for greasing

1 egg

FOR THE CARAMEL

1 cup + 3½ tablespoons
superfine sugar

2 tablespoons water

1¼ cups heavy cream

6½ tablespoons unsalted
butter, at room temperature

2 eggs

1 teaspoon *fleur de sel* salt

1 Prepare the sweet flaky pastry dough: Split the vanilla bean in half (if using) and scrape out the seeds, then mix with the superfine sugar. Sift the flour directly onto a work surface, add the butter, and rub in with your fingertips until the mixture resembles fine bread crumbs. Make a well in the center of the mixture. Add the egg and pour in the vanilla sugar. Use your fingertips to combine all the ingredients, without kneading too much. Smooth out the dough with the palm of your hand, then shape it into a ball. Flatten it slightly between both hands, wrap it in plastic wrap, and let it rest for at least 30 minutes in the refrigerator.

2 Preheat the oven to 350°F. Grease ten to twelve 4-inch mini tart pans. Remove the dough from the refrigerator and roll it out to a thickness of 1⁄16 inch. Use the dough to line the pans. Prick the bottom of each pastry shell with a fork, cover with a piece of nonstick parchment paper, add some pie weights, and bake blind (*see page 475*) for 5 minutes. Remove the weights and paper and bake for another 5 minutes.

3 Prepare the caramel: Put the sugar and measured water into a heavy saucepan and bring to a boil over high heat. When the caramel starts to color at the edges, swirl the saucepan gently and regularly to mix it. Meanwhile, heat the cream in another saucepan. When the caramel darkens, carefully add the simmering cream. Whisk well. Remove from the heat and let cool, then stir in the butter, eggs, and salt. Whisk well.

4 Reduce the oven temperature to 300°F. Pour the caramel mixture into the bottom of the pastry shells and bake for 15–20 minutes. Let them cool, then refrigerate for 2 hours.

TIP

Be careful not to overcook the caramel, because this will make it bitter.

CHOCOLATE
tart

Serves 4–6

Preparation time: 15 minutes

Dough resting time: 30 minutes

Cooking time: 20–25 minutes

INGREDIENTS

FOR THE SWEET FLAKY PASTRY DOUGH

1 egg

⅓ cup confectioners' sugar

2 tablespoons ground almonds

A pinch of salt

¾ cup + 2 tablespoons all-purpose flour, plus extra for dusting

4 tablespoons unsalted butter, cut into small pieces

FOR THE GANACHE

9 oz semisweet chocolate, broken into pieces

1¼ cups heavy cream

1 Prepare the sweet flaky pastry dough: In a large bowl, whisk the egg using a fork. Add the confectioners' sugar, ground almonds, and salt. Stir vigorously with a wooden spoon until the mixture is frothy and pale.

2 Sift in all the flour and stir quickly with a spatula. Pick up small portions of the dough and flatten each one between your fingers. It should not stick together; it should crumble into small grains, like sand. Transfer the contents of the bowl onto a floured work surface. Sprinkle the pieces of butter over the dough, then knead by hand until the butter is mixed in. Shape the dough into a ball, wrap it in plastic wrap, and let it rest in the refrigerator for at least 30 minutes.

3 Preheat the oven to 340°F. Roll out the dough to a thickness of 1/16 inch. Use it to line an 8¾-inch round fluted tart pan. Prick the bottom with a fork, then cover it with nonstick parchment paper and add some pie weights. Bake for 20–25 minutes, removing the paper and weights after 10 minutes. Remove the tart shell from the oven and let cool.

4 Prepare the ganache: Put the chocolate into a large bowl. Bring the cream to a boil in a small saucepan and pour it over the chocolate. Cover the bowl for 5 minutes, then whisk well. Pour the mixture into the bottom of the tart. Place in the refrigerator until you are ready to serve.

TIP

The ganache can be used to ice a cake—beat it while it's still cold to lighten it. You can also flavor it with a liqueur of your choice, one tablespoon of instant coffee, or two pinches of grated tonka bean.

LEMON MERINGUE *mini tarts*

Makes 6 mini tarts	Preparation time: 35 minutes	Dough resting time: 30 minutes	Cooking time: 35–40 minutes

1½ sticks (6 oz) cold unsalted butter, plus extra, melted, for greasing

¾ cup + 1 tablespoon confectioners' sugar

3 unwaxed lemons

4 egg whites

5 eggs

1 tablespoon cornstarch

1 vanilla bean

1½ cups + 1½ tablespoons all-purpose flour, plus extra for dusting

1⅓ cups superfine sugar

INGREDIENTS

FOR THE PASTRY DOUGH

1 vanilla bean

⅓ cup superfine sugar

1½ cups + 1½ tablespoons all-purpose flour

1 stick (4 oz) cold unsalted butter, cut into pieces, plus extra for greasing

1 egg

FOR THE LEMON CREAM

3 unwaxed lemons

3½ tablespoons unsalted butter

4 eggs

1 cup superfine sugar

1 tablespoon cornstarch

1 tablespoon water

FOR THE MERINGUE

4 egg whites

¾ cup confectioners' sugar

1 Prepare the sweet flaky pastry dough: Split the vanilla bean in half and scrape out the seeds. In a bowl, mix the vanilla seeds with the superfine sugar.

2 Sift the flour directly onto a work surface. Add the butter and rub in with your fingertips until the mixture resembles fine bread crumbs.

3 Make a well in the center of the mixture. Break the egg into it and pour in the vanilla sugar mixture. Rub in with your fingertips until well combined, but without kneading too much.

4 Press the dough together, then shape into a ball. Wrap it in plastic wrap and let it rest for at least 30 minutes.

5 Brush 6 fluted mini tart pans (or a 10¼-inch round tart pan with a removable bottom) with the melted butter. Roll the dough out on a work surface using a rolling pin, cut out disks of the correct size, and use them to line the pans.

6 Preheat the oven to 400°F. Prepare the lemon cream: Zest the lemons. Squeeze out the lemon juice. In a small saucepan, melt the butter over low heat.

7 Whisk the eggs with the superfine sugar until the mixture is pale. Stir in the cornstarch diluted in the measured water, butter, and lemon juice and zest. Mix well.

8 Pour the lemon cream over the bottom of the dough. Bake the mini tarts for 35–40 minutes, then remove from the oven and let cool. Remove the mini tarts from the pan and put onto an ovenproof plate.

9 Prepare the meringue topping: Whip the egg whites into stiff peaks while gradually adding the confectioners' sugar.

10 Turn on the broiler to high. Spread the meringue over the mini tarts, using a spatula to create attractive peaks.

11 Slide the mini tarts under the broiler for 2–3 minutes, until they achieve a nice color (or lightly brown them with a chef's torch). Let the mini tarts cool before serving.

WHITE CHOCOLATE
mini tarts

Makes 10–12 mini tarts

Preparation time:
15 minutes

Dough resting time:
30 minutes

Cooking time:
35 minutes

Refrigeration time:
3 hours

INGREDIENTS

FOR THE SWEET FLAKY PASTRY DOUGH

2 cups all-purpose flour

1 stick + 3 tablespoons (5½ oz) unsalted butter, at room temperature, cut into small pieces, plus extra for greasing

1 egg

⅓ cup superfine sugar

FOR THE FILLING

8 oz white chocolate, broken into pieces

1¼ cups light cream

3 egg yolks

1 Prepare the sweet flaky pastry dough: Sift the flour directly onto a work surface, then add the butter. Rub in with your fingertips until the mixture resembles fine bread crumbs. Make a well in the center. Break an egg into it and add the superfine sugar. Use your fingertips to mix everything together, but without kneading too much. Smooth out the dough, shape it into a ball, flatten it slightly between your hands, and wrap it in plastic wrap. Let it rest for at least 30 minutes in the refrigerator.

2 Preheat the oven to 350°F. Grease 10–12 mini tart pans, 4 inches in diameter. Remove the pastry dough from the refrigerator and roll it out to a thickness of ¹⁄₁₆ inch. Line the pans with the dough. Prick the dough with a fork, cover with nonstick parchment paper, and fill with pie weights. Bake blind (*see* page 475) for 5 minutes. Remove the parchment paper and weights, then bake for another 5 minutes.

3 Prepare the filling: Put the chocolate into a large bowl. Bring the cream to a boil in a small saucepan and pour it over the chocolate. Cover for 5 minutes, then whisk well. Fold in the egg yolks while continuing to whisk.

4 Reduce the oven temperature to 250°F. Pour the chocolate mixture into the bottom of the prepared mini tart pans and bake for 25 minutes.

5 Let the mini tarts cool to room temperature before putting them into the refrigerator for at least 3 hours.

Serving suggestion

Dust the mini tarts with a little cocoa powder. Serve the mini tarts cold with mixed berries.

BANANA CHOCOLATE
tart

Serves 4–6

Preparation time: 10 minutes

Cooking time: 20 minutes

Refrigeration time: 2 hours

INGREDIENTS

1¾ tablespoons unsalted
butter, for greasing

1 sheet of ready-to-bake all-
butter puff pastry (about 8 oz)

FOR THE FILLING

6 oz bittersweet cooking
chocolate, broken into pieces

1¼ cups light cream

A handful of slivered almonds

3 bananas

1 Preheat the oven to 350° F. Grease a 6¼ × 12-inch rectangular tart pan. Unroll the dough, place it in the pan, peel away the paper, and fold the edges over. Prick the dough with a fork, replace the paper, then top it with pie weights. Bake for about 20 minutes, or until golden.

2 Prepare the filling: Put the chocolate into a large bowl. Bring the cream to a boil in a small saucepan and pour it over the chocolate. Cover for 5 minutes, then whisk well.

3 Lightly toast the almonds in a skillet while continuously stirring. Slice the bananas. Sprinkle two-thirds of the banana slices across the bottom of the precooked pastry, then pour the chocolate cream on top.

4 Decorate the top of the tart with the remaining banana slices and the toasted slivered almonds. Refrigerate for 2 hours before serving.

VARIATION

Do not be afraid to make this tart in a variety of shapes;
for example, you can use 6 small 3¼-inch pans to make mini tarts.

10 secrets OF A *successful tart*

1 Keep the ingredients in the refrigerator until just before preparing the dough, which should be kneaded as little as possible.

2 Let the dough rest in the refrigerator before rolling it out. This will make it less elastic and keep it from shrinking in the oven. It should rest for a minimum of 30 minutes, but it's even better to let it rest overnight.

3 Before rolling out dough that has just been refrigerated, let it rest at room temperature for 15 minutes; this will prevent it from cracking.

4 To prevent the dough from sticking to the work surface, flour your hands and the rolling pin instead of the dough. You can also roll it out between two sheets of nonstick parchment paper.

5 Never use porcelain pie plates; they will cause the bottom of the tart to become soggy.

6 After lining the pan with the dough, refrigerate it for 20 minutes (or freeze it for 10 minutes) before adding the filling.

7 Blind bake (*see* page 475) tart dough before adding a moist filling so that the bottom of the tart doesn't become soggy. For particularly liquid fillings, blind bake the dough twice: first for 10 minutes with pie weights, then for 5 minutes after having made it impermeable with an egg wash.

8 After baking, remove the tart from the pan and place it on a wire rack so that it cools without becoming soggy.

9 The best advice for removing a tart from the pan without problems—use a pan with a removable bottom.

10 To give fruit tarts a shiny look, brush them with a thin layer of slightly warmed apricot jam (without chunks) mixed with a little warm water.

BRAIDED EDGES

Let the dough spill over the edge of the pie pan by ¾ inch, then add the filling. Cut out ½-inch-wide strips of dough using a pastry wheel or pizza cutter. Braid them around the edge of the pie pan. Fold the excess dough around the perimeter, forming folds every ¾–1¼ inches.

PATTERNED EDGE

Cut the dough from the edge of the dish to remove the excess. Cut out shapes of your choice and arrange them around the edge of the tart dish, fastening them with beaten egg whites as you go.

THE FINISHES THAT MAKE ALL THE
difference

Let the final touch on your tart **"wow"** your guests. You'll need a tart pan with a flat edge and a second store-bought rolled sheet of dough, or an additional half portion of dough if you're making it from scratch.

CRENELLATED EDGE

Cut the dough from the edge of the dish to remove the excess. Cut out every other ½ inch of dough. Fold each resulting strip of dough back onto itself.

RIPPLED EDGE

Roll out the first sheet of dough onto a pie plate. Add the filling. Cut out ½-inch-wide strips from a second sheet of dough. Weave the strips above and below each other over the tart.

FLAVORED
pastry

Flavoring pastry dough adds complexity to a tart. Here are some flavoring ideas:

- **Cinnamon, ginger, or allspice** (especially good in fruit tarts).

- **Citrus zests** (lemon or lime, orange, grapefruit).

- **Cocoa powder** (for a chocolate or coffee tart).

- **Ground almonds or hazelnuts, dry coconut flakes** (great for any tart).

- 1–2 drops of **essential oils,** such as lemon oil, sweet orange, or lavender.

MASCARPONE
tart

Serves 6

Preparation time: 20 minutes

Dough resting time: 30 minutes

Cooking time: 40 minutes

INGREDIENTS

FOR THE FLAKY PASTRY DOUGH

1½ cups + 1½ tablespoons
all-purpose flour

A pinch of salt

2 tablespoons superfine
sugar (optional)

7 tablespoons cold unsalted
butter, cut into small pieces,
plus extra for greasing

5 tablespoons cold water

FOR THE CREAM

1 unwaxed lemon

4 eggs

½ cup superfine sugar

1 tablespoon vanilla
sugar (*see* page 13)

1 cup mascarpone cheese

½ cup ground almonds

1 Prepare the flaky pastry dough: Pour the flour into a large bowl. Make a well in the center and add the salt, superfine sugar (if using), and butter. Rub in with your fingertips until the mixture resembles fine bread crumbs. Add the measured water to bring the ingredients together, then work the mixture until you have a pliable dough. Shape it into a ball and let it rest for at least 30 minutes in the refrigerator.

2 Preheat the oven to 350°F. Grease an 11-inch round tart pan. Roll out the dough and use it to line the pan.

3 Prepare the cream: Zest the lemon. Set aside half the zest and chop the remainder into small pieces. In a large bowl, beat the eggs with the sugars until frothy, then fold in the mascarpone, chopped lemon zest, and ground almonds. Mix well.

4 Pour the mixture over the dough. Bake the tart for 40 minutes. Decorate the top of the tart with the reserved lemon zest and serve warm or cold.

VARIATION

Replace the mascarpone cheese with the same amount of cream cheese.

SAINT TROPEZ
tart

Serves 6

Preparation time: 45 minutes

Dough resting time: 3 hours

Cooking time: 40 minutes

INGREDIENTS

½ small (⅔ oz) cake fresh yeast or
1¾ teaspoons active dry yeast

2 tablespoons milk, slightly warmed

1½ cups + 1½ tablespoons
all-purpose flour

3 eggs

2 tablespoons superfine sugar

2 tablespoons orange blossom water

4½ tablespoons unsalted butter, at
room temperature, cut into small
pieces, plus extra for greasing

A pinch of salt

2½ tablespoons granulated sugar

FOR THE CRÈME PÂTISSIÈRE

1 vanilla bean

2 cups milk

3 egg yolks

⅓ cup superfine sugar

½ cup all-purpose flour

FOR THE BUTTERCREAM

1 egg yolk

2 tablespoons superfine sugar

1 teaspoon water

1 stick (4 oz) unsalted butter, at
room temperature, cut into pieces

1 Dissolve the yeast in the warm milk, then add ⅓ cup of the flour. Set aside in a warm place for 1 hour. Sift the remaining flour into a large bowl, make a well in the center, and pour in 2 beaten eggs, the superfine sugar, orange blossom water, butter, and salt. Work the dough with your hands, then mix in the yeast. Knead for 10–15 minutes, shape the dough into a ball, and let it rest in a warm place for at least 2 hours.

2 Preheat the oven to 350°F. Grease an 11-inch round tart pan. Roll out the dough and use it to line the pan. Beat the remaining egg and brush over the dough. Sprinkle the granulated sugar on top and bake for 30 minutes.

3 Prepare the crème pâtissière: Split the vanilla bean in half lengthwise and scrape out the seeds. Pour the milk into a saucepan and add the vanilla bean and seeds. Bring to a boil and remove from the heat. Let it cool, leaving the bean in place. Meanwhile, in a large bowl, whisk the egg yolks with the superfine sugar for 2 minutes. Pour in the flour and beat until smooth.

4 Remove the vanilla bean from the milk and pour the milk into the large bowl, stirring constantly. Return the mixture to the saucepan and let it thicken over medium heat, while continuing to stir, for 5 minutes. Remove the pan from the heat and let cool.

5 Prepare the buttercream: Beat the egg yolk. In a small saucepan, heat the superfine sugar and measured water until simmering. Immediately pour this syrup onto the egg yolk while beating continuously, then gradually mix in the butter. Stir for a few minutes. Gradually add the crème pâtissière to the buttercream.

6 Remove the cake from the pan and cut it in half horizontally. Spread the combined creams over the bottom half, then cover with the top half of the cake. Serve cold.

VARIATION

Replace the buttercream with ⅔ cup heavy cream whisked
with a teaspoon of vanilla sugar (*see* page 13).

PARISIAN
flan

Serves 6–8

Preparation time:
30 minutes

Dough resting time:
30 minutes

Cooking time:
1¼ hours

Refrigeration time:
3 hours

INGREDIENTS

FOR THE FLAKY PASTRY DOUGH

1½ cups + 1½ tablespoons
all-purpose flour

A pinch of salt

2 tablespoons superfine
sugar (optional)

7 tablespoons cold unsalted
butter, cut into small pieces,
plus extra for greasing

5 tablespoons cold water

FOR THE CREAM

1⅔ cups milk

1½ cups + 1 tablespoon water

4 eggs

1 cup + 1 tablespoon
superfine sugar

¼ cup store-bought flan mix

1 Prepare the flaky pastry dough: Pour the flour into a large bowl, make a well in the center, and add the salt, sugar (if using), and butter. Rub in with your fingertips until the mixture resembles fine bread crumbs. Add the measured water to bring the ingredients together, then work the mixture until you have a pliable dough. Shape it into a ball, wrap it in plastic wrap, and let it rest in the refrigerator for at least 30 minutes.

2 Preheat the oven to 375°F. Grease an 8¾-inch round tart pan. Roll out the dough to a thickness of 1⁄16 inch, use it to line the pan, and refrigerate.

3 Meanwhile, prepare the cream: Heat the milk and measured water in a saucepan. In another saucepan, beat the eggs, superfine sugar, and flan mix, then gradually pour the mixture into the boiling water and milk, stirring continuously, with a whisk. Wait for the mixture to come to a boil again before removing the saucepan from the heat. Pour the mixture into the prepared tart and bake for 1 hour.

4 Let the flan cool before refrigerating it for 3 hours.

ORANGE
cheesecake

Serves 6	Preparation time: 30 minutes	Cooking time: 5 minutes	Refrigeration time: 4 hours

¾ cup + 1½ tablespoons
heavy cream

2 cups cream cheese

1 unwaxed orange,
plus extra orange
slices to decorate

5 tablespoons
unsalted butter

4½ oz butter
cookies

2 eggs

3 gelatin
sheets

⅓ cup superfine
sugar

1 Prepare the crust: Melt the butter over low heat.

2 Break the cookies into pieces, put the pieces into a blender to reduce them to crumbs, and mix the crumbs in with the butter.

3 Place a pastry ring, 8 inches in diameter and 1¼–1½ inches deep, onto a round serving dish. Pour in the crust mixture, then use a spatula to pack it in tightly. Refrigerate.

4 Prepare the filling: Soak the gelatin sheets in warm water.

5 Zest the orange and chop the zest into pieces.

6 Squeeze the orange and heat the juice in a small saucepan.

7 Wring the gelatin sheets between your hands, add them to the saucepan, and let them slowly dissolve.

8 Separate the egg whites from the yolks. Whisk together the egg yolks, sugar, and orange zest.

9 Add the cream cheese, heavy cream, and orange juice. Whisk until the mixture is smooth and even.

10 Whip the egg whites into soft peaks, then carefully fold them into the orange juice mixture.

11 Pour the filling into the pastry ring and refrigerate for at least 4 hours. Serve chilled with orange slices on top.

BAKED VANILLA
cheesecake

Serves 6

Preparation time:
20 minutes

Cooking time:
1¼ hours

Refrigeration time:
12 hours

INGREDIENTS

Fresh fruit or a fruit
coulis, to serve

FOR THE CRUST

5 oz butter cookies or
speculoos (1½ cups crumbs)

4 tablespoons unsalted butter,
at room temperature

FOR THE FILLING

3 eggs

⅓ cup superfine sugar

1½ teaspoons vanilla
sugar (*see* page 13)

2 cups cream cheese

⅔ cup heavy cream

1 vanilla bean

1 The day before, preheat the oven to 250°F. Prepare the cheesecake crust: Crush the cookies into crumbs, then mix them with the butter. Use your fingers to press the mixture into a 7–8-inch springform pan, pushing it up against the sides as much as possible. Refrigerate.

2 Prepare the filling: In a large bowl, beat the eggs, superfine sugar, and vanilla sugar until frothy. Fold in the cream cheese and cream. Split the vanilla bean in half, scrape out the seeds, and add them to the bowl. Stir until creamy.

3 Pour the batter into the pan. Bake for 1¼ hours, making sure the cheesecake doesn't brown.

4 Let the cheesecake cool at room temperature before refrigerating overnight. Remove the springform ring just before serving. Serve chilled with fresh fruit or a fruit coulis.

TIP

Don't use a pastry ring or a regular tart pan with a removable bottom. Only a hinged springform pan can prevent the mixture from escaping. Resting overnight is essential to let the cheesecake become creamy.

APPLE
crisp

Serves 6

Preparation time: 20 minutes

Cooking time: 45 minutes

INGREDIENTS

Crème fraîche, to serve (optional)

FOR THE CRUMB TOPPING

1 cup all-purpose flour

6½ tablespoons unsalted butter, at room temperature, cut into pieces, plus extra for greasing

⅓ cup + 1 tablespoon superfine sugar

A pinch of salt

FOR THE FILLING

10 apples (about 3¼ lb), peeled, cored, and diced

2 tablespoons raisins (optional)

½ teaspoon ground cinnamon

1 Prepare the crumb topping: Pour the flour into a bowl and add the butter, superfine sugar, and salt. Rub in with your fingertips until the mixture resembles fine bread crumbs.

2 Preheat the oven to 300°F. Generously grease a baking dish. Sprinkle the apple across the bottom of the greased dish. Add the raisins (if using), sprinkle the cinnamon on top, then cover the fruit with the crumb topping

3 Bake for 45 minutes, making sure the surface does not brown too much. Serve the apple crisp hot, in its baking dish, with a scoop of crème fraîche, if using.

APPLE AND RASPBERRY
crisp

Serves 6

Preparation time: 15 minutes

Cooking time: 30–40 minutes

INGREDIENTS

6 tablespoons unsalted butter, cut into pieces, plus extra for greasing

5–6 apples, peeled, cored, and coarsely diced

4 cups raspberries

½ cup packed light brown sugar

¾ cup all-purpose flour

Crème fraîche, to serve

1 Preheat the oven to 350°F. Grease an 11–12-inch-long oven dish and place the apples in the bottom. Add the raspberries on top.

2 Combine the sugar and flour in a bowl, then add the butter. Rub in with your fingertips until the mixture resembles fine bread crumbs. Sprinkle the crumb topping over the apple-and-raspberry mixture and bake for 30–40 minutes. Serve warm or cold with crème fraîche.

Crèmes & mousses

MINI CREAM
cups

Serves 6

Preparation time: 10 minutes

Cooking time: 10 minutes

Refrigeration time: 3 hours

INGREDIENTS

2 cups milk

1 vanilla bean

1 cup superfine sugar

2 eggs + 6 yolks

2 cups heavy cream

1 Pour the milk into a saucepan. Split the vanilla bean in half lengthwise and add it to the milk. Bring to a boil, then remove from the heat and let stand for a few minutes to infuse.

2 Meanwhile, beat the sugar with the whole eggs and egg yolks until dissolved. Incorporate the cream. Remove the vanilla bean from the milk, then slowly pour the egg mixture into the saucepan.

3 Put the saucepan over low heat and stir until the mixture has thickened. When the cream coats the back of a spoon, pour it into 6 small cups and refrigerate for at least 3 hours before serving.

VARIATION

You can also flavor this cream with coffee or chocolate. Dilute cocoa powder
in the milk (1 tablespoon per cup) or instant coffee in a little water (1 teaspoon
per cup). Add these flavors to the cream as you pour it into the cup.

VANILLA
pudding

Serves 4–6

Preparation time: 20 minutes

Cooking time: 40 minutes

INGREDIENTS

1 vanilla bean
4¼ cups whole milk
⅔ cup superfine sugar
4 eggs

1 Split the vanilla bean in half lengthwise and scrape out the seeds. Bring the milk and sugar to a boil, then add the vanilla bean and seeds.

2 Preheat the oven to 400°F. In a large bowl, beat the eggs thoroughly with a whisk.

3 Remove the vanilla bean from the milk. Gradually add the boiling milk to the eggs, stirring continuously.

4 Pour the mixture into 4–6 ovenproof ramekins, about 3¼–4 inches in diameter. Place in a bain-marie (*see* page 494) and bake for 40 minutes. Make sure the pudding is cooked through by piercing it with a knife; the knife should come out clean. Let it cool and keep refrigerated until serving.

CRÈME
caramel

Serves 4-6

Preparation time:
25 minutes (over 2 days)

Steeping time:
12 hours

Cooking time:
45 minutes

Refrigeration time:
12 hours

INGREDIENTS

1 vanilla bean
4¼ cups whole milk
4 eggs + 3 egg yolks
1 cup superfine sugar

FOR THE CARAMEL
¼ cup water
½ cup superfine sugar
A few drops of lemon juice

1 Split the vanilla bean in half lengthwise and scrape out the seeds. Bring the milk to a boil and add the vanilla bean and seeds. Refrigerate and steep for 12 hours. Remove the vanilla bean and bring the milk to a boil again.

2 In a large bowl, whisk the whole eggs and egg yolks with the superfine sugar for 30 seconds. While continuing to stir, add the boiling milk. Strain and let rest while you prepare the caramel.

3 Preheat the oven to 265°F. Prepare the caramel: In a heavy saucepan, bring the measured water, superfine sugar, and lemon juice to a boil over high heat. When the caramel starts to color around the edges, gently and rhythmically swirl the saucepan to mix the contents. When the caramel has browned, quickly use it to lightly coat 4-6 ramekins. Divide the contents of the large bowl evenly among the ramekins. Place in a bain-marie (*see* page 494) and bake for 45 minutes.

4 Let the crème caramels cool to room temperature, then cover and refrigerate for 12 hours.

5 Carefully remove the caramels from the ramekins, running the point of a sharp knife around the edge of each one to loosen it. Turn out the crème caramels onto a serving dish. Serve cold.

VARIATION

You can make this in a single soufflé mold; just cook for 1 hour 10 minutes.

CRÈME
brûlée

Serves 4

**Preparation time:
20 minutes**

Cooking time: 1 hour

**Refrigeration time:
4 hours**

INGREDIENTS

1 vanilla bean
1 cup milk
1¼ cups heavy cream
4 egg yolks
⅓ cup superfine sugar

FOR THE CARAMEL

3 tablespoons packed
light brown sugar

1 Split the vanilla bean in half lengthwise and scrape out the seeds. Pour the milk and cream into a heavy saucepan and add the vanilla bean and seeds. Bring to a boil, then remove from the heat and let stand.

2 Preheat the oven to 215°F. In a large bowl, beat the egg yolks and superfine sugar. Add the contents of the saucepan and whisk again. Divide the cream mixture among 4 ovenproof porcelain ramekins. Place in a bain-marie (*see* page 494) and bake for 1 hour.

3 Let the crème brûlées cool completely before refrigerating for at least 4 hours (you could even make them the night before).

4 Turn on the broiler to high. Sprinkle brown sugar on top of the crèmes and caramelize them by placing them under the broiler for a few minutes, monitoring continuously. Serve warm or cold.

TIP

You can caramelize the crèmes with a chef's torch, which can be found in most kitchen stores, or a blowtorch, which is sold in DIY stores.

VARIATION

For an even richer crème brûlée, replace part
or all of the milk with heavy cream.

DARK CHOCOLATE
crème brûlée

Serves 8

**Preparation time:
15 minutes**

Cooking time: 1 hour

Refrigeration time: 12 hours

INGREDIENTS

FOR THE CRÈME BRÛLÉE

8 egg yolks

¾ cup + 2 tablespoons
superfine sugar

2 cups whole milk

2 cups heavy cream

7 oz bittersweet chocolate
(70 percent cocoa solids),
coarsely chopped

FOR THE CARAMEL

3 tablespoons packed
light brown sugar

1 The day before, prepare the crème brûlée: Beat together the egg yolks and superfine sugar. Bring the milk and cream to a boil in a saucepan. Add the chocolate. When the mixture is smooth, pour it over the egg-and-sugar mixture and mix well.

2 Preheat the oven to 215°F. Divide the cream among 8 ovenproof porcelain ramekins. Place in a bain-marie (*see* page 494) and bake for 1 hour. Let them cool before refrigerating overnight.

3 The following day, remove the crèmes from the refrigerator and turn on the broiler to high. Sprinkle the brown sugar over the crèmes and caramelize by placing them under the broiler for a few minutes, monitoring continuously. Serve warm or cold.

FLOATING
islands

| Serves 4 | Preparation time: 20 minutes | Cooking time: 30 minutes | Refrigeration time: 40 minutes |

1 vanilla
bean

8 eggs

3⅓ cups milk

A pinch
of salt

1¾ cups superfine
sugar

Lemon juice or white
wine vinegar

INGREDIENTS

8 eggs

A pinch of salt

1¼ cups superfine sugar

3⅓ cups milk

1 vanilla bean

FOR THE CARAMEL

½ cup superfine sugar

2 tablespoons water

Lemon juice or
white wine vinegar

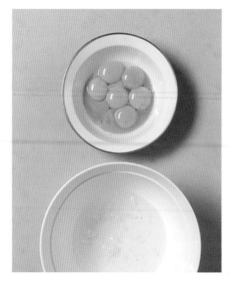

1 Preheat the oven to 350°F. Separate the egg whites from the egg yolks.

2 Whip the egg whites into stiff peaks with the pinch of salt. Gradually add ¼ cup of the sugar.

3 Pour the egg whites into an 8¾-inch fluted Bundt pan or, if unavailable, a round pan. Place the pan in a baking pan filled with warm water.

4 Bake in the oven for 30 minutes, until the top begins to brown. Let cool completely.

5 Meanwhile, prepare the crème anglaise: In a large bowl, beat the egg yolks and remaining 1 cup of sugar until the mixture is pale.

6 Split the vanilla bean in half lengthwise and scrape out the seeds. Bring the milk and vanilla bean and seeds to a boil in a small saucepan. Carefully pour the boiling milk over the egg-and-sugar mixture, stirring continuously.

7 Reheat the mixture over low heat without letting it boil, stirring continuously with a wooden spoon until thickened. Remove the vanilla bean.

8 Pour the mixture into 4 cups and refrigerate for about 40 minutes, until completely cooled.

9 Remove the cooked egg whites from the pan, cut into pieces, and place on top of the crème anglaise in the cups.

10 Prepare the caramel: Melt the sugar, the measured water, and a little lemon juice or white wine vinegar over low heat, then slightly increase the heat.

11 When the syrup starts to boil, lift the saucepan and swirl it every so often. Drizzle the caramel, still boiling, over the cooked egg whites. Refrigerate until you're ready to serve.

ZABAGLIONE

Serves 4

Preparation time: 15 minutes

Cooking time: 2–3 minutes

INGREDIENTS

4 egg yolks

⅓ cup superfine sugar

1 cup dry white wine
(or champagne)

Rind of 1 unwaxed lemon,
removed in strips

Cookies or fresh fruit, to serve

1 In a heat-resistant bowl, mix together the egg yolks, superfine sugar, wine, and lemon rind. Place the bowl over a slightly simmering bain-marie (*see* page 494) and beat vigorously by hand or with an electric mixer until the mixture becomes frothy and doubles in volume. The water shouldn't touch the bottom of the bowl.

2 Remove the bowl from the bain-marie and whisk for another 30 seconds. Remove the lemon rind and serve immediately in cups or glasses. Pair with cookies or fresh fruit.

Serving
suggestion
———
This Italian cream can be
served as an accompaniment
or topping for puddings,
rice desserts, poached
fruit, or ice cream.

VARIATION
———
You can also prepare the zabaglione with a sweet wine, such
as a Sauternes or Marsala, with port, or with a mixture of
white wine and liqueur (Armagnac, cognac, rum).

BLANCMANGE

Serves 4–6 | Preparation time: 20 minutes (over 2 days) | Almond milk resting time: 12 hours | Refrigeration time: 4–5 hours

INGREDIENTS

6 gelatin sheets

1 drop bitter almond extract

½ cup superfine sugar

1⅔ cups cold heavy cream

1¾ cups mixed berries of your choice, to serve

FOR THE ALMOND MILK

1 cup water

1½ cups ground almonds

1 The day before, prepare the almond milk: Bring the measured water and ground almonds to a boil in a saucepan. Blend the mixture with a handheld immersion blender while still hot, then filter it using a fine mesh strainer, pressing down with a spatula to extract all the milk. Refrigerate overnight.

2 The following day, soften the gelatin sheets in a bowl of cold water for 10 minutes, then drain.

3 In a small saucepan, heat one-quarter of the almond milk. Add the bitter almond extract and gelatin sheets, mix well to melt them completely, then pour the contents of the saucepan into the rest of the almond milk and stir. Add the superfine sugar and mix until dissolved.

4 Whip the cream to soft peaks, then carefully add it to the mixture using a rubber spatula. Pour this mixture into a 7-inch round charlotte cake pan or 4–6 molds and refrigerate for 4–5 hours.

5 Briefly submerge the pan or individual molds in hot water, then turn over the blancmange onto a serving dish. Decorate it with mixed berries before serving.

TIP

Don't add more than one drop of bitter almond extract, because this would give the dessert an unpleasant flavor.

Serve the blancmange with a mixed berry coulis (*see* page 488) or a peach coulis.

Serving
suggestion

VARIATION

Replace the almond milk with coconut milk and the bitter
almond extract with a pinch of ground ginger.

COCONUT AND RED BERRY
panna cotta

Serves 4

Preparation time: 30 minutes

Cooking time: 5 minutes

Refrigeration time: 4 hours

INGREDIENTS

3 gelatin sheets

¾ cup + 2 tablespoons coconut milk

1 cup light cream

¼ cup superfine sugar

1 vanilla bean

FOR THE COULIS

3¼ cups red berries of your choice—one type or a mixture (strawberries, red currants, raspberries, or wild strawberries)

⅓ cup confectioners' sugar

1 Soften the gelatin sheets by soaking them in a bowl of cold water for about 10 minutes.

2 Pour the coconut milk, cream, and sugar into a saucepan. Split the vanilla bean lengthwise and scrape out the seeds with a small knife. Add the seeds to the saucepan, mix well, and bring the contents to a boil. Remove from the heat, cover, and let rest for a few minutes to infuse.

3 Drain the gelatin sheets, then add them to the saucepan. Mix well. Pour the mixture into 4 glasses and refrigerate for 4 hours.

4 Prepare the coulis: Hull the strawberries and stem the red currants, if using. Pulse the fruit in a blender with the confectioners' sugar, then strain using a fine mesh strainer. Thin the coulis with a little water, if necessary (depending on the type of fruit used). Divide the coulis among the 4 glasses of panna cotta, decorate with red berries, and serve cold.

VARIATION

You can replace the red berries with mango.

RICE AND CARAMEL
cake

Serves 4–6

Preparation time: 30 minutes

Cooking time: 1 hour 20 minutes

INGREDIENTS

FOR THE RICE PUDDING

1 vanilla bean

3¾ cups whole milk

⅓ cup superfine sugar

½ cup short-grain rice

3½ tablespoons unsalted butter

3 eggs

A pinch of salt

FOR THE CARAMEL

¼ cup cold water

⅔ cup superfine sugar

A few drops of lemon juice

¼ cup hot water

1 Prepare the rice pudding: Split the vanilla bean in half lengthwise. In a large, heavy saucepan, bring the milk, split vanilla bean, superfine sugar, and rice to a boil. Reduce the heat, cover, and simmer gently for 30–40 minutes. When the rice is cooked, add the butter and stir, then let cool.

2 Separate the egg whites from the yolks. Remove the vanilla bean from the rice and add the egg yolks, mixing well. Whip the egg whites into stiff peaks with the salt, then gradually fold them into the rice.

3 Preheat the oven to 400°F. Prepare the caramel: Pour the measured cold water and the superfine sugar into a heavy saucepan. Add the lemon juice and boil over high heat. When the caramel starts to brown at the edges, gently and rhythmically swirl the saucepan to mix the contents. When the caramel is golden, pour half of it into an 8-inch fluted charlotte pan, turning the pan to distribute the caramel evenly on all sides.

4 Reheat the rest of the caramel, add the measured hot water, and boil for 2 minutes, until liquid. Let cool.

5 Pour the rice mixture into the pan and pack it in tightly. Place it in the oven in a bain-marie (*see* page 494) with hot water. Bake for 45 minutes.

6 Let the cake cool, then remove it from the pan and place it on a serving dish. Pour the liquid caramel over the cake.

CITRUS
rice pudding

Serves 4 | Preparation time: 30 minutes | Cooking time: 40 minutes

INGREDIENTS

FOR THE CITRUS PEEL

2 unwaxed oranges

1 unwaxed grapefruit

¾ cup + 2 tablespoons water

½ cup packed light brown sugar

FOR THE RICE PUDDING

1 vanilla bean

4¼ cups whole milk

½ cup superfine sugar

½ short-grain rice

2 egg yolks

FOR THE WHIPPED CREAM

⅔ cup cold heavy cream

1 Prepare the citrus peel: Remove the orange and grapefruit rinds without cutting into the pith. Chop into thin slivers. Submerge these in a saucepan of boiling water for 2 minutes, then drain. Change the water in the saucepan, bring it to a boil, and repeat the process. Drain the citrus peel.

2 Slowly bring the measured water to a boil in a saucepan with the brown sugar, stirring until the sugar is completely dissolved. Submerge the citrus peel in this syrup, simmer for 10 minutes, then remove them with a slotted spoon. Let cool before chopping them into small pieces.

3 Prepare the rice pudding: Split the vanilla bean in half lengthwise. In a large, heavy saucepan, bring the milk to a boil with the split vanilla bean, superfine sugar, and rice. Reduce the heat, cover, and cook gently for 30–40 minutes. Let it cool, then add the egg yolks. Mix well. Let the mixture cool completely.

4 Prepare the whipped cream: Whip the cream to soft peaks. Carefully mix it in with the candied citrus peel (reserving some for decoration) and rice, then pour the dessert into a large bowl. Refrigerate until you're ready to serve. Sprinkle with the reserved citrus peel pieces before serving.

RASPBERRY TAPIOCA
pudding

Serves 4

Preparation time: 20 minutes

Cooking time: 20 minutes

Refrigeration time: 3 hours

INGREDIENTS

2⅓ cups almond milk
2 tablespoons agave syrup
⅓ cup tapioca pearls
¾ cup slivered almonds
1⅔ cups raspberries

1 Heat the almond milk and agave syrup in a small saucepan. When the mixture is hot, add the tapioca pearls and cook over low heat for about 20 minutes, until the tapioca is translucent and the mixture has thickened.

2 Toast the almonds in a skillet.

3 Remove the tapioca from the heat and carefully add the raspberries and slivered almonds to the saucepan, reserving some of each for decoration. Pour the cream mixture into small glasses and refrigerate for 3 hours. Just before serving, sprinkle the reserved slivered almonds and raspberries on top.

THE TOP 8

quick + easy

RECIPES

POUND CAKE
PAGE 18

PAGE 88

**EXTRA-CHOCOLATY
CHOCOLATE CAKE**

**PINEAPPLE UPSIDE-DOWN
CAKE**
PAGE 68

4

DOUBLE CHOCOLATE MUFFINS
PAGE 372

5

DRIED FRUIT MENDIANTS
PAGE 380

6

RASPBERRY AND PISTACHIO FINANCIERS
PAGE 382

7

FRENCH BUTTER COOKIES
PAGE 416

8

MERINGUE WITH BERRIES AND CREAM
PAGE 238

ORANGE AND RAISIN
semolina cake

Serves 4

Preparation time: 25 minutes

Cooking time: 20 minutes

INGREDIENTS

½ cup raisins

A drizzle of orange blossom water

4¼ cups whole milk

1 cup superfine sugar

¾ cup fine semolina flour

3 eggs

1 Soften the raisins in the orange blossom water. Heat the milk with ½ cup of the sugar, then immediately pour in all the semolina flour and whisk without stopping until the mixture has thickened. Beat the eggs and add them to the semolina. Mix in the raisins and orange blossom water.

2 Preheat the oven to 350°F. Heat the remaining sugar in a saucepan with a few drops of water, then let it caramelize. Pour the caramel into an 8¾-inch charlotte mold, making sure it coats the sides.

3 Pour in the semolina mixture and bake for 20 minutes. Let the cake cool, then remove it from the mold.

RICE
pudding

Serves 6–8

Preparation time: 30 minutes

Cooking time: 55–65 minutes

INGREDIENTS

4¼ cups milk

½ cup superfine sugar

½ vanilla bean

A pinch of salt

¾ cup short-grain rice

3½ tablespoons unsalted butter, plus extra for greasing

6 eggs

⅓ cup fine bread crumbs

1 Preheat the oven to 425°F. In an ovenproof saucepan, heat the milk with the superfine sugar, vanilla bean, and a pinch of salt. Add the rice and butter, stir, and slowly bring to a boil. Cover, then place the saucepan in the oven and cook for 25–30 minutes.

2 Meanwhile, separate the egg whites from the yolks. Whip the egg whites into stiff peaks.

3 Remove the pan from the oven and gently stir in the egg yolks one by one. Then slowly incorporate the egg whites.

4 Reduce the oven temperature to 350°F. Grease an 8¾-inch round pan (or 6–8 ovenproof ramekins, about 3¼–4 inches in diameter) and sprinkle with bread crumbs. Pour the mixture into the pan or ramekins, place in a bain-marie (*see* page 494), and bake for 30–35 minutes (20–25 minutes for the ramekins).

Serving suggestion

This pudding can be served with a mixed berry coulis (*see* page 488).

VARIATION

To make a chocolate rice pudding, add ¾ cup grated semisweet chocolate to the rice pudding when you remove it from the oven the first time, then mix well until the chocolate has melted.

RASPBERRY
mousse

Serves 4

Preparation time: 15 minutes

Refrigeration time: 2 hours

INGREDIENTS

2 gelatin sheets

⅔ cup cold heavy cream

1⅔ cups raspberries, plus extra
for decorating

⅔ cup confectioners' sugar

1 Soak the gelatin sheets in cold water for 5–10 minutes. Meanwhile, using an electric mixer, whip the cold cream to soft peaks. Mix the raspberries with the confectioners' sugar.

2 Squeeze out the gelatin and place in the microwave for 20 seconds to melt. Mix it into the raspberry coulis.

3 Gently mix the whipped cream with the raspberry coulis and divide among individual serving cups or bowls. Cool for at least 2 hours in the refrigerator. Just before serving, decorate with fresh raspberries.

LIME
mousse

Serves 6

Preparation time: 30 minutes

Cooking time: 10 minutes

Refrigeration time: 4 hours

INGREDIENTS

4 unwaxed limes
6 eggs
½ cup superfine sugar
2 cups cold heavy cream
¾ cup confectioners' sugar
A pinch of salt

1 Finely grate the zest from the limes. Cut the limes in half, juice them, and pour the juice into a saucepan.

2 Separate the egg whites from the yolks.

3 Add the superfine sugar and lime zest to the saucepan (reserving some zest for decoration) and slowly bring to a boil. When the first bubbles appear, remove the saucepan from the heat and pour its contents onto the egg yolks, beating vigorously. Return the mixture to the saucepan and slowly heat it, stirring continuously, until thickened. Remove it from the heat and let cool.

4 Whip the cold cream into firm peaks until it sticks to the whisk. Add the confectioners' sugar, mix well, and carefully fold into the lime cream.

5 Whip the egg whites into stiff peaks with a pinch of salt. Carefully fold them into the prepared mixture, scooping as you stir so the mousse doesn't deflate.

6 Pour into a large bowl or into 6 smaller bowls. Refrigerate for 4 hours. Serve cold, decorated with the reserved lime zest.

CINNAMON AND BANANA
mousse

Serves 4

Preparation time: 10 minutes

Refrigeration time: 1 hour

INGREDIENTS

1 unwaxed lime

4 large, ripe bananas,
peeled and sliced

¼ cup mascarpone cheese

⅓ teaspoon ground cinnamon

3 egg whites

A pinch of salt

¼ cup superfine sugar

1 Juice the lime and drizzle it over the banana slices. Blend the bananas with the mascarpone cheese and cinnamon until finely pureed.

2 In a large bowl, whip the egg whites with a pinch of salt, adding the sugar halfway through. Continue whipping until the egg whites become firm and velvety. Use a rubber spatula to fold them into the puree carefully.

3 Divide the mousse among 4 small bowls and refrigerate for 1 hour. Serve cold.

VARIATION

To make a delicious banana and ginger mousse, replace the mascarpone with 3–4 tablespoons coconut milk and replace the cinnamon with the same quantity of ground ginger.

DOUBLE CHOCOLATE
mousse

Serves 4–6 | Preparation time: 15 minutes | Cooking time: 5 minutes | Refrigeration time: 4 hours

INGREDIENTS

1¾ oz bittersweet chocolate
(at least 60 percent cocoa
solids), broken into pieces

3½ oz milk chocolate,
broken into pieces

5¾ tablespoons unsalted
butter, cut into pieces

4 eggs

2½ tablespoons superfine sugar

⅓ cup + 1½ tablespoons
crème fraîche

1 Melt both chocolates and the butter in a saucepan over a bain-marie (*see* page 494) over low heat, stirring continuously, until the mixture is smooth. Remove it from the heat and let cool. The mixture should have the consistency of a smooth, thick cream.

2 Separate the egg whites from the yolks. Whip the egg whites into soft peaks, adding the sugar halfway through.

3 Add the egg yolks and crème fraîche to the melted chocolate. Mix well.

4 Quickly mix 2 tablespoons of the egg whites into the chocolate cream to lighten it. Carefully fold in the remaining egg whites, scooping as you stir to avoid deflating the mousse.

5 Pour the mixture into a large bowl, cover, and refrigerate for at least 4 hours.

pastry-making TIPS and shortcuts

1 FOLDING IN THE *egg whites*

Start by mixing one-quarter of the whipped egg whites into the mixture to soften it. Put some energy into the whisking. Add the rest of the egg whites in two or three stages with a spatula, folding from the center of the bowl and moving toward the edges. Stop folding when there are no more visible egg whites, otherwise the mixture may begin to lose volume.

2 WELL-DISTRIBUTED *filling*

Many cook books recommend adding flour when adding raisins, but this doesn't really make a difference. What does work is incorporating a filling (dried fruit, fruit pieces, chocolate chips) into the batter, then letting it rest for 30 minutes in the refrigerator. Next, transfer the batter to the greased and floured pan and bake immediately. As it bakes, the batter will start to set before the fruit has time to sink to the bottom.

3 A SUCCESSFUL *Chantilly cream*

The fat content in cream is what makes Chantilly set, so it's imperative that you use either heavy cream (35 percent fat content) or whipping cream (30 percent fat content). It also needs to be cold, as does the bowl. Put it into the freezer 15 minutes before use. For a firmer Chantilly that is dense and holds well, add a little mascarpone cheese (60 percent fat content); use 1 heaping tablespoon for 1¼–2 cups of cream. Whip everything in a cold bowl. When whipped, the cream will keep its texture for about 2 hours in the refrigerator.

Whipped cream or Chantilly cream?
Whipped cream is heavy cream that has been whisked to incorporate air. It's plain instead of sweet and is often added to other preparations, such as mousses. Chantilly cream is a sweetened whipped cream, which is used most often as a topping for desserts.

4 ROUNDED
madeleines

To give your madeleines a nice rounded shape, prepare the batter the day before and keep it refrigerated overnight, or for at least 2 hours. Grease your madeleine pans before pouring in the batter and quickly put them into the oven. The madeleines will rise due to the sudden change in temperature between the cold batter and the hot oven.

5 A NICE CRACK
in your cakes

As cakes bake, a random crack can form on top as the batter rises in the oven. To be sure you end up with a nice, centered and even crack, score the top of the cake with a knife after it's been baking for 10 minutes. Make sure you score it through the thin layer of film that has begun to form, then continue to bake the cake normally. The air in the cake will escape through the scored crack.

6 EASILY WHIPPED
egg whites

Egg whites are easier to whip when they are at room temperature. The eggs can also be kept for up to 4 days in a sealed container. Arm yourself with a large mixer. If the eggs are due to be cooked, it's best to separate the egg whites from the yolks 2–3 days ahead of time and store them in the refrigerator in sealed bowls. Egg whites "broken" by the cold will yield a smooth peak that won't spread out during baking.

7 A PERFECT
bake

For evenly and thoroughly baked cakes, cook them at a lower temperature than indicated and for longer. For example, for a cake that is supposed to be baked for 40 minutes at 350°F, try baking it at 325°F for 50–60 minutes. This way, the sides will be less dry and less cooked, and the middle will be baked to perfection.

CHOCOLATE MOUSSE
with candied orange peel

Serves 4

Preparation time: 15 minutes

**Cooking time:
about 15 minutes**

**Refrigeration time:
a minimum of 3 hours**

INGREDIENTS

1 unwaxed orange

⅔ cup superfine sugar

½ cup water

2 eggs

⅓ cup + 1½ tablespoons
light cream

6 oz semsiweet chocolate,
coarsely grated

A pinch of salt

1 Grate the zest from the orange and then squeeze out the juice. In a small saucepan, heat the orange juice with the sugar and the measured water. Add the zest (reserving some for decoration) and simmer for about 10 minutes, until the zest is translucent. Drain the zest.

2 Separate the egg whites from the yolks. Bring the cream to a boil in a saucepan, then pour it into a large bowl and add the chocolate. Stir briskly with a wooden spoon. When the chocolate is completely melted, add the egg yolks, one by one, stirring continuously until well combined.

3 Using an electric mixer, whip the egg whites to soft peaks with a pinch of salt. Fold them into the chocolate mixture, carefully scooping as you stir to avoid deflating the mousse. Add the orange zest. Pour the mousse into small ramekins and refrigerate for at least 3 hours. Decorate with the reserved orange zest before serving.

WHITE CHOCOLATE
mousse

Serves 4–6 | Preparation time: 10 minutes | Refrigeration time: 3 hours

INGREDIENTS

4 oz white chocolate,
coarsely chopped
1¾ cup cold heavy cream

1 Slowly melt the chocolate with ½ cup of the cream in a large bowl over a bain-marie (*see* page 494). The water shouldn't simmer or touch the bottom of the bowl.

2 Let the mixture cool to room temperature. In a bowl, whip the remaining cold cream. Gradually fold the whipped cream into the white chocolate, carefully scooping the mixture with a rubber spatula.

3 Pour the mousse into small cups or into a serving dish. Refrigerate for 3 hours.

Serving
suggestion

Enjoy this mousse with
a red berry coulis
(*see* page 488).

VARIATION

Add 1 tablespoon instant coffee diluted in 1 teaspoon
water to the cream or add 2 tablespoons Amaretto.

CHOCOLATE
marquise

Serves 4–6 | Preparation time: 20 minutes | Cooking time: 3–4 minutes | Refrigeration time: 12 hours

INGREDIENTS

3 eggs

7 oz semisweet chocolate, broken into small pieces

1 stick (4 oz) unsalted butter

A pinch of salt

⅔ cup confectioners' sugar

4–6 Cape gooseberries (ground cherries), to decorate

1 The day before, separate the egg whites from the yolks. Melt the chocolate and butter over a bain-marie (*see* page 494) or in the microwave.

2 Remove the bowl from the bain-marie and mix the contents well. Let it cool, then whisk in the egg yolks briskly.

3 Whip the egg whites into stiff peaks with the salt, adding the confectioners' sugar halfway through. Add to the chocolate mixture, carefully scooping the mixture with a rubber spatula as you stir.

4 Pour the mixture into ramekins or into a cake pan. Refrigerate the marquises for 12 hours before serving each decorated with a Cape gooseberry.

GRANDMA'S
chocolate pudding

Serves 6

Preparation time: 10 minutes

Cooking time: 25 minutes

Refrigeration time: 2 hours

INGREDIENTS

6 egg yolks

¾ cup superfine sugar

1 tablespoon cornstarch

1¾ cups milk

1½ cups light cream

1 cup shaved or grated
semisweet chocolate

1 teaspoon vanilla extract

1 In a heavy saucepan, whisk the egg yolks with the sugar until the mixture becomes frothy and light. Add the cornstarch, then the milk and cream while continuing to stir.

2 Put the saucepan over low heat and stir the cream constantly until thickened, without letting it boil.

3 Remove from the heat and add the chocolate and vanilla extract. Mix well. Pour the cream into serving cups. Let them cool, cover, and refrigerate for at least 2 hours.

Serving suggestion

Sprinkle shelled, chopped, and lightly toasted pistachios on the top of each pudding.

CHOCOLATE CHESTNUT
verrines

Makes 4–6 verrines

Preparation time: 15 minutes

Cooking time: 3 minutes

INGREDIENTS

4 small store-bought meringue shells, broken into small pieces

FOR THE CHOCOLATE SAUCE

3½ oz bittersweet chocolate (70 percent cocoa solids), coarsely chopped

⅓ cup + 1½ tablespoons heavy cream

FOR THE CHESTNUT CREAM

¾ cup + 1½ tablespoons chestnut cream

⅓ cup + 1½ tablespoons heavy cream

1 Prepare the chocolate sauce: Put the chocolate into a bowl. Bring the cream to a boil in a saucepan, then immediately pour it over the chocolate. Cover for 5 minutes, then whisk well.

2 Prepare the chestnut cream: Using a spatula, vigorously stir the chestnut cream to soften it. Whip the heavy cream into stiff peaks. Carefully fold it into the chestnut cream, without mixing too well, to achieve a marbled effect.

3 Sprinkle the meringue in the bottom of 4–6 small glasses, each with a volume of ½–⅔ cup. Pour in the chocolate sauce, then top with the chestnut cream.

TIP

For added effect, fill the glasses by piping in the chestnut cream.

TIRAMISU

Serves 8

Preparation time: 15 minutes

Refrigeration time: 4 hours

INGREDIENTS

6 eggs

6 tablespoons superfine sugar

2 cups mascarpone cheese

16 ladyfingers

1 cup strong coffee

½ cup Marsala

3 tablespoons unsweetened
cocoa powder

1 Separate the egg whites from the yolks. Whip the egg whites into stiff peaks, gradually adding the sugar halfway through. Whisk the yolks with the mascarpone, then combine the mixtures carefully using a rubber spatula.

2 Dip the ladyfingers into the coffee and Marsala before arranging them across the bottom of individual cups or a large bowl. Cover them with the mascarpone mixture and refrigerate for at least 4 hours.

3 Dust the top with the cocoa powder just before serving.

VARIATION

Replace the Marsala with a coffee liqueur.

Fruit
desserts

CHERRY
clafoutis

| Serves 6 | Preparation time: 15 minutes | Maceration time: 30 minutes | Cooking time: 35–40 minutes |

INGREDIENTS

3⅔ cups pitted black cherries

½ cup superfine sugar

Butter for greasing

⅔ cup all-purpose flour

A pinch of salt

3 eggs

1¼ cups milk

Confectioners' sugar

1 In a large bowl, mix the cherries with ¼ cup of the superfine sugar and let them macerate for at least 30 minutes.

2 Preheat the oven to 350°F. Grease a 9½-inch-long rectangular baking dish or an ovenproof porcelain cake pan.

3 Sift the flour into a large bowl and add the remaining sugar and a pinch of salt. Break the eggs into the middle of the bowl and add the milk. Whisk well.

4 Distribute the cherries across the bottom of the baking dish, then pour in the batter. Bake for 35–40 minutes.

5 Remove the clafoutis from the oven. Let it cool, then dust the top with confectioners' sugar. Serve warm or cold in the baking dish.

VARIATION

You can make the same clafoutis with Mirabelle plums.
Add 2 tablespoons plum brandy to the mixture.

BAKED APPLES
with pistachios

Serves 6 | Preparation time: 15 minutes | Cooking time: 30 minutes

INGREDIENTS

6 apples
¾ cup chopped pistachios
6 teaspoons honey
A little butter

1 Preheat the oven to 350°F. Wash the apples and, using a small knife, dig out a hole in the top of each one. Place the apples in a large ovenproof dish with some water in the bottom.

2 Fill the center of each apple with chopped pistachios and 1 teaspoon of honey. Bake for 30 minutes. Halfway through cooking, baste the apples with the juices from the bottom of the dish and place a dollop of butter on top of each apple to make them caramelize.

APRICOT PEACH
tian

Serves 4 | Preparation time: 20 minutes | Cooking time: 20–25 minutes

INGREDIENTS

4 peaches, peeled,
halved, and pitted

8 apricots, halved and pitted

2 tablespoons honey

A scoop of vanilla ice cream or
apricot sorbet, to serve (optional)

FOR THE ALMOND CREAM

4 tablespoons unsalted butter,
at room temperature

⅓ cup superfine sugar

⅔ cup ground almonds

1 egg yolk

1 tablespoon all-purpose flour

½ teaspoon bitter almond extract

1 Prepare the almond cream: In a bowl, use a wooden spoon to mix together the softened butter, sugar, ground almonds, egg yolk, flour, and almond extract. Spread the almond cream over the bottom of a shallow baking dish.

2 Preheat the oven to 400°F. Cut the peaches and apricots into ¼-inch slices.

3 Arrange the fruit slices on top of the almond cream. Drizzle with the honey. Bake for 20–25 minutes.

4 Serve the tian hot, with a scoop of vanilla ice cream or apricot sorbet, if using.

SPICED PINEAPPLE AND
passion fruit packages

Serves 4

Preparation time: 15 minutes

Cooking time: 20 minutes

INGREDIENTS

1 pineapple, peeled and diced

2 passion fruit

¼ cup packed brown sugar

½ teaspoon ground cinnamon

4 star anise

1 Preheat the oven to 350°F. Cut a sheet of nonstick parchment paper into 4 large rectangles. Divide the diced pineapple equally among the rectangles, then add to each the pulp of ½ a passion fruit, 1 tablespoon brown sugar, a pinch of cinnamon, and 1 star anise.

2 Close the packages tightly and bake for 20 minutes. Serve immediately.

I'M BURSTING
with fruit!

Fruit is sovereign when it comes to dessert ingredients. Fruit takes center stage in a wide range of recipes, from the simplest to the most sophisticated. It also makes it possible to end a meal on a light note. When your fruit starts to become overripe, or if you have a large quantity of them, cooking them will let you enjoy them in the best possible way.

A DELICIOUS
everyday **stir-fry**

Most fruit is delicious when fried, including apple and pear wedges, plums, apricots, peach halves, diced pineapple, and mango slices. You can, for example, combine 1 pear, 1 apple, and a handful of Mirabelle plums or 3–4 regular plums per person. For these proportions, melt 3½ tablespoons unsalted butter in a nonstick skillet and lightly brown the fruit over medium heat. Dust the top with 2–3 tablespoons packed brown sugar until the juice has caramelized and coated the fruit. Serve with a scoop of ice cream or with whipped cream and cookies.

mixed berry
coulis

This is great for when you have a only handful of leftover berries. Blend them with some lemon juice and, if desired, some sugar, to make a delicious coulis. Pair it with fromage blanc (a soft, creamy cheese originating from the north of France) or yogurt.

a traditional
apple dessert

Baked apples are easy and inexpensive to make: Core your apples and, if they're not organic, peel them. Place them in a greased ovenproof dish, sprinkle with spices and dried fruit or nuts (cinnamon, ginger, allspice, cranberries, raisins, marzipan, walnuts, almonds, or chopped hazelnuts), and top with a pat of butter. Bake for about 40 minutes in an oven preheated to 350°F.

I'M BURSTING
with fruit!

Preserves

This is the best way to eat fruit all year round or to use fruit that is about to go bad. What's more, preserves go with almost anything.

PECTIN IS YOUR FRIEND

The success of your preserves will depend on how much pectin your fruit contains. It acts as a natural gelatin and gives preserves a nice, solid texture. Lemon juice helps to activate the pectin during cooking. Apples, citrus fruit, and plums are particularly high in pectin.

WHAT SHOULD THE FRUIT-TO-SUGAR RATIO BE?

Traditionally, jam was made with equal parts fruit (peeled and pitted) and sugar. Nowadays, a lower ratio is preferable: a 60–70 percent fruit-to-sugar ratio is enough, or 3–3½ cups superfine sugar for 2¼ lb of fruit.

JAM, *preserves,* or jelly?

A fruit preparation can only count as preserves if it contains small pieces of fruit. Jams are made with crushed or strained fruit, not with whole fruit or fruit pieces. Marmalade is noted for its pieces of citrus fruit and peel in a transparent jelly. Finally, jelly is made with fruit juice, separated from the pulp, extracted, and carefully filtered.

WHAT ABOUT FRUITS CONTAINING LITTLE PECTIN, SUCH AS STRAWBERRIES OR PEACHES?

Cook the fruit over the course of two days so that it cooks through and loses much of its water. The first day, boil the fruit with the sugar for 15 minutes. Transfer the mixture to a bowl, let it cool, and cover overnight. The following day, cook it again in a jam pan or heavy saucepan for about 30 minutes or until it passes the plate test (*see* below).

CANNING

Use glass jars with good-quality lids. To sterilize them, after washing by hand keep jars and lids in simmering water at 180°F. Or wash and keep them in a dishwasher until ready to use. Fill the jars with boiling preserves, carefully seal them, and place them on a dish towel until completely cold. Store in the refrigerator and use within a couple of weeks.

THE PLATE TEST

Place a plate in the refrigerator ahead of time so it is cold. For the test, drop a little jam onto it and tip it. If the drop runs quickly down the plate, continue cooking it. If it remains in place as the plate tips, the jam is ready for canning.

RECOMMENDED PAIRINGS

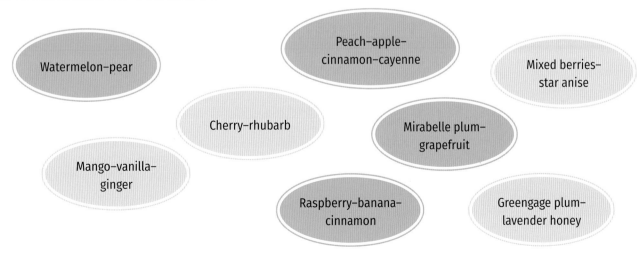

Watermelon–pear

Peach–apple–cinnamon–cayenne

Mixed berries–star anise

Cherry–rhubarb

Mirabelle plum–grapefruit

Mango–vanilla–ginger

Raspberry–banana–cinnamon

Greengage plum–lavender honey

PAN-FRIED
lemon mirabelles

Serves 4

Preparation time: 15 minutes | **Cooking time: 15–20 minutes**

INGREDIENTS

½ vanilla bean

3½ tablespoons water

⅓ cup + 1 tablespoon
superfine sugar

2 teaspoons freshly
squeezed lemon juice

1¾ lb Mirabelle plums,
halved and pitted

1 Split the ½ vanilla bean and scrape out the seeds. In a large nonstick skillet, bring the measured water, sugar, lemon juice, and vanilla bean and seeds to a boil, stirring constantly, until the sugar has completely dissolved.

2 Add the plums and cook over low heat for 10–15 minutes, regularly swirling the pan and basting the plums with their cooking juice.

3 Carefully drain the plums with a slotted spoon and place them in 1 large bowl or in 4 small serving cups. Cook the remaining juice over high heat for 2–3 minutes, until thickened.

4 Pour the syrup onto the plums. Let them cool, then refrigerate before serving.

TIP

When fresh plums are not in season, use frozen Mirabelle plums.

ROASTED SPICED
bananas

Serves 6

Preparation time: 10 minutes

Cooking time: 20 minutes

INGREDIENTS

4 large, ripe bananas, peeled and halved lengthwise

½ teaspoon ground cinnamon

A pinch of ground nutmeg

¼ cup superfine sugar

⅓ cup + 1½ tablespoons freshly squeezed lime juice

⅔ cup freshly squeezed orange juice

3½ tablespoons dark rum (optional)

Lime slices, to decorate

1 Preheat the oven to 410°F. Put the bananas into an ovenproof dish just large enough to fit them and dust them with the cinnamon and nutmeg.

2 Mix the superfine sugar with the citrus juices and stir until completely dissolved. Pour this syrup over the bananas. Bake for 20 minutes, regularly basting the bananas with their cooking juice.

3 At the end of the cooking time, there should be little juice left in the dish. Remove the bananas from the oven and, if using, drizzle with some warm rum, set it on fire, and let it flambé. Serve immediately, decorated with lime slices.

ROASTED FIGS
with almonds

Serves 4

Preparation time: 10 minutes

Cooking time: 10 minutes

INGREDIENTS

12 figs

⅓ cup coarsely chopped almonds

¼ cup honey

A pinch of ground cinnamon

1¾ tablespoons unsalted
butter, melted

Juice of ½ an orange

1 Preheat the oven to 350°F. Arrange the figs in a greased ovenproof dish and, using a small knife, cut a deep X shape into the tops.

2 In a bowl, combine the chopped almonds, honey, and cinnamon.

3 Pour the mixture over the figs and baste them with the butter and orange juice. Bake for 10 minutes. Serve hot.

SPICED PINEAPPLE
millefeuilles

Serves 6

Preparation time: 25 minutes

Cooking time: 20–30 minutes

INGREDIENTS

8 sheets phyllo pastry

7 tablespoons unsalted
butter, melted

Confectioners' sugar

1 vanilla bean

1 pineapple (about 1¾ lb),
peeled, cored, and diced

1 small piece of ginger,
peeled and grated

1 tablespoon finely ground
cardamom seeds

¼ cup packed light brown sugar

¼ cup pistachios, crushed

⅔ cup mixed berry coulis
(optional; *see page 488*)

1 Preheat the oven to 350°F. Line an oven sheet with nonstick parchment paper. Place 2 phyllo dough sheets on top of each other, brush them with a little of the melted butter, and sprinkle some confectioners' sugar on top. Cut out six 4¾-inch disks and place them on the oven sheet. Bake for 3–5 minutes, until golden. Repeat with the remaining 6 sheets.

2 Split the vanilla bean in half lengthwise and scrape out the seeds. Place the pineapple in a large bowl. Add the ginger, cardamom seeds, brown sugar, and vanilla bean and seeds. Mix well.

3 In a skillet, add the remaining melted butter and the pineapple. Cook over medium heat for about 10 minutes, stirring often. Remove the vanilla bean and cardamom pod.

4 Assemble the millefeuilles: Place 2 phyllo pastry disks on each serving dish. Sprinkle with pineapple cubes and pistachios, then cover with another 2 pastry disks, and continue, finishing with 2 pastry disks on top—you should have 8 pastry disks in each stack. Serve drizzled with mixed berry coulis, if using.

Serving suggestion

Decorate with confectioners' sugar, pistachios, and a small bunch of red currants.

PEACH AND ORANGE
caramel crunch

| Serves 4 | Preparation time: 30 minutes | Cooking time: 20 minutes |

1¼ cups freshly squeezed orange juice

7 tablespoons unsalted butter

¼ cup superfine sugar

Zest of ½ unwaxed orange

6 firm peaches

4 sheets brick pastry (feuilles de brick)

Juice of 1 lemon

INGREDIENTS

6 firm peaches

7 tablespoons unsalted butter

Zest of ½ unwaxed orange

¼ cup superfine sugar

1¼ cups freshly squeezed orange juice

Juice of 1 lemon

4 sheets brick pastry (feuilles de brick)

Mint leaves, for decorating

1 Plunge the peaches into a saucepan of boiling water for 30 seconds, then drain and let them cool a little.

2 Peel, halve, and pit the peaches. Cut 4 of the peaches into cubes and the other 2 into quarters.

3 In a skillet, melt 3½ tablespoons of the butter over medium heat. When it begins to froth, add the orange zest, then sprinkle the sugar all over and let it caramelize lightly.

4 Add the peaches and soften them for 1–2 minutes, turning them once carefully to coat them in caramel.

5 Carefully remove the fruit, using a slotted spoon, and set the peach pieces aside.

6 Pour the orange and lemon juices into the skillet and reduce over high heat until syrupy.

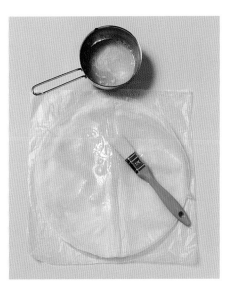

7 Preheat the oven to 350°F. Melt the remaining butter and brush the brick pastry sheets with it.

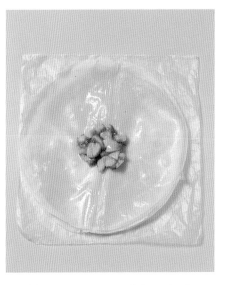

8 Place one-quarter of the cubed peaches in the center of each brick pastry sheet.

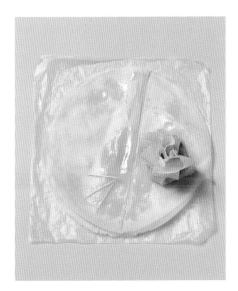

9 Fold into packages and secure each one with a toothpick.

10 Place the packages carefully on a nonstick baking sheet and bake for 6–8 minutes, until golden.

11 Pour the orange caramel onto warm serving dishes, place a peach package on each one, and surround it with the caramelized peach quarters. Decorate with mint leaves before serving.

APPLE–MANGO COMPOTE
with vanilla

Serves 4

Preparation time: 15 minutes

Cooking time: 20–30 minutes

INGREDIENTS

2 vanilla beans

6 apples (preferably
Boskoop or Pink Lady),
peeled, cored, and diced

1 ripe mango, peeled,
pitted, and diced

¼ cup packed light brown sugar

Zest of ½ unwaxed lemon or lime

1 Split the vanilla beans in half lengthwise and scrape out the seeds.

2 Combine the apples, mango, brown sugar, and vanilla seeds and beans in a saucepan. Put over low heat and mix well. Cook gently for 20–30 minutes, until the fruits are well done and easily crushed.

3 At the end of the cooking time, remove the vanilla beans from the mixture. Crush the fruit with a fork or blend it for a smoother texture. Let it cool and sprinkle lemon or lime zest on top before serving.

MERINGUE
with berries and cream

Serves 6 | **Preparation time: 15 minutes**

INGREDIENTS

4½ cups fresh mixed berries

1½ tablespoons
confectioners' sugar

2 tablespoons lemon juice

20 small store-bought
meringues, broken into pieces

1¾ cups crème fraîche

1 Blend one-quarter of the fruit with the confectioners' sugar and lemon juice. If the coulis (sauce) contains seeds, pass it through a small strainer.

2 Fill 6 small cups or glasses by alternating the meringue pieces, cream, remaining fruit, and coulis. Do not stir the cream to mix it through. Serve cold.

TIP

Don't try to make this look pretty or neat. It should be messy, hence the English name for this dish—Eton mess!

PEARS POACHED
in sweet wine

Serves 4

Preparation time: 15 minutes

Cooking time: 45 minutes

INGREDIENTS

1 unwaxed lemon

1 vanilla bean

2 cups pear juice

2 cups sweet white wine

2 cardamom pods

1 cinnamon stick

2 star anise

4 Bartlett pears, not too ripe,
peeled, with the stem retained

1 Use a peeler to remove the rind from the lemon, then squeeze out the juice. Split the vanilla bean in half lengthwise.

2 Pour the pear juice into a saucepan and reduce it over low heat for 15 minutes. Add the wine, spices, and lemon rind, then bring to a simmer for 15 minutes.

3 Meanwhile, douse the pears in the lemon juice. Add them to the syrup and cook over low heat for 15 minutes, turning the pears regularly. Serve them warm with a little of the syrup.

VANILLA PINEAPPLE
carpaccio

Serves 4

Preparation time: 20 minutes

Refrigeration time: 1 hour

INGREDIENTS

1 pineapple (about 2¼ lb)

FOR THE SYRUP
2½ tablespoons superfine sugar
½ cup water
1 vanilla bean

1 Prepare the pineapple: Remove the skin and the "eyes" with the tip of a sharp knife. Cut the flesh into thin slices, ideally using a mandoline. Lay the slices on a large dish, being careful so they do not overlap.

2 Prepare the syrup: Put the superfine sugar and measured water into a heavy saucepan. Split the vanilla bean in half lengthwise and scrape the seeds into the saucepan, using the tip of a small knife. Bring the syrup to a slow boil, swirling the saucepan to distribute the heat evenly until large bubbles start to form.

3 Drizzle the hot syrup over the pineapple slices, cover with plastic wrap, and refrigerate for 1 hour. Serve cold.

PASTRY-MAKING *challenges*

and solutions

My crème anglaise is lumpy

When you pour your hot egg–sugar–milk mixture into the saucepan to be cooked, you should be able to see a fine layer of mousse on top. Then comes a fleeting moment in which this mousse suddenly retracts toward the edges of the saucepan. That's the precise moment when you should stop the cooking by pouring the cream into a large cold bowl. After this stage, the cream will curdle, because the temperature will be above 181°F. If your crème anglaise is still lumpy, blend it for a few seconds with a handheld immersion blender. Out of sight, out of mind!

An unpleasant film ON TOP OF *my creams*

To prevent a film from forming on your crème anglaise or crème pâtissière as it cools, cover it in plastic wrap, placing the plastic wrap directly on the surface. This way, you'll also avoid ending up with a lumpy cream.

My macaron

SHELLS ARE

covered in bubbles

A good macaronage is the key to making successful macarons. Macaronage is the process of adding whipped egg whites to the almond–sugar mixture. Unlike the method used when making cake batter, they should be incorporated vigorously. Don't be afraid to mix them in well, or until the batter forms a ribbon when you lift the spatula. Macaron batter should be more "fluid" than you might think. Here's another trick for smoothing out the surface of your macaron shells: Blend the confectioners' sugar and ground almonds together, then sift everything into a fine powder.

My cake

CAVES IN LIKE

a soufflé

It had risen nicely, it was pretty, and then it went and caved in like a soufflé as it cooled. The problem? Too much baking powder. Try to reduce the quantity by, for example, adding 2 teaspoons instead of a whole envelope.

My pie dough

IS ALWAYS TOO

soft

Forget about ceramic or glass pie plates. Pie dough will never cook correctly in these types of dishes. Opt instead for traditional metal pans, which can be lightly greased before use and won't need to be greased again later. There's a reason why professionals only use these! In a pinch, use a nonstick baking pan.

CITRUS AND MINT
nage

Serves 4

Preparation time: 10 minutes

Refrigeration time: 2 hours

INGREDIENTS

3 grapefruit

3 oranges

10–15 mint leaves, finely chopped

¼ teaspoon grated ginger

2 tablespoons agave syrup

1–2 passion fruit

1 Using a small, sharp knife, peel the grapefruit and oranges, removing any pith. Slide the blade between each membrane and carefully remove the citrus pieces. Put these into a large bowl with the mint, ginger, and agave syrup, then squeeze out any remaining juice and add it to the bowl.

2 Refrigerate for at least 2 hours. Add the passion fruit pulp and serve cold.

TIP

You can also use ground ginger instead of fresh ginger, or even a little ground cinnamon in its place.

POACHED RHUBARB
with vanilla Chantilly cream

Serves 4

Preparation time: 5 minutes

Cooking time: 15 minutes

Resting time: 12 hours

INGREDIENTS

8 rhubarb stalks (about 14 oz), cut into 1-inch pieces
⅔ cup superfine sugar
2 star anise
3 cups boiling water

FOR THE CHANTILLY CREAM
1 vanilla bean
1 cup cold heavy cream
2½ tablespoons confectioners' sugar

1 The day before, cook the rhubarb, superfine sugar, and star anise in the measured water for 15 minutes. Drain the rhubarb, let it cool, and return it to the syrup. Let it rest overnight.

2 The next day, make the Chantilly cream. Split the vanilla bean in half lengthwise, scrape out the seeds, and mix them into the cream. Whip the cream, slowly at first, then on high speed. When it has doubled in volume, add the confectioners' sugar.

3 Pour the rhubarb and syrup into 4 bowls. Serve the Chantilly cream on the side.

WATERMELON AND BASIL
soup

Serves 4

Preparation time: 20 minutes

Cooking time: 5 minutes

Refrigeration time: 2 hours

INGREDIENTS

FOR THE WATERMELON COULIS
¼ watermelon (about 1¾ lb), rind
removed, seeded, and diced
2 tablespoons lemon juice

FOR THE BASIL SYRUP
⅔ cup water
3½ tablespoons superfine sugar
1 tablespoon finely chopped basil

FOR THE DECORATION
A few basil leaves

1 Prepare the watermelon coulis: Refrigerate one-third of the watermelon in a small bowl. Blend the remaining watermelon with the lemon juice until you obtain a smooth and watery sauce.

2 Prepare the basil syrup: In a small saucepan, slowly heat the measured water and superfine sugar, stirring until the sugar has completely dissolved. Bring to a boil, remove from the heat, and add the chopped basil. Cover and let it stand for 10 minutes, then strain. Mix the watermelon coulis with the basil syrup and refrigerate for 2 hours.

3 Right before serving, pour the mixture into 4 serving bowls and top with the reserved watermelon. Decorate each serving with basil leaves and serve cold.

Serving
suggestion

If it's a hot day, add
a few ice cubes to
the bowls.

PAN-FRIED CHERRIES
with honey and pistachios

Serves 4

Preparation time: 10 minutes

Cooking time: 10 minutes

INGREDIENTS

1 tablespoon honey

2 star anise

2⅔ cups pitted cherries

2 tablespoons coarsely
chopped pistachios

1 Heat the honey and star anise in a skillet until the honey becomes frothy. Add the cherries and cook for another 5 minutes while stirring continuously.

2 Deglaze the pan with 1–2 tablespoons water. Place the cherries in small bowls and sprinkle pistachios on top. Serve hot or warm.

Serving suggestion

Serve the cherries with a few spoonfuls of fromage blanc (a soft, creamy cheese from the north of France) or soft sheep cheese.

CHILLED LYCHEES
and raspberries

Serves 4 | Preparation time: 20 minutes | Cooking time: 3 minutes

INGREDIENTS

2½ cups raspberries,
plus a few extra, to decorate

2 tablespoons lemon juice

⅓ cup superfine sugar

1 lb fresh lychees, peeled and
pitted (or 1¾ cups drained
lychees from a can)

1 Puree the raspberries in a blender. Pour the raspberry puree into a saucepan with the lemon juice and superfine sugar. Bring to a boil and cook for about 3 minutes.

2 Pour the mixture into 4 bowls and let cool to room temperature before refrigerating. Serve cold with the lychees and extra raspberries arranged on top.

TIP

If you don't like raspberry seeds getting stuck in your teeth, pass the raspberry puree through a strainer before adding the lychees.

Serving
suggestion

Serve this dessert with a
scoop of vanilla ice cream
or Greek yogurt.

Frozen
desserts

FROZEN BLACK CURRANT
charlotte

Serves 4–6

Preparation time: 40 minutes

Freezing time: 2 hours

Cooking time: 15 minutes

INGREDIENTS

3½ tablespoons black
currant syrup

24 ladyfingers

3 cups black currant sorbet

1⅓ cups fresh or frozen black
currants, plus extra for decorating

Mint sprig, for decorating

FOR THE CRÈME ANGLAISE

½ vanilla bean

2 cups milk

4 egg yolks

⅓ cup superfine sugar

1 Dilute the black currant syrup in half a glass of water. Soak the ladyfingers in the black currant juice, then use some of them to line the bottom and sides of a 7-inch charlotte pan.

2 Add a layer of black currant sorbet, sprinkle with some black currants, and cover with another layer of soaked ladyfingers. Repeat until all the ingredients have been used up. Freeze for at least 2 hours.

3 Meanwhile, prepare the crème anglaise: Split the vanilla bean in half lengthwise. In a small saucepan, bring the milk and vanilla bean to a boil. Remove from the heat and let stand for 20 minutes. In a large bowl, whisk the egg yolks and superfine sugar until the mixture is pale. Remove the vanilla bean from the milk and scrape out its seeds. Bring the milk and vanilla seeds to a boil. Pour the boiling milk onto the egg yolk mixture while stirring continuously with a wooden spoon. Return the mixture to the saucepan over low heat while turning the pan until the cream coats the back of a spoon. Place the saucepan in a large bowl filled with ice water (or pour the cream into a chilled bowl) to stop the cooking. Refrigerate.

4 Remove the charlotte from its pan just before serving. Decorate with the extra black currants and the mint sprig and serve with the crème anglaise on the side.

VARIATION

If serving to only adults, you may want to replace
the syrup with crème de cassis.

APPLE AND ALMOND
semifreddo

| Serves 6 | Preparation time: 45 minutes | Cooking time: 10 minutes | Freezing time: 30 minutes |

INGREDIENTS

1¼ cups crumbled amaretti cookies (or almond macarons)

1 (8¾-inch) sponge cake, preferably homemade (*see* page 478, with the zest of 1 unwaxed lemon added to the dough), sliced horizontally into 3 layers

Confectioners' sugar, for dusting

FOR THE APPLES

4 apples (preferably Boskoop or Pink Lady), peeled, seeded, and diced

⅓ cup superfine sugar

Zest of 1 unwaxed lemon

½ cup sweet wine, such as Muscat

3 tablespoons water

FOR THE FILLING

¾ cup + 1½ tablespoons cold heavy cream

4 egg yolks

⅓ cup superfine sugar

1 Prepare the apples: Cook them in a saucepan over low heat for 10 minutes with the sugar, lemon zest, wine, and measured water. The fruit should be cooked through and the liquid should have evaporated. Mash the apples with a fork. Add the crumbled amaretti cookies.

2 Prepare the filling: Whip the cream. In a small saucepan, whisk the egg yolks and sugar until pale, then place them over a bain-marie (*see* page 494). Whisk them for a few moments, then remove from the heat and keep whisking them until they're cool. Carefully fold in the whipped cream.

3 Mix the cream with the apples and amaretti cookies.

4 Cut out a sheet of nonstick parchment paper the same size as the sponge cake. Place the first layer of cake onto the paper. Use a spatula to spread half the cream mixture on top. Add the next layer of cake and repeat, then cover with the final layer.

5 Freeze the cake for 30 minutes, then refrigerate until ready to eat. Dust with confectioners' sugar just before serving.

FROZEN
strawberry soufflé

Serves 6 | Preparation time: 35 minutes | Freezing time: 12 hours

INGREDIENTS

1⅔ cups strawberries (about 9 oz)
2½ tablespoons superfine sugar
6 egg yolks
1 cup cold heavy cream
1 tablespoon unsweetened
cocoa powder (optional)

FOR THE SYRUP

¾ cup + 1½ tablespoons water
⅓ cup superfine sugar

1 The day before, hull the strawberries and dice them into small pieces. In a large bowl, mix the strawberries with the superfine sugar.

2 Prepare the syrup: In a small saucepan, bring the water and superfine sugar to a boil.

3 In a large bowl, whisk the egg yolks while gradually adding the boiling syrup. Remove from the heat and continue to beat the mixture until completely cold and frothy. Use a spatula to carefully add the strawberries and their juice.

4 Whip the cream and carefully fold it into the mixture.

5 Line the sides of a soufflé pan with nonstick parchment paper. Pour the mixture into the soufflé pan and freeze for at least 12 hours.

6 Before serving, remove the surrounding parchment paper and dust the top of the soufflé with cocoa powder, if using.

CHESTNUT
vacherin

Serves 6–8	Preparation time: 1 hour	Steeping time: 30 minutes
Refrigeration time: 3 hours	Cooking time: 1 hour 40 minutes	Freezing time: 12 hours

Marrons glacés
(candied chestnuts)

2 cups
heavy cream

⅔ cup chestnut
cream

1 vanilla bean

1½ cups superfine
sugar

7 egg yolks

1 cup confectioners'
sugar, plus extra
to decorate

6 egg whites

1¼ cups ground
almonds

⅔ cup
whole milk

½ cup chestnut
spread

Marrons glacés (candied chestnuts), to decorate (optional)

FOR THE ICE CREAM

⅔ cup whole milk

2 cups heavy cream

1 vanilla bean

7 egg yolks

⅓ cup superfine sugar

⅔ cup chestnut cream

½ cup chestnut spread

FOR THE DOUGH

1¼ cups ground almonds

1 cup confectioners' sugar,
plus extra to decorate

6 egg whites

1 cup + 1½ tablespoons
superfine sugar

1 The night before, prepare the chestnut ice cream: Bring the milk and cream to a boil. Split the vanilla bean in half lengthwise, scrape out the seeds, and add both the vanilla bean and seeds to the saucepan. Let steep for 30 minutes, then strain.

2 In a separate saucepan, whisk the egg yolks with the superfine sugar. Add the vanilla milk and cook over low heat until the mixture thickens (it should never reach a boil).

3 Add the chestnut cream and spread. Let it cool and then refrigerate for 3 hours. Churn it in an ice cream maker, then pour it into a springform pan and freeze it.

4 Prepare the dough: Sift the ground almonds and confectioners' sugar into a large bowl.

5 Whip the egg whites into soft peaks with a little of the superfine sugar. When they've puffed up, immediately add all of the remaining sugar. Stir for 1 minute.

6 Using a spatula, fold the almond mixture into the egg whites. Preheat the oven to 325°F.

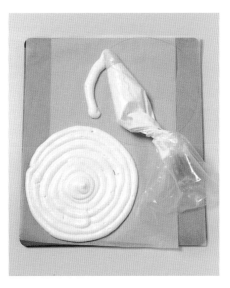

7 Line a baking sheet with nonstick parchment paper and draw two 8-inch circles onto the paper. Fill a pastry bag fitted with a ½-inch tip with the egg white mixture and pipe the mixture into the traced circles, drawing a spiral from the outside in.

8 Bake for 30 minutes, then immediately reduce the oven temperature to 275°F and bake for another 1 hour. Let the meringue disks cool completely before removing them from the baking sheet.

9 The following day, place a meringue disk on a serving plate. Spread the chestnut ice cream on top of the disk.

10 Place the other disk on top of the ice cream.

11 Dust confectioners' sugar on top and decorate with marrons glacés, if using.

PEAR AND BLACK CURRANT
frozen delight

Serves 6

Preparation time: 35 minutes

Draining time: 1 hour

Freezing time: 3½ hours

INGREDIENTS

1½ cups cold cottage cheese

4½ cups fresh or frozen black currants, stems removed

Juice of 1 lemon

2 pears, peeled, cored, and diced

⅔ cup superfine sugar

⅓ cup + 1½ tablespoons water

⅔ cup cold mascarpone cheese

1 Put the cottage cheese into a colander lined with 2 layers of paper towels and drain for 1 hour.

2 Put the black currants into a blender and mix, then strain the resulting coulis through a strainer.

3 Drizzle the lemon juice over the diced pears.

4 In a small saucepan, heat the sugar and measured water over low heat, stirring until the sugar has completely dissolved. Bring to a boil, then remove from the heat at the first sign of bubbles. Add two-thirds of the coulis and mix.

5 Vigorously beat the drained cottage cheese with the mascarpone cheese, then add them to the black currant syrup and mix well. Pour half the mixture into a 7-inch round cake pan and freeze for 30 minutes.

6 When the mixture has set sufficiently, cover it with the diced pears, then pour the rest of the black currant cream on top of the pears and freeze again for at least 3 hours.

7 Remove the dessert from the mold and wait 15 minutes before cutting into it. Serve with the remaining coulis.

Serving
suggestion

Decorate this dessert with
some cookies, fruit pieces,
and mixed berries.

PROFITEROLES

Makes 30 profiteroles

Preparation time: 40 minutes

Cooking time: 30 minutes

INGREDIENTS

FOR THE CHOUX PASTE

¼ cup water

¼ cup + 1 tablespoon whole milk

1 teaspoon fine sea salt

1 teaspoon superfine sugar

3½ tablespoons unsalted butter

½ cup + 1 tablespoon
all-purpose flour

2 eggs

FOR THE CHOCOLATE SAUCE

⅓ cup + 1½ tablespoons
heavy cream

7 oz semisweet chocolate,
finely chopped

FOR THE FILLING

Vanilla ice cream
(or other flavor of your choice)

1 Prepare the choux paste: Pour the measured water and milk into a saucepan with the salt, sugar, and butter. Bring to a boil while stirring, then immediately add all of the flour. Stir vigorously with a spatula until the paste becomes smooth and even. Continue to stir for 2–3 minutes after it starts to detach from the sides and bottom of the saucepan to thicken it. Remove from the heat and let cool. Add the eggs, one at a time, while continuing to stir the mixture. Use a spatula to regularly lift the mixture as you stir. When it falls off the spatula in ribbons, it's ready.

2 Preheat the oven to 410°F. Line a baking sheet with nonstick parchment paper. Put the paste into a pastry bag fitted with a smooth tip and pipe 30 walnut-size dough balls onto the baking sheet. Bake for 7 minutes, then reduce the temperature to 340°F and bake for another 15 minutes. To make sure the pastry is cooked through, gently press down on a choux bun with your finger. It shouldn't give. If it does, continue to bake.

3 Prepare the chocolate sauce: Bring the cream to a boil, pour it over the chocolate, and mix well.

4 Slice off the top of each choux bun. Fill the choux buns with vanilla ice cream and cover with the tops. Place the profiteroles in a serving dish or in individual serving bowls. Top them with the warm chocolate sauce. Serve immediately.

ITALIAN
cassata

Serves 8

Preparation time: 15 minutes

Cooking time: 15 minutes

Freezing time: 4 hours

INGREDIENTS

½ cup crushed nuts: Almonds, walnuts, pistachios, and so on, mixed or just 1 type

4 cups ice cream of your choice (chocolate, vanilla, strawberry)

⅓ cup water

⅓ cup + 1 tablespoon superfine sugar

5 egg yolks

2 cups heavy cream

¼ cup diced candied fruit

1 Toast the almonds (not the walnuts or pistachios) for about 5 minutes in a dry skillet, stirring continuously. Remove the ice cream from the freezer.

2 In a small saucepan, bring the measured water and superfine sugar to a boil. In a large bowl, beat the egg yolks while gradually adding the boiling syrup. Beat the mixture until it's completely cooled and frothy. Whip the cream and carefully fold it into the mixture. Add the nuts and candied fruit.

3 Using a spatula, spread the ice cream along the sides and bottom of a 7-inch charlotte pan. Pour in the prepared mixture and freeze for 4 hours.

4 Before serving the cassata, run the pan under hot water for a few seconds, then flip the dessert onto a serving dish.

VARIATION

A cassata can be made with myriad fillings: candied fruit, fresh fruit, lemon zest, chocolate chips, pine nuts, layers of sponge cake, and many more. You can also flavor it with 3 tablespoons rum, maraschino, or orange blossom extract. For an even more authentic cassata, replace half the cream with 1 cup ricotta cheese.

FROZEN CHOCOLATE PARFAIT
with caramelized almonds

 Serves 4 | Preparation time: 30 minutes | Freezing time: 6 hours | Cooking time: 5 minutes

INGREDIENTS

7 oz semisweet chocolate,
broken into pieces

½ cup superfine sugar

¼ cup water

3 egg yolks

3½ tablespoons unsalted butter,
at room temperature, cut
into pieces

1 cup cold heavy cream

½ cup slivered almond

2 tablespoons packed
light brown sugar

1¾ oz white chocolate shavings

1 Melt the semisweet chocolate over a bain-marie (*see* page 494). Heat the sugar in a saucepan with the measured water until it becomes a syrup.

2 Use an electric mixer to beat the egg yolks while simultaneously adding the syrup. Continue beating until the mixture is pale, then add the chocolate and butter and beat the mixture again.

3 Whip the cream and carefully fold it into the chocolate mixture. Pour the chocolate cream into a 6 × 3¼-inch cake pan and cover it with plastic wrap. Freeze for at least 6 hours.

4 Toast the almonds in a skillet, dust them with brown sugar, and let them caramelize. Pour the almonds and caramel onto a sheet of nonstick parchment paper and let cool.

5 Remove the parfait from its pan, running the pan under hot water for a few seconds, if necessary. Sprinkle the caramelized almonds and white chocolate shavings on top. Serve immediately.

Keeping cool in
THE SUMMER

What can be nicer than a fresh and light dessert or snack on a hot summer day? Here are some quick recipe ideas for treating yourself without spending hours in the kitchen.

The right tools

Homemade ice cream and sorbets require special equipment: the ice cream maker and the centrifuge. These will help you make high-quality desserts with less sugar than what's found in store-bought products, not to mention the fact that you have the option of pairing a wider range of ingredients. Ice cream makers include a freezer bowl that must be placed in the freezer several hours before each use. The centrifuge, which is heavier and more expensive, comes with its own source of cold.

1

2

WHAT IF I DON'T HAVE AN
ice cream
maker or a centrifuge?

It's still possible to make ice cream. The basic ingredients are the same: a fruit coulis or puree and syrup for sorbets, and a crème anglaise base for ice creams. Put your mixture into a covered container in the freezer, stir it a few times at the start of the freezing process, cut it into pieces, and zap it in a blender.

3

4

Keeping cool in THE SUMMER

Nice cream piña colada ①

Serves 4 · Preparation time: 5 minutes

2½ cups frozen, diced pineapple, plus 1 slice fresh pineapple, diced · ¾ cup coconut milk · ⅓ cup white rum (optional)
2 tablespoons brown sugar · Zest of 1 unwaxed lime

1 Put all the ingredients except for the fresh pineapple and lime zest into a blender. Start by pulsing them, then blend continuously until the texture is creamy. Serve the nice cream immediately, sprucing it up with the fresh, diced pineapple and lime zest, or freeze it in a freezer tray—in which case you should remove it from the freezer 10 minutes before serving.

A "nice cream" is a **quick and easy ice cream** made without a centrifuge or ice cream maker. Instead, it's made with frozen fruit placed directly in a blender. You often find them made from ripe bananas, because these make them creamy, but any fruit will do. The result is a versatile ice cream that has a texture similar to "Italian" ice cream. It's best when served immediately.

Mango–lime ② *sorbet*

Serves 4 · Preparation time: 10 minutes
Cooking time: 5 minutes · Resting time: 3 hours

⅔ cup water · 1 unwaxed lime · ¼ cup superfine sugar
2 ripe mangoes, plus ½ to serve

1 Prepare a syrup with the measured water, zest and juice of the lime, and sugar. Bring it to a boil for 5 minutes, then let it cool.

2 Blend the mango pulp with the warm syrup, then refrigerate for at least 2 hours.

3 Put the mixture into an ice cream maker or centrifuge. Pour the ice cream into a freezer tray and freeze for about 1 hour so that it hardens again. Serve with fresh mango slices.

Mixed berry granita ③

> Serves 4 · Preparation time: 10 minutes
> Freezing time: 3 hours and 20 minutes

2½ tablespoons superfine sugar · A little lemon juice
2 cups mixed berries (or ¾ cup mixed berry coulis)
⅓ cup + 1½ tablespoons water

1 Prepare a syrup by combining the sugar, lemon juice, and fruit with the measured water. Pour it into a metal bowl and place it in the freezer.

2 After 20 minutes, scrape the surface with a fork and return it to the freezer. Repeat this operation 2 or 3 times until the whole sorbet is in flakes. Expect this to take about 3 hours in total. Serve the granita immediately to preserve the correct texture.

PARTY granitas!

- Omit the lemon juice and substitute the water with the same amount of champagne.

- Serve the granita in glasses topped with mixed berry skewers.

- For a presentation worthy of a good cocktail party, decorate the glasses by dipping the rims in lemon juice and sugar.

Fruit ice pops ④

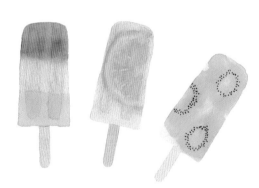

> Preparation time: 10 minutes · Freezing time: 3 hours

Mango: 2 ripe mangoes
A little lemon juice · 1 teaspoon superfine sugar
Strawberry: 1⅔ cups strawberries
A little lemon juice
Lemon: Syrup made with ¼ cup lemon juice,
¾ cup superfine sugar, and 1¼ cups water

1 Blend your chosen ingredients to obtain a smooth coulis. To make lemon ice pops, prepare the syrup beforehand and let it cool.

2 Slip in a few pieces of fruit, then place the mixture in ice pop molds. Freeze for 3 hours.

TIP
To make it easier to remove the ice pops from their molds, briefly run them under hot water.

PEACH
Melba

Serves 4

Preparation time: 30 minutes | **Cooking time: 15 minutes**

INGREDIENTS

1 cup raspberries

4 peaches, preferably white

3 cups vanilla ice cream

FOR THE SYRUP

1 vanilla bean

2 cups water

1¼ cups superfine sugar

1 For the raspberry sauce: Crush the raspberries in a blender to make a sauce.

2 Plunge the peaches in boiling water for 30 seconds, immediately run them under cold water, then peel them.

3 Prepare the syrup: Split the vanilla bean in half lengthwise and scrape out the seeds. Bring the measured water, superfine sugar, and vanilla bean and seeds to a boil for 5 minutes. Plunge the peaches into the syrup and cook over low heat for 7–8 minutes, turning them often. Drain the peaches and let them cool completely, then halve and pit them.

4 Cut the peaches into wedges and divide them among 4 dessert glasses. Drizzle with the raspberry sauce and top with scoops of vanilla ice cream.

VARIATION

You can make a pear Melba using the same recipe
and poaching the pears in the vanilla syrup.

BELLE HÉLÈNE
pears

Serves 6 | **Preparation time: 45 minutes** | **Cooking time: 20–30 minutes**

INGREDIENTS

6 Bartlett pears, peeled, with the stem left on

¼ cup water

4 oz semisweet chocolate, broken into pieces

¼ cup heavy cream

4 cups vanilla ice cream

FOR THE SYRUP

2 cups water

1¼ cups superfine sugar

1 Prepare the syrup: Bring the measured water and sugar to a boil.

2 Prepare the pears: Cook the pears in the syrup for 20–30 minutes. When softened, drain and refrigerate them.

3 Bring the ¼ cup of measured water to a boil. Put the chocolate into a saucepan and pour the boiling water on top, mixing well until the chocolate has melted. Add the cream.

4 Place a pear in each serving dish and cover in hot chocolate sauce, then serve a scoop of vanilla ice cream alongside.

MANDARIN ORANGE
sorbet

Serves 8

Preparation time: 30 minutes

Freezing time: 3½ hours

INGREDIENTS

16 mandarin oranges
⅓ cup superfine sugar
⅓ cup hot water
1 egg white

1 Slice the tops off 8 of the mandarin oranges with a bread knife, then scoop out the pulp with a sharp-edge spoon, being careful to avoid piercing the rind. Freeze the hollowed-out mandarin oranges and their tops.

2 Strain the pulp through a strainer, pressing down on it with a spatula. Squeeze the remaining mandarin oranges to obtain 3⅓ cups juice.

3 Dissolve the sugar in the measured water. Add the syrup to the juice and transfer to a plastic container. Freeze for at least 3 hours.

4 About 30 minutes before serving, whip the egg white with a fork. Using a large knife, dice the sorbet into small cubes. Blend the cubes in a food processor, gradually adding two-thirds of the egg white. Stop when you've obtained a pale and frothy sorbet. Scoop the sorbet into the hollowed-out mandarin oranges. Replace the mandarin tops and freeze for 30 minutes before serving.

VARIATION

You can make this recipe with lemons, oranges, or
grapefruit, using their juices to prepare the sorbet.

BAKED
Alaska

| Serves 6 | Preparation time: 1½ hours | Cooking time: 30 minutes |

1 teaspoon
vanilla extract

4 cups vanilla
ice cream

3 tablespoons
unsalted butter

Confectioners' sugar

3 egg whites

⅓ cup + 1½ tablespoons
Grand Marnier®

4 eggs

1½ cups superfine
sugar

1 cup +
2 tablespoons
all-purpose
flour

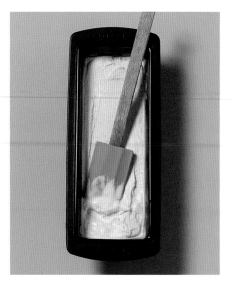

1 Let the vanilla ice cream soften slightly before scooping it into a loaf pan. Place it back in the freezer until just before needed. Preheat the oven to 400° F.

2 Line a baking sheet with nonstick parchment paper. Prepare the batter: Sift the flour into a bowl. Melt the butter in a saucepan and let it cool.

3 In a mixing bowl, combine the eggs and superfine sugar. Place over a simmering bain-marie (*see* page 494) and begin to whisk. Continue to stir until the mixture has thickened.

4 Remove the bowl from the bain-marie and use an electric mixer to beat the mixture until completely cooled. Put 2 tablespoons of this mixture into a small bowl and add the butter. Gradually sprinkle the sifted flour into the mixing bowl, then combine with the contents of the small bowl.

5 Pour the sponge batter into the lined baking sheet and bake for 15 minutes. Use the knife test to make sure the cake is fully cooked by inserting the blade into it, which should come out clean. Let the cake cool.

6 Cut out 2 rectangles of sponge the same size as the loaf pan. Increase the oven temperature to 485° F.

7 Prepare the meringue: Whip the egg whites into soft peaks, adding half the sugar. When doubled in volume, pour in the rest of the sugar and the vanilla extract.

8 Prepare the syrup: Bring the sugar and measured water to a boil. Let it cool, then add half the liqueur. Place 1 sponge rectangle on an ovenproof plate. Use a brush to soak it in syrup.

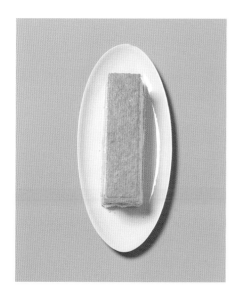

9 Just before serving, turn on the broiler. Scoop the vanilla ice cream onto the sponge and cover it with the other sponge rectangle. Use a spatula to spread half the meringue on top until smooth.

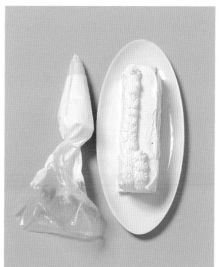

10 Fill a pastry bag fitted with a star-shaped tip with the remaining meringue and use it to decorate the top of the dessert. Dust the top with confectioners' sugar and place the dessert under the broiler for 3 minutes with the door open.

11 Heat the rest of the liqueur in a small saucepan. Set it on fire and pour it over the dessert. Let it flambé in front of your guests and serve immediately.

MANGO
sorbet

Makes about 4 cups sorbet | **Preparation time: 10 minutes** | **Freezing time: 3–4 hours**

INGREDIENTS

2 lb 10 oz ripe mangoes,
peeled, pitted, and diced

1 lemon or lime

¼ cup superfine sugar

⅓ cup + 1½ tablespoons hot water

1 Put the mangoes into a blender or food mill and puree; it should yield 3 cups of puree. Juice the lemon or lime.

2 Melt the sugar in the measured water.

3 Whisk the mango puree with the lemon or lime juice. Add sugar syrup to taste (some mangoes are so naturally sweet that no sugar will be needed). Refrigerate for at least 3 hours before churning it in an ice cream maker.

TIP

If you don't have an ice cream maker, put the mixture in the freezer, mix it in a food processor after 2 hours, then freeze it again for another 2 hours.

VARIATION

Lime zest makes a nice addition to this sorbet.

MINT
ice cream

Makes about 4 cups of ice cream

Preparation time: 20 minutes

Infusion time: 20 minutes

Freezing time: 4 hours

INGREDIENTS

2 cups whole milk

1 cup heavy cream

6¼ cups chopped
fresh mint leaves

6 egg yolks

⅔ cup superfine sugar

Fresh mint leaves, to decorate

1 In a saucepan, bring the milk and cream to a boil. Remove from the heat, add the chopped mint, and let stand for 20 minutes, covered. Strain.

2 In another saucepan, whisk the egg yolks with the sugar. Pour the infused milk into the saucepan and cook over low heat (without bringing it to a boil), stirring with a wooden spoon, until thickened (the mixture should reach 181°F).

3 Immediately pour the cream into a large bowl placed over ice to stop the cooking process. Let it cool, then refrigerate for at least 3 hours before churning it in an ice cream maker.

4 If you don't have an ice cream maker, put the mixture into the freezer, mix it in a food processor after 2 hours, then put it back in the freezer for another 2 hours. Serve in individual dessert bowls, decorated with fresh mint leaves.

LEMON
granita

Makes about 4 cups of granita | **Preparation time: 15 minutes** | **Freezing time: about 3 hours**

INGREDIENTS

3 unwaxed lemons
½ cup superfine sugar
3⅓ cups water

1 Finely grate the zest of 1 lemon. Juice all 3 lemons, retaining the pulp; you should have about ⅔ cup of juice.

2 In a large bowl, dissolve the superfine sugar in the measured water and add the lemon zest, juice, and pulp. Mix well and freeze.

3 After 1½ hours, remove the mixture from the freezer and mix it up with a fork. Place it back in the freezer until the ice has completely hardened.

VARIATION

You can substitute lemons with limes and drizzle a
dash of vodka over the granita before serving.

FRENCH
chocolate float

Serves 6 | **Preparation time: 20 minutes** | **Cooking time: 5 minutes**

INGREDIENTS

3 cups water

⅓ cup superfine sugar

6 oz bittersweet chocolate
(67 percent cocoa solids),
coarsely chopped

⅓ cup unsweetened
cocoa powder

¾ cup + 1½ tablespoons
cold heavy cream

3 cups chocolate ice cream

Semisweet chocolate flakes
(optional; *see* page 52)

1 Put a large bowl into the freezer for 15 minutes.

2 Meanwhile, prepare the chocolate beverage: Bring the measured water and sugar to a boil. Add the chocolate and cocoa powder, whisking vigorously by hand. Remove from the heat and blend with a handheld blender for 3 minutes. Let the mixture cool before refrigerating.

3 Pour the cream into the chilled bowl and whip it into stiff peaks, then scoop it into a pastry bag with a fluted tip.

4 Just before serving, place 2 scoops of ice cream per person in 6 tall glasses. Pour the cold chocolate beverage over the ice cream. Top with a rosette of whipped cream. Sprinkle with chocolate shavings, if using. Serve immediately with a straw and an ice cream spoon.

VARIATION

To make a French coffee float, use 3 cups cold
strong coffee and coffee ice cream.

Celebration *cakes*

PRALINE
Paris~Brest

Serves 6

Preparation time: 40 minutes

Cooking time: 40 minutes

INGREDIENTS

Confectioners' sugar, for dusting

FOR THE CHOUX PASTE

⅓ cup + 1½ tablespoons
whole milk

½ teaspoon salt

1 teaspoon superfine sugar

5½ tablespoons unsalted butter

¾ cup + 1 tablespoons
all-purpose flour

3 eggs + ½ an egg, if needed

1 egg yolk for the egg wash

3 tablespoons slivered almond

FOR THE PRALINE CREAM

1 cup milk

1 stick (4 oz) unsalted butter

1 egg + 1 egg yolk

2½ tablespoons superfine sugar

¼ cup cornstarch

¾ cup ground praline

1 Prepare the choux paste by following the steps on page 476.

2 Preheat the oven to 375°F. Pour the batter into a pastry bag fitted with a smooth tip. Line a baking sheet with nonstick parchment paper and trace an 8-inch circle on it. Line the edge of the circle with a crown of eight 1½-inch choux dollops placed close together.

3 Brush the crown of choux with egg yolk mixed with a little water and sprinkle the top with slivered almonds. Bake for 30 minutes without opening the oven door. Let the choux cool in the closed oven.

4 Prepare the praline cream: Bring the milk to a boil. Divide the butter in half, then dice one half and put the other half into a large bowl. Beat one whole egg with the egg yolk, sugar, and cornstarch. Pour the boiling milk on top, whisk well, and return the mixture to the heat, stirring constantly, until it returns to a boil. Add the diced butter and mix well. Pour the cream into a dish, cover it with plastic wrap so that it touches the cream, and let it cool. Work the ground praline into the remaining unsalted butter. Using an electric mixer, mix the praline butter into the cooled cream.

5 Cut the choux crown in half horizontally. Scoop the cream into a pastry bag fitted with a fluted tip and pipe it onto the choux. Top the crown with its "hat" and refrigerate until serving. Dust with confectioners' sugar before enjoying.

TIP

Assemble the cake immediately before serving.

CHOUX BUNS
with Chantilly cream

Makes 12 choux buns

Preparation time:
30 minutes

Cooking time:
45–50 minutes

INGREDIENTS

Confectioners' sugar, for dusting

FOR THE CHOUX PASTRY

⅓ cup + 1½ tablespoons
whole milk

½ teaspoon salt

1 teaspoon superfine sugar

5½ tablespoons unsalted butter

⅓ cup water

¾ cup + 1 tablespoon
all-purpose flour

3 eggs + ½ an egg, if needed

1 egg yolk for the egg wash

FOR THE CHANTILLY CREAM

2 vanilla beans

1 cup cold heavy cream

2 tablespoons
mascarpone cheese

2 tablespoons
confectioners' sugar

1 Preheat the oven to 375°F. Prepare the choux paste: Put the milk, salt, sugar, butter, and measured water into a saucepan. Bring to a boil while stirring with a spatula. Immediately add all of the flour and stir vigorously with a wooden spoon until smooth (the batter should be coming away from the sides of the saucepan). Continue to stir for 1–2 minutes to "cook it down."

2 Pour the batter into a large bowl, add 1 egg, and mix well. Repeat with each egg. Continue to stir until the batter forms a ribbon when you lift it with the spoon. If it's still a little dry, beat the fourth egg and add it gradually while continuing to stir until the ribbon forms.

3 Pour the batter into a pastry bag fitted with a fluted or smooth tip. Line a baking sheet with nonstick parchment paper and pipe out the batter in little balls of 2–2½ inches, spacing them out enough to let them spread during cooking.

4 Brush the choux balls with the egg yolk mixed with a little water. Bake for 35–40 minutes. Let the choux cool on a wire rack.

5 Prepare the Chantilly cream: Split the vanilla beans in half lengthwise and scrape out the seeds. Whip the cream with the mascarpone cheese, confectioners' sugar, and vanilla seeds.

6 Use a pastry bag to liberally fill the choux buns with the Chantilly cream. To add the filling, you can either cut the tops off the choux buns or make holes in the bottom and fill them with cream. Dust with confectioners' sugar before serving.

TIP

You can fill the choux buns ahead of time, but not too far in advance or they will probably become soggy.

THE TOP 8
RECIPES TO MAKE
with children

1

YOGURT CAKE
PAGE 16

2

3

BANANA BREAD
PAGE 54

CHOCOLATE AND MIXED BERRY ROULADE
PAGE 72

4

APPLE AND RASPBERRY CRISP

PAGE 152

5

WHITE CHOCOLATE MOUSSE

PAGE 200

6

LEMON GRANITA

PAGE 294

7

FRANGIPANE GALETTE DES ROIS

PAGE 342

8

BLUEBERRY AND LEMON MUFFINS

PAGE 374

SAINT-HONORÉ
cake

Serves 6–8 | Preparation time: 1¼ hours | Cooking time: 40 minutes

INGREDIENTS

7 oz all-butter puff pastry

FOR THE CRÈME PÂTISSIÈRE
½ vanilla bean
1½ cups milk
4 egg yolks
⅓ cup + 1½ tablespoons
superfine sugar
¼ cup + 1½ teaspoons cornstarch

FOR THE CHOUX PASTE
3½ tablespoons water
3½ tablespoons milk
½ teaspoon salt
½ teaspoon superfine sugar
3 tablespoons unsalted butter
½ cup all-purpose flour
2 eggs

FOR THE CARAMEL
½ cup superfine sugar
2 teaspoon white wine vinegar

FOR THE CHANTILLY CREAM
1¼ cups cold heavy cream
1 tablespoon vanilla sugar (*see* page 13)

1 Prepare the crème pâtissière: Split the ½ vanilla bean and scrape out the seeds. In a saucepan, bring the milk and vanilla bean and seeds to a boil. In a bowl, whisk the egg yolks with the superfine sugar and add the cornstarch. Remove the vanilla bean from the saucepan. Mix a little of the boiling milk into the contents of the bowl, then pour the contents into the saucepan. Cook, stirring continuously, until thickened. Remove from the heat and let cool.

2 Preheat the oven to 410°F. Line 2 baking sheets with nonstick parchment paper.

3 Prepare the choux paste: Bring the water, milk, salt, superfine sugar, and butter to a boil in a large, heavy saucepan. Sift in the flour and stir vigorously with a wooden spoon until the batter is smooth and even. When it begins to separate from the sides, reduce the heat and continue to stir for 2–3 minutes to "cook it down." Remove the pan from the heat and let it cool a little. Add the eggs while stirring continuously.

4 Roll out the puff pastry into a 9½-inch disk. Prick the disk with a fork and place it on a lined baking sheet. Scoop the choux paste into a pastry bag fitted with a ½-inch tip and pipe the paste onto the disk in a spiral, starting ½ inch from the edge. Pipe eighteen ¾-inch choux balls onto the second baking sheet. Bake for 5 minutes, then reduce the temperature to 340°F. After 10 minutes, remove the choux balls from the oven and bake the puff pastry for another 10 minutes. Let them cool.

5 Scoop the crème pâtissière into a pastry bag, pierce the bottom of each choux ball, and fill with the cream.

6 Prepare the caramel (*see* page 489). Dunk the choux balls in the caramel and place them close together around the outer edge of the puff pastry disk.

7 Make the Chantilly cream: Whip the cream with the vanilla sugar. Scoop it into a pastry bag fitted with a fluted tip and use it to fill the spaces between the choux balls.

VARIATION

Add strawberries or raspberries to the center of the
cake before covering it with Chantilly cream.

CHOCOLATE
religieuses

Makes 12 religieuses | **Preparation time: 45 minutes** | **Cooking time: 40 minutes**

INGREDIENTS

FOR THE CHOCOLATE CREAM

6 egg yolks

¾ cup superfine sugar

⅓ cup cornstarch

2 cups milk

5¼ oz semisweet chocolate,
broken into small pieces

3½ tablespoons
mascarpone cheese

FOR THE CHOUX PASTE

½ cup water

½ cup + 1½ tablespoons
whole milk

1 teaspoon fine sea salt

1 tablespoon superfine sugar

7 tablespoons unsalted butter

1 cup + 2 tablespoons
all-purpose flour

4 eggs

FOR THE TOPPING

1 quantity chocolate
glaze (*see* page 486)

1 Prepare the chocolate cream: In a bowl, whisk the egg yolks with the superfine sugar, then incorporate the cornstarch. Bring the milk to a boil in a heavy saucepan. Mix a little of the boiling milk into the contents of the bowl, then pour the contents into the saucepan. Cook, stirring continuously, until thickened. Remove it from the heat and whisk in the chocolate. Let the mixture cool before adding the mascarpone cheese. Refrigerate.

2 Preheat the oven to 410°F. Line 2 baking sheets with nonstick parchment paper. Prepare the choux paste: Bring the measured water, milk, salt, superfine sugar, and butter to a boil in a large, heavy saucepan. Sift in the flour and stir vigorously with a wooden spoon until the batter becomes smooth and even. When it begins to separate from the sides, reduce the heat and continue to stir for 2–3 minutes to "cook it down." Remove the pan from the heat and let it cool a little. Add the eggs, one at a time, while stirring continuously.

3 Scoop the paste into a pastry bag fitted with a smooth tip and pipe twelve 2-inch choux balls onto one baking sheet and twelve ¾-inch choux balls onto the other.

4 Bake the large and small choux balls for 5 minutes, then reduce the heat to 340°F. After about 10 minutes, remove the smaller choux balls from the oven. Bake the larger choux balls for about another 10 minutes. Let them cool.

5 Scoop the chocolate cream into a small pastry bag, pierce the bottom of each choux ball, and fill with the cream.

6 Dip each choux ball into the frosting, wipe away any excess frosting, and place the choux balls on a plate. Wait a few minutes before placing the small choux balls on top of the large ones.

VARIATION

Use praline cream instead of chocolate cream (*see* page 300).

FRAISIER

| Serves 6 | Preparation time: 30 minutes | Cooking time: 15 minutes |

1 (8¾-inch) sponge cake

1½ sticks (6 oz) unsalted butter

4 egg yolks

1 cup milk

2 tablespoons Kirsch

¾ cup superfine sugar

1 egg

1 pound strawberries

Confectioners' sugar, for decorating

¼ cup all-purpose flour

1 (8¾-inch) sponge cake
1 lb strawberries
Confectioners' sugar, for dusting

FOR THE BUTTERCREAM

1½ sticks (6 oz) unsalted butter,
at room temperature
2 tablespoons water
⅓ cup superfine sugar
1 egg + 1 egg yolk
1 tablespoon Kirsch

FOR THE CRÈME PÂTISSIÈRE

3 egg yolks
¼ cup superfine sugar
¼ cup all-purpose flour
1 cup milk

FOR THE KIRSCH SYRUP

2½ tablespoons superfine sugar
⅓ cup + 1½ tablespoons water
1 tablespoon Kirsch

1 Prepare the buttercream: Work the softened butter until pale and creamy with a wooden spoon.

2 In a small saucepan, bring the measured water and sugar to a boil over low heat. Let the syrup cook until it reaches a rolling boil (248°).

3 Beat 1 whole egg and 1 egg yolk together in a large mixing bowl until pale and frothy.

4 When the syrup is ready, drizzle it over the eggs while beating fast. Continue beating until the mixture has completely cooled, then add the butter while continuing to beat. Add the Kirsch.

5 Prepare the crème pâtissière: Beat the egg yolks with the sugar. Add the flour.

6 Bring the milk to a boil, then add it, still boiling, to the egg mixture while stirring continuously. Pour the cream into a saucepan and cook it over low heat until thickened. Remove it from the heat.

7 Beat the buttercream and add half the crème pâtissière, setting the remainder aside.

8 Prepare the Kirsch syrup: Combine the superfine sugar, measured water, and Kirsch. Cut the sponge cake in half horizontally and, using a brush, soak each half in the Kirsch syrup.

9 Set some strawberries aside for the decoration. Place 1 half of the sponge cake in a round pan, cut side up. Spread half the cream over it.

10 Hull a few strawberries and cut them in half. Stand them up along the sides of the pan, cut side out. Dice the remaining fruit and place them in the center of the cake. Cover with cream.

11 Place the other soaked sponge cake half on top and press down to set it in place. Keep refrigerated. Remove the pan to serve. Dust with confectioners' sugar and decorate with the reserved strawberries.

MOCHA
cake

Serves 4

Preparation time: 40 minutes

Cooking time: 20 minutes

Refrigeration time: 3 hours

INGREDIENTS

FOR THE SPONGE CAKE
2 eggs

⅓ cup + 1 tablespoon superfine sugar

1½ tablespoons unsalted butter, plus extra for greasing

½ cup + 1½ tablespoons all-purpose flour

⅓ cup ground hazelnuts

FOR THE BUTTERCREAM
1¼ sticks (5 oz) unsalted butter, softened

1¼ cups confectioners' sugar

1 teaspoon coffee extract

FOR THE RUM SYRUP
⅓ cup superfine sugar

3½ tablespoons water

2 tablespoons rum

FOR THE TOPPING
1 cup blanched hazelnuts

1 Preheat the oven to 350°F. Prepare the sponge cake (*see* page 478), adding the ground hazelnuts. Grease a baking sheet with a lip, spread the sponge batter on top, and bake for 12–15 minutes. Flip the sponge onto a clean dish towel, let it cool completely, then cover it with another dish towel and refrigerate it for 1 hour.

2 Prepare the buttercream: Beat the butter with an electric mixer until pale and creamy, then gradually sift in the confectioners' sugar. Flavor it with the coffee extract, then continue to beat for another 5 minutes, until the cream is pale and fluffy.

3 Prepare the rum syrup: Bring the sugar and measured water to a boil. Let it cool and add the rum.

4 Put the hazelnuts onto a baking sheet and toast them under a preheated hot broiler for 5 minutes. Coarsely chop them.

5 Cut the sponge into 3 equal-size rectangles. Divide the buttercream into 5 equal parts. Brush 1 rectangle with rum syrup, spread one-fifth of the buttercream over it with a spatula, and sprinkle one-quarter of the hazelnuts on top. Place another rectangle on top and repeat until all the rectangles have been used up.

6 Use a long knife to cut the cake into 4 pieces. Use a spatula to spread buttercream along the sides of the cakes, then press the rest of the hazelnuts into the sides.

7 Put the remaining cream into a pastry bag fitted with a fluted tip and pipe rosettes onto the cakes. Refrigerate the mocha cakes for 2 hours before serving.

COFFEE
cake

Serves 6–8

Preparation time: 45 minutes

Cooking time: 45 minutes

Refrigeration time: 2 hours

INGREDIENTS

FOR THE BATTER

¾ cup + 2 tablespoons ground hazelnuts

⅓ cup ground almonds

⅓ cup blanched almonds, ground

1¼ cups confectioners' sugar

4 teaspoons all-purpose flour

6 egg whites

A small pinch of salt

FOR THE BUTTERCREAM

2 eggs + 2 egg yolks

3½ tablespoons water

⅔ cup superfine sugar

1 tablespoon coffee extract

2¼ sticks (9 oz) unsalted butter, softened

FOR THE TOPPING

1½ cups slivered almonds

1 Prepare the batter: Combine the ground hazelnuts and ground almonds with the confectioners' sugar and flour. Whip the egg whites into stiff peaks with a pinch of salt. Carefully fold them into the dry mix.

2 Preheat the oven to 265°F. Line 2 baking sheets with nonstick parchment paper. Using a pencil and a plate, trace three 8¾-inch circles on the nonstick parchment paper. Scoop the batter into a pastry bag fitted with a No. 8 piping tip and pipe it in a spiral onto the traced circles, starting from the edge and working toward the center. Bake for about 45 minutes. Put the slivered almonds into the oven on another baking sheet at the same time as the cakes and remove them after 15 minutes. When the disks have cooled, peel the paper off.

3 Prepare the buttercream: Beat the eggs and egg yolks in a large bowl with a handheld mixer. Bring the measured water and superfine sugar to a boil over low heat. Heat the syrup until it reaches a rolling boil (248°F), then drizzle it, still boiling, onto the eggs while beating continuously. Continue to beat lightly until the mixture has completely cooled, then add the coffee extract. Whisk in the butter.

4 Spread buttercream over the first cake disk using a spatula, then place the second disk on top and cover it with more buttercream. Place the third disk on top. Top with the slivered almonds. Refrigerate for 2 hours before serving.

BLACK FOREST
gâteau

Serves 8

Preparation time:
45 minutes

Cooking time:
30 minutes

Resting time:
1 hour

Refrigeration time:
1 hour

INGREDIENTS

FOR THE KIRSCH CHERRIES

2¾ cups canned cherries

⅓ cup + 1½ tablespoons Kirsch

FOR THE SPONGE

7 tablespoons unsalted butter, at room temperature, plus extra for greasing

1⅓ cups + 2 tablespoons all-purpose flour

⅓ cup unsweetened cocoa powder

2½ teaspoons baking powder

6 eggs

¾ cup + 1 tablespoon confectioners' sugar

1 tablespoon vanilla sugar (*see page 13*)

FOR THE CHANTILLY CREAM

¾ cup + 1½ tablespoons cold heavy cream

1 tablespoon vanilla sugar (*see page 13*)

FOR THE TOPPING

Candied cherries

Tempered chocolate shavings (*see page 487*)

1 Drain the cherries, then macerate them in the Kirsch while you prepare the cake.

2 Preheat the oven to 350°F. Grease a springform cake pan. Prepare the sponge: Sift the flour with the cocoa powder and baking powder. Separate the egg whites from the yolks. In a large bowl, beat the butter with the egg yolks and sugars until creamy. Fold in the sifted mixture and stir until smooth and even. Whip the egg whites into stiff peaks and carefully fold them into the mixture with a rubber spatula.

3 Pour the batter into the pan and bake for 30 minutes. Let the sponge cool in the pan for at least 1 hour.

4 Remove the cake from the pan and slice it horizontally into 3 layers. Set the top layer aside. Spread the cherries and Kirsch over the 2 remaining layers.

5 Whip the heavy cream and add the vanilla sugar halfway through. Reserve one-quarter of the whipped cream and spread the remaining whipped cream over the cherries, then assemble the cake.

6 Pipe rosettes of Chantilly cream onto the top of the cake and decorate with the candied cherries and chocolate shavings. Refrigerate the gâteau for at least 1 hour before serving.

VARIATION

Replace the cherries with fresh raspberries and
the Kirsch with raspberry liqueur.

CHOCOLATE AND VANILLA
Bavarian

| Serves 4–6 | Preparation time: 1 hour | Cooking time: 10–15 minutes | Refrigeration time: 6 hours |

3 egg yolks

⅓ cup superfine sugar

1¼ cups milk

½ vanilla bean

1¼ cups cold heavy cream

3 gelatin sheets

2½ oz semisweet chocolate (at least 55 percent cocoa solids), plus extra to decorate

1 CUP - 250ml

1 Prepare the crème anglaise: Split the vanilla bean in half lengthwise. In a small saucepan, bring the milk to a boil with the vanilla bean. Remove from the heat and let stand for 15–20 minutes.

2 In another saucepan, combine the egg yolks and sugar. Beat well. Remove the vanilla bean from the milk and scrape out its seeds. Bring the milk to a boil again.

3 Carefully pour the boiling milk over the egg mixture, stirring continuously. When the mixture has thickened, place the saucepan in a bowl filled with cold water to stop the cooking.

4 Prepare the Bavarian cream: Dissolve the gelatin sheets in a bowl of cold water, then drain.

5 Divide the warm crème anglaise between 2 bowls, then add the chocolate to one and stir it in to melt it.

322

6 Divide the gelatin equally between the two bowls and stir it in to melt it.

7 Whip the cream, then divide it between the 2 bowls of cream.

8 Grease an 8–8¾-inch-long rectangular cake pan or individual dessert molds with oil. Pour in the chocolate cream. Refrigerate for about 30 minutes.

9 Cover with the vanilla cream. Let it set again by refrigerating it for 4–5 hours.

10 Run the pan under hot water for a few seconds. Remove the Bavarian from the pan and place it on a serving dish.

11 For the decoration: Spread some melted semisweet chocolate onto a nonstick baking sheet and refrigerate for 15 minutes. Break into shards and sprinkle over the Bavarian along with chocolate candies of your choice.

CHOCOLATE
charlotte

Serves 8

Preparation time: 30 minutes

Refrigeration time: 12 hours

INGREDIENTS

24 ladyfingers

Mixed red berries and
whipped cream, to serve

FOR THE SYRUP

½ cup superfine sugar

1 tablespoon unsweetened
cocoa powder

¾ cup plus 1½ tablespoons water

FOR THE CREAM

10½ oz bittersweet chocolate
(70 percent cocoa solids)

1¼ sticks (6 oz) unsalted butter

6 eggs

A pinch of salt

⅓ cup superfine sugar

1 The day before, prepare the syrup: Combine the superfine sugar and cocoa powder in a saucepan, gradually add the measured water, then bring to a boil for about 1 minute while stirring continuously. Pour the syrup into a bowl and let it cool.

2 Quickly dunk the ladyfingers in the syrup and arrange them on the bottom and around the sides of a 7-inch charlotte pan. Refrigerate.

3 Prepare the cream: In a large bowl, melt the chocolate and butter over a bain-marie (*see* page 494). Remove the bowl from the bain-marie, whisk well, and let cool. Separate the egg whites from the yolks. Add 4 egg yolks to the chocolate cream, one at a time.

4 Whip all the egg whites into stiff peaks with a pinch of salt, adding the sugar halfway through. Carefully fold them into the mixture with a rubber spatula.

5 Pour the mixture into the pan and refrigerate until the following day. When you're ready to serve, remove the charlotte from the pan and place on a serving dish.

6 Serve with mixed red berries and whipped cream.

VARIATION

Replace the cocoa powder in the syrup with
2 drops mint or orange extract.

FESTIVE CAKES FOR CHILDREN

Children's birthdays are great excuses for indulging in life's small pleasures, which invariably start in the kitchen. Add a twist to those classic chocolate or yogurt cakes by topping them with a dreamy or trendy decoration that will be sure to thrill your guests!

CRUNCHY *chocolate* NESTS

Makes 12 nests • Preparation time: 30 minutes
Cooking time: 5 minutes • Resting time: 1 hour

7 oz semisweet chocolate, broken into pieces
6 tablespoons unsalted butter
⅔ cup confectioners' sugar
7 cups cornflakes
1 package of mini sugar-coated chocolate candies

1 Melt the chocolate and butter in the microwave. Add the confectioners' sugar and cornflakes and mix well.

2 Place paper liners into a cupcake pan. Divide the mixture among them. Pack it down with a small spoon and press down in the middle to create the shape of a nest. Refrigerate for 1 hour.

3 Fill the nests with mini chocolate candies before serving.

GOLDFISH
in a bowl

Serves 6–8 children • Preparation time: 40 minutes
Cooking time: 40 minutes

Butter, for greasing
½ cup plain yogurt
2 cups superfine sugar
1½ level teaspoons vanilla sugar (*see* page 13)
4 eggs
4 cups all-purpose flour
2½ teaspoons baking powder
½ cup sunflower oil

FOR THE DECORATION
¾ cup + 2 tablespoons cream cheese
2 tablespoons confectioners' sugar
1 package mini sugar-coated chocolate candies
1 package strawberry gummy candies
3 cups hulled and sliced strawberries
1 small package sugar-coated chocolate candies

1 Preheat the oven to 350°F. Grease an 8¾-inch round cake pan. Put the yogurt into a bowl.

2 Add the sugars and eggs and whisk well. Sift in the flour and baking powder. Mix well and add the oil.

3 Pour the mixture into the cake pan. Bake for 40 minutes. Let it cool completely at room temperature before removing it from the pan.

4 To decorate the cake, cut a 2-inch-wide triangle out of the cake (as if you were cutting out a small slice) and place it on the other side of the cake, with the rounded end facing out, to make the fish tail.

5 Combine the cream cheese with the confectioners' sugar and cover the cake with it. Smooth it out with a spatula.

6 Decorate the head of the goldfish with red and pink mini sugar-coated chocolate candies, then place a strawberry gummy candy as the eye.

7 Arrange the strawberries over the body of the fish, all in the same direction, to make fish scales. Place some pink mini chocolate candies between each strawberry.

8 Cover the whole tail with strawberry gummy candies. Add chocolate candies to the serving dish to mimic bubbles.

STRAWBERRY
charlotte

Serves 6–8

Preparation time: 35 minutes

Refrigeration time: 4 hours

INGREDIENTS

6 gelatin sheets

1 lb strawberries, hulled

⅓ cup + 1 tablespoon
superfine sugar

1¼ cups cold heavy cream

24 ladyfingers

⅓ cup + 1½ tablespoons
strawberry syrup, diluted with
⅓ cup + 1½ tablespoons water

Confectioners' sugar, for dusting

1 Soak the gelatin sheets in a bowl of cold water.

2 Set aside the best-looking strawberries for the decoration and blend the others, making sure to maintain some of their texture. Carefully drain the gelatin sheets. In a small saucepan, lightly heat one-quarter of the strawberry puree with the superfine sugar until the sugar has dissolved, then add the gelatin and stir. Fold in the remaining puree.

3 Whip the cream and carefully fold it into the mixture with a rubber spatula.

4 Briefly dunk the ladyfingers into the diluted syrup, arrange some of them around the sides of an 8¾-inch charlotte pan, then scoop in the strawberry mousse. Cover with the remaining ladyfingers and refrigerate for 4 hours.

5 To remove the charlotte from the pan, briefly run the pan under hot water and flip the cake onto a serving dish. Top with the remaining strawberries and dust with confectioners' sugar.

VARIATION

You can make the same recipe with ripe peaches or apricots.

PEAR
charlotte

| Serves 6-8 | Preparation time: 1 hour | Cooking time: 20-25 minutes | Refrigeration time: 6-8 hours |

INGREDIENTS

8 gelatin sheets
2 tablespoons pear brandy
3½ tablespoons heavy cream
24 ladyfingers
Raspberries, to decorate

FOR THE PEARS

4¼ cups water
2½ cups superfine sugar
8 pears (about 3¼ lb),
peeled, halved, and cored

FOR THE CRÈME ANGLAISE

½ vanilla bean
3½ tablespoons milk
6 egg yolks
⅓ cup superfine sugar

1 Prepare the pears: In a large saucepan, bring the measured water and superfine sugar to a boil. Gently simmer the pears in the syrup for 10 minutes over low heat. Drain the pears and preserve the syrup. Blend two pear halves into a puree and cut the rest into thin slices.

2 Prepare the crème anglaise (*see* page 483). Soak the gelatin sheets in cold water. Drain the gelatin sheets, then add them to the still warm crème anglaise.

3 When the crème anglaise has cooled, add the pear brandy and pear puree. Whip the cream and fold it into the mixture, stirring carefully.

4 Dunk the ladyfingers in the pear syrup and arrange some of them around the sides of an 8-inch charlotte pan. Scoop a layer of cream on top, add a layer of pear slices (reserve a few for the decoration), then add another layer of cream. Repeat until the pan is filled, then finish with the remaining ladyfingers. Cover the pan with plastic wrap and refrigerate for 6-8 hours.

5 Quickly run the pan under hot water before flipping the charlotte onto a serving dish. Top with the reserved sliced pears and a few raspberries.

| TIP |

When pears are not in season, you can use preserved pears instead.

easy chocolate ÉCLAIRS

Makes about 12 éclairs (depending on the size of the piping tip)	Preparation time: 45 minutes	Cooking time: 35 minutes	Refrigeration time: 1 hour

2 cups milk

10½ oz semisweet chocolate, coarsely chopped

6 egg yolks

½ cup superfine sugar

⅓ cup all-purpose flour

½ cup + 1½ tablespoons all-purpose flour

4 tablespoons unsalted butter

1 teaspoon superfine sugar

¼ cup water

⅓ cup whole milk

2 eggs

1 teaspoon fine sea salt

3½ oz bittersweet chocolate

⅓ cup + 1 tablespoon confectioners' sugar

2 tablespoons unsalted butter

1 Prepare the chocolate cream: In a small saucepan, bring the milk to a boil.

2 In a large bowl, beat together the egg yolks and sugar.

3 Add the flour and whisk until the mixture has become smooth.

4 Carefully add the boiling milk to the mixture, stirring continuously.

5 Thicken the cream by warming it over low heat. Remove it from the heat at the first sign of boiling.

6 Add the chocolate to the still warm cream in 3 or 4 handfuls.

7 Prepare the choux paste: In a small saucepan, combine the measured water with the milk. Add the salt, sugar, and butter and bring to a boil, stirring continuously.

8 Immediately add all of the flour. Stir with a spatula until the dough becomes smooth and even.

9 When the dough begins to separate from the sides of the saucepan, continue to stir for 2–3 minutes to "cook it down."

10 Place the dough in a large bowl. Add the eggs, one at a time, mixing well after each one. Continue to work the dough. Preheat the oven to 375° F.

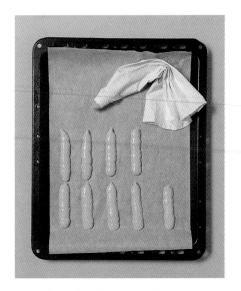

11 Place the choux paste in a pastry bag fitted with a large, smooth tip. On a baking sheet covered in nonstick parchment paper, pipe the dough into 4¾-inch-long strips.

12 Bake the choux for 20 minutes, leaving the oven door slightly open after the first 7 minutes. Place the éclairs on a wire rack to cool.

13 Prepare the glaze: Melt the chocolate over a bain-marie (*see* page 494). Use a large bowl, because you will need to dunk the éclairs into the glaze.

14 Add the confectioners' sugar to the melted chocolate and mix it in quickly.

15 Add the butter and stir with a spatula until it has melted and the mixture becomes smooth.

16 Make three holes on top of each éclair. You can use a small pastry bag tip for this, if you want.

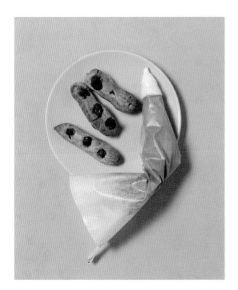

17 Place the chocolate cream in a pastry bag with a smooth tip and fill the éclairs through the holes. Do this carefully to avoid breaking the éclairs.

18 Scrape off any excess cream with a flat knife.

19 Dunk each éclair into the glaze and let the excess drip off before plating. Sprinkle the éclairs with dried fruits and nuts to decorate, if using. Refrigerate for 1 hour to let the glaze set.

RUM BABAS

Serves 6

Preparation time: 45 minutes

Dough resting time:
30 minutes

Cooking time: 25–30 minutes

INGREDIENTS

FOR THE LEAVENING
¼ small (⅔-oz) cake fresh yeast or
scant 1 teaspoon active dry yeast

FOR THE BABA DOUGH
3½ tablespoons unsalted butter,
plus extra for greasing
1 cup all-purpose flour
A pinch of salt
⅔ cup superfine sugar
2 eggs

FOR THE SYRUP
1¼ cups superfine sugar
2 cups water
1 vanilla bean
⅓ cup + 1½ tablespoons rum

TO SERVE
Whipped cream
Golden sugar crystals

1 Prepare the leavening: Dissolve the yeast in a bowl with 1 tablespoon warm water. Let it rest.

2 Meanwhile, prepare the baba dough: Melt the butter and let it cool. In a large bowl, sift in the flour and add the salt, superfine sugar, and 1 egg. Stir with a wooden spoon. Add the leavening and mix well. Add the remaining egg. Work the dough until it becomes soft and pliable. Pour in the melted butter and mix well.

3 Grease 6 small baba pans. Fill each baba pan three-quarters full with the dough. Cover and let them rise for 30 minutes in a warm place.

4 Preheat the oven to 400°F. Bake the babas for 15–20 minutes.

5 Meanwhile, prepare the syrup: In a heavy saucepan, dissolve the superfine sugar in the measured water over low heat. Split the vanilla bean in half lengthwise and add it to the syrup, bring to a boil, and let cook for a few moments before removing from the heat.

6 Remove the babas from their pans while still warm. When cooled, dip them in the warm syrup until bubbles stop coming out of them. Set the syrup aside and drain the babas on a wire rack. Place them in individual serving bowls.

7 Just before serving, mix the rum with ⅓ cup of the remaining syrup and drizzle the mixture over the babas. Serve with whipped cream and decorate with golden sugar crystals.

VARIATION

Replace half the water in the syrup with orange
juice and the rum with Grand Marnier.

SURPRISE *cakes*

You don't have to tackle complex, time-consuming recipes to impress your guests. A simple cake made with a few tricks and twists will make just as good an impression when you cut into it.

BLUEBERRY AND CREAM CHEESE *zebra cake*

> **Serves 8 • Preparation time: 30 minutes**
> **Cooking time: 40 minutes**

1 stick (4 oz) lightly salted butter, melted, plus extra for greasing • 1⅔ cups all-purpose flour, plus extra for dusting • 4 extra-large eggs, at room temperature • 1 cup superfine sugar • ½ cup heavy cream • 1 teaspoon baking powder • 1¾ cups blueberries • ⅓ cup + 2 tablespoons cream cheese

1 Preheat the oven to 340°F. Grease and flour a 10-inch round cake pan.

2 In a large bowl, beat the eggs and sugar with an electric mixer until the mixture doubles in volume. Add the cream and mix well. Sift in the flour and baking powder and mix again. Add the melted butter. The texture of the batter should be smooth and soft.

3 Blend the blueberries and pass them through a strainer to remove the skins. Mix half the batter with the blueberry puree and the other half with the cream cheese.

4 Scoop 3 tablespoons of the cream cheese batter into the center of the baking pan. Let it expand into a 3¼-inch disk. Pour 3 tablespoons of the blueberry batter on top. Repeat until all the ingredients have been used up.

5 Bake for 40 minutes. Halfway through the cooking time, cover the pan with aluminum foil to keep the top of the cake from browning too much. Let it cool before removing it from the pan.

TRICK OF THE TRADE

Make sure the batter spreads into round and even disks in the center of the pan. If needed, tilt the pan to help the spread of the batter.

CHOCOLATE SPREAD
surprise cake

Serves 8 • Preparation time: 40 minutes
Cooking time: 65 minutes

1½ sticks (6 oz) lightly salted butter, melted, plus extra for greasing • 2½ cups all-purpose flour, plus extra for dusting • 6 extra-large eggs, at room temperature • 1⅓ cups superfine sugar • 4 teaspoons vanilla sugar (*see* page 13) • ¾ cup heavy cream • 1 teaspoon baking powder • ¾ cup chocolate-hazelnut spread

1 Preheat the oven to 325°F. Line a baking sheet with nonstick parchment paper. Grease and flour a 10¼-inch-long rectangular cake pan.

2 In a large bowl, use an electric mixer to beat the eggs and sugars. Add the cream and mix well. Sift in the flour and baking powder and mix well. Mix in the melted butter. The batter should be smooth and soft.

3 Mix half the batter with the chocolate-hazelnut spread. Spread it evenly onto the baking sheet, then smooth it out with a spatula. Tap the sheet to eliminate any air bubbles. Bake for 15 minutes. Let cool, then cut out some shapes with a pastry cutter. Increase the oven temperature to 340°F.

4 Pour one-quarter of the vanilla batter into the pan. Line up the shaped chocolaty cake pieces along the center of the pan, making sure they touch each other. Cover with the remaining vanilla batter, filling the pan by two-thirds. Smooth out the top.

5 Bake for 50 minutes. Let the cake cool before removing it from the pan.

FRANGIPANE
galette des rois

Serves 6

Preparation time: 20 minutes

Refrigeration time: 30 minutes

Cooking time: 40 minutes

INGREDIENTS

1 lb 6 oz all-butter puff pastry

1 egg

1 lucky charm

FOR THE FRANGIPANE CREAM

5¾ tablespoons unsalted
butter, at room temperature

⅔ cup confectioners' sugar

1 medium egg

¾ cup + 1½ tablespoons
ground almonds

1 Prepare the frangipane cream: In a large bowl, whisk the butter, confectioners' sugar, and egg until creamy, then add the ground almonds.

2 Line a baking sheet with nonstick parchment paper. Split the block of puff pastry in half and roll out each section into a disk about 1/16 inch thick. Place 1 of the pastry disks on the baking sheet.

3 Beat the egg and brush some of it over the disk. Spread the frangipane cream on top and place the lucky charm a couple of inches away from the edge. Place the other disk on top and seal the edges. With a sharp knife, draw some decorative grooves on the dough without piercing it. Refrigerate for 30 minutes.

4 Preheat the oven to 485°F. Brush the pastry with the remaining egg. Put the baking sheet into the oven, reduce the temperature to 400°F, and bake for 40 minutes. Serve warm.

TIP

Don't use store-bought rolled pie dough, because it will be too thin for this recipe. Look for all-butter puff pastry blocks in the frozen or refrigerated section of your local grocery store (if frozen, let it defrost overnight in the refrigerator). You can also buy it fresh online.

VARIATION

Melt 3½ oz semisweet chocolate with 3½ tablespoons
heavy cream and add it to the frangipane.

BORDELAISE
cake of kings

 Makes 1 large brioche | **Preparation time: 30 minutes** | **Dough resting time: 3 hours** | **Cooking time: 25 minutes**

INGREDIENTS

3 tablespoons lightly salted butter

1 small (⅔ oz) cake fresh yeast or 3½ teaspoons active dry yeast

⅓ cup warm milk

2 cups + 1½ tablespoons all-purpose flour, plus extra for dusting

¼ cup superfine sugar

Zest of 1 unwaxed orange

½ teaspoon fine salt

1 egg + 1 egg yolk for glazing

⅔ cup chopped candied fruit of your choice

Sugar crystals, for decorating

1 Melt the butter. Crumble the yeast into the warm milk and let it rest for 15 minutes. Combine the flour, sugar, orange zest, and salt in a large bowl. Beat the whole egg, add it to the bowl, then pour the melted butter into the mixture and stir it in quickly. Add the milk and mix until the dough is even and elastic.

2 Knead the dough for 5 minutes on a floured work surface (adding more flour if the dough sticks too much). Put it into a bowl, cover with a clean dish towel, and let rise for 2 hours in a warm place.

3 When the dough has doubled in volume, knead it again quickly (it's normal for it to deflate at this point) and mix in the candied fruit (reserving some for the topping). Roll the dough into a ball, place it on a baking sheet lined with nonstick parchment paper, make a large hole in the middle, and carefully stretch it out into the shape of a crown.

4 Add a few drops of cold water to the egg yolk and brush some of it onto the top of the brioche. Let the dough rise again for 1 hour in a warm place. The dough will inflate and increase in volume, which is why the hole in the crown should be large at first.

5 Preheat the oven to 340°C. Brush more egg yolk onto the brioche and sprinkle sugar crystals on top. Bake for 20–25 minutes, until the brioche is lightly golden. Top with the reserved candied fruit and some more sugar crystals. Serve warm or cold.

CHOCOLATE
praline log

Serves 8 | Preparation time: 45 minutes | Cooking time: 10 minutes | Refrigeration time: 2½ hours

INGREDIENTS

⅓ cup ground praline

FOR THE DACQUOISE
⅔ cup confectioners' sugar
1 cup ground hazelnuts
3 egg whites
2½ tablespoons superfine sugar

FOR THE CHOCOLATE MOUSSE
1 gelatin sheet
7 oz semisweet chocolate
1½ cups cold heavy cream

FOR THE PRALINE MOUSSE
6 oz chocolate praline
2 tablespoons lightly salted butter
¾ cup + 1½ tablespoons
cold heavy cream
2 tablespoons ground praline

1 Preheat the oven to 350° F. Prepare the dacquoise: Sift together the confectioners' sugar and ground hazelnuts. Whip the egg whites into stiff peaks. Add the superfine sugar and continue to whip. Carefully fold the egg whites into the hazelnut mixture.

2 Using a pastry bag fitted with a smooth tip, pipe a 12-inch-long strip of dough (or the length of a yule log pan) onto a baking sheet covered in nonstick parchment paper. Bake for 10 minutes, then let cool.

3 Prepare the chocolate mousse: Soak the gelatin in a bowl of cold water. Melt the chocolate over a bain-marie (*see* page 494). Heat 3½ tablespoons of the heavy cream, remove it from the heat, and add the drained gelatin. Add the cream to the chocolate and mix well. Whip the remaining cream and carefully fold it into the chocolate.

4 Fill the bottom of a yule log pan with chocolate mousse and sprinkle with half the ground praline. Refrigerate for 30 minutes.

5 Prepare the praline mousse: Melt the chocolate praline over a bain-marie and add the butter. Whip the cream and carefully fold it into the melted mixture. Scoop this over the chocolate mousse and cover it with the dacquoise. Refrigerate for 2 hours. To serve, turn out the chocolate praline log so that the dacquoise is on the bottom and sprinkle the top with ground pralines.

Mixed berry
MILLEFEUILLE

| Serves 6 | Preparation time: 35 minutes (not counting the puff pastry) | Cooking time: 40 minutes |

3 egg yolks

¼ cup confectioners' sugar, plus extra to decorate

¼ cup all-purpose flour

¼ cup superfine sugar

14 oz all-butter puff pastry, fresh or frozen

1 cup cold heavy cream

1 cup milk

Sucre VANILLÉ
100% NATUREL
à l'extrait naturel de Vanille

½ teaspoons vanilla sugar

4 cups mixed berries of your choice

⅓ cup mixed berry preserves

INGREDIENTS

14 oz all-butter puff
pastry, fresh or frozen

¼ cup confectioners' sugar,
plus extra to decorate

4 cups mixed berries
of your choice

1 cup cold heavy cream

⅓ cup mixed berry preserves

FOR THE CRÈME PÂTISSIÈRE

3 egg yolks

¼ cup superfine sugar

1½ teaspoons vanilla
sugar (*see page 13*)

¼ cup all-purpose flour

1 cup milk

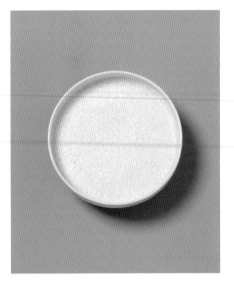

1 Prepare the crème pâtissière: In a large bowl, beat the egg yolks with the sugars, then incorporate the flour. Bring the milk to a boil, then pour it over the mixture, stirring continuously.

2 Pour the crème pâtissière into a saucepan and thicken it by cooking it over low heat and whisking continuously for about 5 minutes. Remove it from the heat and pour it into a large bowl.

3 Preheat the oven to 410°F. Roll out the puff pastry into a large ⅛-inch-thick rectangle. Place it on a baking sheet.

4 Bake for 10 minutes, then reduce the temperature to 350°F. Dust the top of the pastry with confectioners' sugar. Place a sheet of nonstick parchment paper and then a second baking sheet on top to prevent the pastry from puffing up. Bake for another 20–25 minutes.

5 Remove the pastry from the oven and let it cool. Cut out a cardboard rectangle and use it as a guide to trace and cut 3 rectangles of the same size from the pastry with a bread knife.

6 Sort the mixed berries, reserving a handful to decorate.

7 Whip the cream.

8 Carefully fold the whipped cream into the crème pâtissière. Refrigerate until you're ready to serve.

9 Assemble the millefeuille just before serving: Place a pastry rectangle on a serving dish, spread the preserves on top, then cover it with half the crème pâtissière. Place half the berries on top in neat rows.

10 Repeat this step, then top with the last pastry rectangle.

11 Decorate with confectioners' sugar and the reserved fruit. (You can also serve it with a mixed berry coulis; *see* page 488.) Serve immediately.

PRUNE
trifle cake

 Serves 6–8

 Preparation time:
30 minutes

 Maceration time:
2 hours

 Cooking time:
5 minutes

 Refrigeration time:
6 hours

INGREDIENTS

1 cup perfumed tea,
preferably Earl Grey

1¾ cups pitted soft Agen prunes
(dried plums)

2 tablespoons Cognac
or Armagnac

20 ladyfingers

Orange zest, to decorate

FOR THE CRÈME PÂTISSIÈRE

⅓ cup superfine sugar

4 egg yolks

⅓ cup + 1 tablespoon
all-purpose flour

1½ cups milk

1 Prepare the tea. Macerate the prunes in the tea and liqueur for 2 hours.

2 Prepare the crème pâtissière: In a large bowl, beat the superfine sugar and egg yolks until the mixture is pale. Quickly add the flour. Bring the milk to a boil in a heavy saucepan and carefully pour it over the mixture, whisking until smooth. Pour the mixture into the saucepan and let thicken over low heat, stirring constantly with a wooden spoon. Remove from the heat at the first sign of bubbles and pour it into a large bowl. Let cool.

3 Drain the prunes and pour the tea into a bowl. Dip one-quarter of the ladyfingers in the tea, one at a time, then arrange them along the bottom of an 8¾-inch-long rectangular cake pan (or individual pans). Add one-third of the crème pâtissière and one-third of the prunes. Repeat twice, ending with a layer of ladyfingers.

4 Cover the trifle cake in plastic wrap and refrigerate for 6 hours. Remove from the pan and decorate with orange zest before serving.

VARIATION

This recipe is also good with dried apricots and Amaretto.

SAVARIN WITH MIXED BERRIES
and Chantilly cream

Serves 4–6

Preparation time: 25 minutes

Dough resting time: 30 minutes

Cooking time: 20–25 minutes

INGREDIENTS

¾ small (⅔ oz) cake fresh yeast or
2½ teaspoons active dry yeast
1¼ cups cake flour
½ teaspoon vanilla extract
1 tablespoon acacia honey
1 teaspoon salt
Zest of ¼ unwaxed lemon
5 eggs
4 tablespoons unsalted butter, at room
temperature, plus extra for greasing

FOR THE SYRUP
¾ cup superfine sugar
⅔ cup water
1 vanilla bean
⅓ cup + 1½ tablespoons rum

FOR THE CHANTILLY CREAM
1 cup cold heavy cream
2 tablespoons confectioners' sugar
1½ teaspoons vanilla sugar (*see* page 13)

FOR THE DECORATION
1⅓ cups hulled strawberries,
plus a few extra, sliced
1½ tablespoons superfine sugar
2 tablespoons lemon juice
2 cups raspberries
1 cup fresh red currants (optional)
Confectioners' sugar

1 Crumble the yeast into a bowl. Add the flour, vanilla extract, honey, salt, lemon zest, and 1 egg. Mix with a wooden spoon, then add the remaining eggs, one by one. Work the dough until it comes away from the sides of the bowl. Mix in the butter and work it again until the dough comes away from the sides of the bowl and is pliable, smooth, and shiny. Grease an 8–8¾-inch savarin pan or ring cake mold. Pour the dough into the pan and let it rise for 30 minutes in a warm place.

2 Preheat the oven to 400°F. Bake the savarin for 20–25 minutes. Remove the savarin from the pan and let it cool on a wire rack. Place it in a deep serving dish.

3 Prepare the syrup: Split the vanilla bean in half lengthwise and scrape out the seeds. Bring the measured water and sugar to a boil in a saucepan with the vanilla bean and its seeds. Boil for 2 minutes. When the syrup has cooled a little, pour it over the savarin. Let it cool, then drizzle the rum on top.

4 Prepare the Chantilly cream: Beat the cream, adding the sugars halfway through.

5 Prepare the decoration: Blend the strawberries with the superfine sugar and lemon juice, then add a little cold water to obtain the consistency of a coulis.

6 Just before serving, pile the Chantilly cream in the middle of the savarin and top with the raspberries, red currants (if used), and reserved strawberries. Drizzle with the strawberry coulis or serve it on the side.

RASPBERRY
Pavlova

Serves 4

Preparation time: 20 minutes

Cooking time: 1 hour

INGREDIENTS

3¼ cups raspberries, chilled
Mint leaves, to decorate

FOR THE MERINGUE
3 egg whites
A pinch of salt
⅔ cup superfine sugar
1 teaspoon cornstarch
1 teaspoon raspberry vinegar

1 Preheat the oven to 300°F. Line a baking sheet with nonstick parchment paper. Prepare the meringue: Whip the egg whites into stiff peaks with the salt until they stick to the whisk. Add the sugar, cornstarch, and raspberry vinegar. Whip for another 30 seconds.

2 Using a brush, slightly moisten the nonstick parchment paper with water. Scoop the egg whites onto the nonstick parchment paper in 1½–2-inch disks. Make a hollow in the middle of each disk with the back of a wet spoon. Bake for 1 hour.

3 Remove the meringues from the oven and let them cool slightly. Turn them over, carefully peel off the nonstick parchment paper, and let them cool completely.

4 Just before serving, place the fresh raspberries in the meringue hollows and decorate with mint leaves.

MONT-BLANC

Serves 4

Preparation time: 1 hour

Cooking time: 1 hour

INGREDIENTS

FOR THE MERINGUE
2 egg whites

⅔ cup superfine sugar

FOR THE CHESTNUT CREAM
3 tablespoons unsalted butter, at room temperature

¾ cup + 1½ tablespoons chestnut cream

⅔ cup chestnut spread

3½ tablespoons rum

FOR THE CHANTILLY CREAM
¾ cup + 1½ tablespoons cold heavy cream

1½ teaspoons vanilla sugar (*see* page 13)

FOR THE DECORATION
Marrons glacés (candied chestnuts), coarsely chopped

Confectioners' sugar

1 Preheat the oven to 215°F. Line a baking sheet with nonstick parchment paper. Prepare the meringue: In a large bowl, whip the egg whites into stiff peaks, gradually adding the superfine sugar halfway through. Whip until the egg whites are firm and velvety. Place the meringue in a pastry bag fitted with a ½-inch tip.

2 Pipe four 3¼-inch meringue disks onto the nonstick parchment paper, piping in a spiral from the outside in. Bake for 1 hour, leaving the oven door slightly ajar, if possible.

3 Prepare the chestnut cream: Whisk the butter with the cream in a bowl, then add the chestnut spread and rum, whisking until the mixture is smooth. Put it into a pastry bag fitted with a small, smooth tip.

4 Prepare the Chantilly cream: Whip the cold cream, adding the vanilla sugar halfway through.

5 Remove the meringues from the paper. Place a dollop of Chantilly cream on top of each meringue and pipe the chestnut cream on top in spirals. Sprinkle with the chopped marrons glacés and dust the top with confectioners' sugar.

VARIATION

Use chestnut liqueur instead of rum.

RASPBERRY
soufflé

 Serves 6 | Preparation time: 20 minutes | Macerating time: 10 minutes | Cooking time: 35 minutes

INGREDIENTS

Butter, for greasing

1 cups + 2½ tablepsoons superfine sugar, plus extra for dusting

1½ cups raspberries

4 eggs + 2 egg whites

2 cups milk

½ cup all-purpose flour

A pinch of salt

1 Grease an 8-inch charlotte pan (or 4 individual ramekins) and dust with sugar. Place the pan or ramekins in the refrigerator.

2 Combine the raspberries with 1½ tablespoons of the superfine sugar in a container and let them macerate in the refrigerator for 10 minutes. Separate the egg whites from the egg yolks.

3 Bring the milk to a boil in a saucepan. In a large bowl, beat the egg yolks with ¾ cup of the sugar until the mixture is pale. Add the flour, mix well, then pour in the boiling milk while continuing to beat. Pour this mixture back into the saucepan and cook over medium heat, stirring, for 4–5 minutes. Remove the cream from the heat and add the raspberries.

4 Preheat the oven to 400°F. Whip the egg whites into stiff peaks with the salt. When they begin to hold, immediately pour in all of the remaining sugar and continue to beat for another 2 minutes to obtain a thick meringue. Carefully fold this into the cream with a spatula.

5 Fill the pan (or ramekins) three-quarters full. Bake the soufflés for 30 minutes without opening the door. Serve immediately.

VARIATION

You can substitute raspberries with strawberries.
Because these are more delicate to cook with, pick ones
that are slightly firm and especially fragrant.

GRAND MARNIER
soufflé

Serves 6

Preparation time: 15 minutes | **Cooking time: 12 minutes**

INGREDIENTS

5 tablespoons unsalted butter,
plus extra for greasing

1 cup milk

⅓ cup + 1 tablespoons
all-purpose flour

3 eggs

2 tablespoons Grand Marnier

⅓ cup superfine sugar,
plus extra for dusting

1½ teaspoons vanilla
sugar (*see* page 13)

Confectioners' sugar, for dusting

1 Melt the butter in a large saucepan. Bring the milk to a boil in a second saucepan. When the butter starts to froth, add the flour. Whisk well, then immediately add all of the boiling milk. Bring to a boil, then reduce the heat and cook for 5 minutes, stirring continuously, to "cook down" the mixture.

2 Separate the egg whites from the yolks. Away from the heat, add the egg yolks to the previous mixture, along with the liqueur.

3 Preheat the oven to 400°F. Grease individual ramekins and dust them with superfine sugar.

4 Beat the egg whites into soft peaks, gradually adding the sugars halfway through. Continue to beat until the mixture is satiny. Carefully fold the egg white mixture into the previous mixture with a rubber spatula. Pour the batter into the ramekins and bake for 12 minutes. Serve immediately, dusted with confectioners' sugar.

VARIATION

You can also use a buttered, dusted 7-inch soufflé dish for this recipe.
If you choose to do so, the baking time will be 20 minutes.

Chocolate
SOUFFLÉ

| Serves 6 | Preparation time: 20 minutes | Cooking time: 30 minutes |

unsalted butter, for greasing

1 tablespoon unsweetened cocoa powder

5 oz bittersweet chocolate (70 percent cocoa solids)

2 tablespoons cornstarch

¼ cup superfine sugar

5 eggs

INGREDIENTS

5 oz bittersweet chocolate
(70 percent cocoa solids)

5 eggs

3 tablespoons cornstarch

unsalted butter, for greasing

A pinch of salt

¼ cup superfine sugar

1 tablespoon unsweetened
cocoa powder

1 Break the chocolate into small pieces.

2 Separate the egg whites from the egg yolks.

3 Put the chocolate into a saucepan and place it over a bain-marie that isn't too hot (*see* page 494). Melt the chocolate slowly, stirring occasionally.

4 Remove the melted chocolate from the bain-marie. Let it cool and add the egg yolks, one by one, mixing well after each one.

5 Dust the surface with cornstarch and mix it in quickly.

6 Preheat the oven to 400° F. Grease a large soufflé pan.

7 Whip the egg whites into stiff peaks with a pinch of salt, adding the sugar halfway through. Whip until the mixture is satiny.

8 Mix 2 tablespoons of the egg white mixture briefly into the chocolate cream to lighten it.

9 Carefully fold the remaining egg white mixture into the chocolate, lightly scooping along the sides from the bottom up.

10 Pour the mixture into the pan and bake for 25 minutes. Make sure the soufflé is cooked by piercing it with a knife; the knife should come out with barely moist crumbs.

11 Lightly dust the surface of the soufflé with cocoa powder and serve immediately.

Cookies
& small cakes

PISTACHIO, HONEY,
and almond cakes

Makes 8–10 small cakes | **Preparation time: 15 minutes** | **Cooking time: 20 minutes**

INGREDIENTS

3½ tablespoons salted butter
+ extra for greasing

½ cup + 1½ tablespoons whole-
wheat flour blended with ½ cup +
1½ tablespoons all-purpose flour
(or 1 cup + 2 tablespoons chestnut
flour), plus extra for dusting

⅓ cup + 1 tablespoon
shelled pistachios

2 eggs

¼ cup superfine sugar

⅓ cup + 1½ tablespoons
fermented milk (or liquid yogurt)

2 teaspoons baking powder

2 tablespoons chestnut honey

A pinch of salt

½ cup ground almonds

Slivered almonds, to decorate

1 Preheat the oven to 350°F. Grease some mini cake pans and dust them with flour (unless the pans are silicone). In a small saucepan, melt the salted butter over medium heat. Using a food processor, grind the pistachios into a powder.

2 In a large bowl, whisk the eggs with the superfine sugar, melted butter, and fermented milk. Sift in the flour and baking powder and continue to whisk.

3 Pour in the chestnut honey and add the salt, ground almonds, and ground pistachios. Mix together energetically.

4 Pour the batter into the pans, decorate with slivered almonds, and bake for 20 minutes.

DOUBLE CHOCOLATE
muffins

Makes 8–10 muffins | **Preparation time: 10 minutes** | **Cooking time: 12 minutes**

INGREDIENTS

6 tablespoons unsalted butter,
at room temperature

⅔ cup superfine sugar

1 egg

¾ cup milk

1½ cups + 1½ tablespoons
all-purpose flour

1 tablespoon unsweetened
cocoa powder

1 teaspoon baking powder

A pinch of salt

½ cup semisweet chocolate chips
(or coarsely chopped
semisweet chocolate)

1 Preheat the oven to 350°F. Line a muffin pan with paper baking liners. In a large bowl, whisk the butter and superfine sugar until the mixture is pale. Add the egg and milk.

2 Sift the flour with the cocoa powder and baking powder and add the salt. Add the dry ingredients to the wet mixture along with the chocolate chips.

3 Pour the batter into the cupcake liners and bake for 12 minutes. Serve warm.

BLUEBERRY AND LEMON
muffins

Makes 10–12 muffins | Preparation time: 20 minutes | Cooking time: 20 minutes

INGREDIENTS

2 cups all-purpose flour

2½ teaspoons baking powder

½ teaspoon baking
soda (optional)

A pinch of salt

¾ cup + 1½ tablespoons milk

2 eggs

⅔ cup superfine sugar

1 stick (4 oz) unsalted butter,
melted, plus extra for greasing

1 teaspoon vanilla extract

Zest of 1 unwaxed lemon,
finely grated

1 cup blueberries

1 Preheat the oven to 350°F. Line a muffin pan with paper baking liners. In a large bowl, combine the flour, baking powder, baking soda (if using), and the salt. Mix well. Warm up the milk.

2 In another large bowl, beat the eggs with the superfine sugar until the mixture is pale, then add the melted butter, vanilla extract, and lemon zest. Pour into the flour mixture and stir the batter without overworking it, while gradually adding the warm milk. Carefully fold in the blueberries.

3 Divide the batter among the baking liners and bake for about 20 minutes, monitoring them carefully; the muffins should be puffy and golden.

CHOCOLATE AND ORANGE
cookies

Makes 50 cookies | **Preparation time: 15 minutes** | **Cooking time: 10–15 minutes per batch**

INGREDIENTS

1⅓ cups all-purpose flour

½ teaspoon baking powder

6 tablespoons unsalted butter,
at room temperature

⅔ cup confectioners' sugar

1 egg + 1 egg white

Zest of ¼ unwaxed orange

3 oz bittersweet chocolate
(70 percent cocoa solids),
coarsely chopped

1 Preheat the oven to 375°F. Line a baking sheet with nonstick parchment paper. Sift the flour with the baking powder.

2 In a large bowl, whip the butter with the confectioners' sugar until creamy. Add the egg, egg white, and orange zest, then the sifted flour.

3 Melt the chocolate in a saucepan over a bain-marie (*see* page 494). Add it to the batter and mix well. Pour the batter into a pastry bag with a No. 10 piping tip. Pipe dollops of batter onto the baking sheet. Bake for 10–15 minutes. Let the cookies cool on a wire rack.

SNACK TIME

Whether it's the weekend, Wednesday afternoon, or a vacation day, it's always a good time to prepare a snack with the kids and spend some time together at the kitchen table. Love of food and family are what make these moments so special.

CHOCOLATE *crêpes*

Serves 6 children • Preparation time: 10 minutes
Cooking time: 20–30 minutes • Resting time: 1 hour

2 cups all-purpose flour • ½ cup unsweetened cocoa powder
2 cups milk • 3 eggs • 3 tablespoons vegetable oil
1½ tablespoons superfine sugar
3½ oz semisweet chocolate

1 Combine the flour and cocoa powder in a large bowl. Make a well in the center and gradually pour in the milk. Fold in the flour using a spatula, making sure there are no lumps. Beat the eggs, add them to the bowl, and mix well, then incorporate the oil and sugar. Let the batter rest for at least 1 hour.

2 Melt the chocolate over a bain-marie (*see* page 494). Cook the crêpes for a few minutes on each side in a hot nonstick skillet. Serve with the melted chocolate.

French toast
FRIES

Serves 4 children • Preparation time: 15 minutes
Cooking time: 2 minutes

5 slices of stale country-style bread
2 eggs • ¾ cup + 1½ tablespoons milk
3 tablespoons superfine sugar • Butter

1 Cut the bread into large strips. In a bowl, combine the eggs, milk, and 2 tablespoons of the sugar.

2 Melt a piece of butter in a large skillet. Dip the bread strips in the egg mixture, then place them in the frothy butter. Let them brown lightly on each side.

3 Place the fries on a plate and dust them with the remaining sugar.

Chocolate
HAZELNUT SPREAD

Makes 1 jar • Preparation time: 20 minutes
Cooking time: 5 minutes

7 oz semisweet chocolate, broken into pieces
1 stick (4 oz) lightly salted butter, cut into pieces
½ cup chopped hazelnuts
1¾ cups sweet condensed milk
3 tablespoons hazelnut paste
2 teaspoons hazelnut oil

1 Melt the chocolate and butter pieces over a bain-marie (*see* page 494).

2 In a large bowl, combine the condensed milk with the hazelnut paste and hazelnut oil. Add the melted chocolate-and-butter mixture, then the chopped hazelnuts. Mix well to obtain a smooth and shiny paste.

3 Pour the chocolate hazelnut spread into a jar. Let the mixture cool before sealing the jar.

IN DEFENSE *of fruit*

If your kid struggles to get through the day without candy, try making them a fun, fruit-based snack instead.

Fruit skewers: Vary the ingredients based on the season and your child's preference. Serve them with chocolate sauce or Chantilly cream and watch them disappear.

Watermelon pizza: Cut a thick disk of watermelon to make the pizza crust and serve it on a plate topped with banana slices, blueberries, strawberry pieces, or shaved coconut. Slice it and serve.

DRIED FRUIT
mendiants

Makes 20 mendiants | **Preparation time: 10 minutes** | **Cooking time: 5 minutes**

INGREDIENTS

7 oz semisweet chocolate (or milk chocolate), broken into pieces

20 toasted hazelnuts (or almonds or pecans)

20 unsalted pistachios

20 large raisins

10 strips candied orange peel, halved

1 Line a baking sheet with nonstick parchment paper. Melt the chocolate over a bain-marie (*see* page 494). Use a spatula to stir until smooth (it should remain liquid).

2 Spoon out 5 small dollops of chocolate onto the nonstick parchment paper. Pat down each dollop with the back of the spoon.

3 Place 1 hazelnut, 1 pistachio, 1 raisin, and 1 piece of candied orange peel on top of each dollop of chocolate. Repeat until all the ingredients have been used up. Let the mendiants cool down in a cool place (about 64°F) before removing them from the parchment paper with a spatula.

TIP

You can make your mendiants come out crispy and shiny if you use a candy thermometer; the temperature of the melted chocolate should be about 122°F. Let it cool to 84°F over a cold bain-marie before heating it again to 88°F. Then spoon out the mixture.

RASPBERRY AND PISTACHIO
financiers

Makes 15 financiers

Preparation time: 15 minutes

Cooking time: 15–20 minutes

INGREDIENTS

7 tablespoons unsalted butter, plus extra for greasing

⅓ cup + 1 tablespoon all-purpose flour

½ cup ground almonds

¾ cup superfine sugar

1 teaspoon vanilla powder

A pinch of salt

4 egg whites

⅔ cup chopped pistachios

1 cup raspberries

1 Preheat the oven to 350°F. Grease the cups of a financier pan.

2 Melt the butter in a saucepan. Sift in the flour, then add the ground almonds, sugar, vanilla powder, and salt. Add the egg whites and whisk well. Add the melted butter and chopped pistachios. Divide the batter among the cups of the financier pan, filling them three-quarters full.

3 Top the financiers with the raspberries and press them down lightly so that they sink into the batter. Bake for 15–20 minutes. Remove them from the pan and let cool on a wire rack.

MADELEINES

Makes 12 madeleines | **Preparation time: 10 minutes** | **Cooking time: 15 minutes**

INGREDIENTS

7 tablespoons unsalted butter,
plus extra for greasing

¾ cup + 1 tablespoon
all-purpose flour

1 teaspoon baking powder

2 eggs

⅔ cup superfine sugar

1 teaspoon grated zest from
an unwaxed lemon

1 Preheat the oven to 425°F. Lightly grease a madeleine pan. Sift together the flour and baking powder. Melt the butter in a small saucepan, then let it cool.

2 In a large bowl, whisk the eggs with the superfine sugar for 5 minutes, until frothy. Gradually add the flour mixture, then the melted butter and lemon zest, stirring continuously.

3 Divide the batter among the cups of the madeleine pan, filling them two-thirds full. Bake for 5 minutes, then reduce the temperature to 400°F and bake for another 10 minutes. Remove the madeleines from the pan while still warm and let cool.

VARIATION

Replace the lemon zest with 1 tablespoon orange blossom water.

CUPCAKES

⅔ cup milk

2 sticks +
3 tablespoons
(9½ oz) unsalted
butter, at room
temperature

2 eggs

1¼ cups
confectioners'
sugar

1¾ cups
all-purpose flour

A few drops of
food coloring
(optional)

1 teaspoon
baking powder

¾ cup superfine
sugar

Sweets, edible
flowers, etc.

1 teaspoon
vanilla extract

386

INGREDIENTS

1 stick + 3 tablespoons (5½ oz)
unsalted butter, at room temperature

¾ cup superfine sugar

2 eggs

1¾ cups all-purpose flour

1 teaspoon baking powder

2 pinches of salt

150ml milk

FOR THE FROSTING

1 stick (4 oz) unsalted butter,
at room temperature

1 teaspoon vanilla extract

1¼ cups confectioners' sugar

A few drops of food
coloring (optional)

FOR THE DECORATION

Sweets or edible flowers

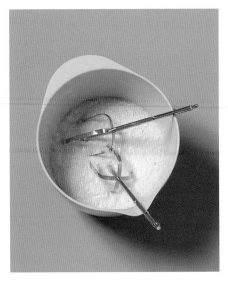

1 Preheat the oven to 350°F. In a large bowl, beat the butter, superfine sugar, and eggs with an electric mixer for about 3 minutes.

2 Sift together the flour, baking powder, and salt.

3 Add this mixture to the large bowl in 2 stages, alternating with the milk, while stirring continuously.

4 Line 2 cupcake pans with paper baking liners.

5 Fill the paper baking liners three-quarters full with batter.

6 Bake for 20 minutes. A toothpick stuck into the middle of a cupcake should come out clean. Let the cupcakes cool on a wire rack.

7 Prepare the frosting: Whip the butter with the vanilla extract using an electric mixer on medium speed until the mixture becomes creamy.

8 Gradually add the confectioners' sugar and continue to beat for about 3 minutes, until the frosting is nice and satiny.

9 Add the food coloring, if using, counting out 10 drops for a pastel color. Use the frosting immediately or refrigerate it, then let stand at room temperature for 30 minutes and whip again right before using it.

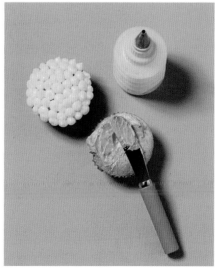

10 Frost the cupcakes with a butter knife or a pastry bag.

11 Decorate with candies or edible flowers, as you prefer.

COCONUT
macaroons

Makes 20 macaroons | **Preparation time: 20 minutes** | **Cooking time: 10 minutes**

INGREDIENTS

1½ cups superfine sugar

A pinch of salt

5 egg whites

3½ cups unsweetened
shredded dry coconut

1 teaspoon vanilla powder

1 Preheat the oven to 485°F. Line a baking sheet with nonstick parchment paper.

2 Place a large bowl over a bain-marie (*see* page 494) over low heat. Pour in the superfine sugar, salt, and egg whites.

3 Whisk continuously until the sugar has dissolved and the mixture is warm. Pour in the shredded coconut and vanilla powder and mix well. Remove from the heat.

4 With a small spoon, scoop out the batter onto the baking sheet and shape it into small mounds. Alternatively, transfer the mixture to a pastry bag with a fluted piping tip and pipe dollops of the mixture onto the baking sheet. Space the macaroons evenly on the baking sheet, leaving plenty of space between them. Bake for about 10 minutes.

5 Remove the macaroons from the oven and let cool before peeling them away from the parchment paper.

CANELÉS

 Makes 12 canelés | Preparation time: 25 minutes | Cooking time: 50 minutes | Infusion time: 15 minutes

INGREDIENTS

1 vanilla bean

3½ tablespoons milk

3½ tablespoons unsalted
butter, plus extra for greasing

2 eggs + 2 egg yolks

2 cups confectioners' sugar

1 tablespoon aged rum
(or orange blossom water)

¾ cup + 1 tablespoon
all-purpose flour

1 Split the vanilla bean in half lengthwise and scrape out the seeds. Bring the milk to a boil in a saucepan with the vanilla bean and its seeds. Remove from the heat and let it steep, covered, for 15 minutes.

2 Preheat the oven to 400°F. Generously grease the cups of a canelé pan. Melt the butter. Combine the eggs and egg yolks with the confectioners' sugar and whisk until the mixture is pale. Add the melted butter and the rum. Incorporate the flour and then thin out the batter with the vanilla-steeped milk.

3 Fill the cups of the canelé pan three-quarters full. Bake for 45 minutes. Remove the canelés from the pan as soon as they're out of the oven. Serve cold.

TIP

Enjoy these little Bordeaux cakes as soon as you can; they're best eaten on the day they're made.

VISITANDINE
cakes

Makes 40 cakes

Preparation time: 20 minutes

Refrigeration time: 1 hour

Cooking time: 8–10 minutes per batch

INGREDIENTS

⅓ cup all-purpose flour

1½ sticks + 1 tablespoon (6½ oz) unsalted butter, plus extra for greasing

⅔ cup superfine sugar

1⅓ cups ground almonds

4 egg whites

1 Sift the flour. Melt the butter slowly over a bain-marie (*see* page 494) or in the microwave. Combine the sugar and ground almonds. Add the flour, then gradually fold in 3 of the egg whites and mix well. Add the melted butter when it's barely warm. In a separate bowl, whip the last egg white into soft peaks and carefully fold it into the mixture.

2 Grease some small barquette or oval baking molds. Pour the batter into the molds, filling each two-thirds full. Refrigerate for at least 1 hour.

3 Preheat the oven to 425°F. Bake the visitandine cakes for 8–10 minutes. They should be golden on the outside and moist on the inside. Remove them from their pans while still warm.

TIP

You may need to cook this recipe in several batches, depending on the size of your oven and the number of baking pans you use. To remove the cakes easily from the pans, lightly tap the pans on the table before flipping them.

LANGUE DE CHAT
cookies

Makes 45 cookies

Preparation time: 20 minutes

Cooking time: 4–5 minutes per batch

INGREDIENTS

1 stick (4 oz) unsalted butter, at room temperature

1½ teaspoons vanilla sugar (*see* page 13)

⅓–½ cup superfine sugar, according to taste

2 eggs

1 cup all-purpose flour

1 Preheat the oven to 400°F. Line a baking sheet with nonstick parchment paper.

2 In a large bowl, combine the butter and sugars and mix well with a wooden spoon. Add the eggs, one at a time. Sift the flour, immediately pour all of it into the mixture, and mix well.

3 Place the batter in a pastry bag with a ¼-inch piping tip and pipe 2-inch strips of batter onto the nonstick paper, leaving a gap of ¾ inch between each strip.

4 The cookies won't fit on a single baking sheet. Bake each batch for 4–5 minutes. When the cookies have cooled, keep them in a sealed container.

COLORFUL
mini meringues

Makes 30 mini meringues | **Preparation time: 30 minutes** | **Cooking time: 1½ hours**

INGREDIENTS

3 egg whites

A pinch of salt

½ cup superfine sugar

1 cup confectioners' sugar

Food coloring

Essential oils (orange, lemon) or extracts (bitter almond, coffee, vanilla)

1 Preheat the oven to 215°F. Line a baking sheet with nonstick parchment paper. In a large bowl, use an electric mixer to beat the egg whites into stiff peaks with the salt. Immediately add all of the superfine sugar and continue to beat on low speed for a few moments. Slowly add the confectioners' sugar. The meringue should be dense and shiny.

2 Divide the meringue among several bowls. Use food coloring and extracts to color and flavor each portion according to your preference.

3 Transfer the colored meringue mixtures to pastry bags with fluted tips. Pipe pretty rosettes onto the baking sheet, leaving plenty of room between them.

4 Dry out the meringues in the oven for 1½ hours, until they are firm and dry to the touch. Let them cool on a wire rack.

MINI ORANGE AND ALMOND
cakes

Makes 10–12 cakes | **Preparation time: 20 minutes** | **Cooking time: 20–22 minutes**

INGREDIENTS

2 unwaxed oranges

4 eggs

A pinch of salt

1 cup superfine sugar

2 cups ground almonds

⅓ cup all-purpose flour

Butter for greasing

6 tablespoons orange marmalade

½ cup almonds

1 Preheat the oven to 350°F. Grease 10–12 small oval molds. Grate the zest of 1 orange. Juice both oranges. Separate the egg whites from the yolks. Whip the egg whites into stiff peaks with the salt.

2 In a large bowl, beat the egg yolks and superfine sugar until the mixture is pale. Add the ground almonds and orange juice and zest. Incorporate the flour, then fold in the egg whites with a rubber spatula.

3 Pour the batter into the molds and bake for 10 minutes. Reduce the temperature to 325°F and bake for another 10–12 minutes. Let the cakes cool, remove them from their molds, and spread the marmalade on top. Decorate with the almonds.

MINI WALNUT
delights

Makes 8–10 cakes | **Preparation time: 20 minutes** | **Cooking time: 20–22 minutes**

INGREDIENTS

Butter, for greasing

1 cup walnut halves

3 eggs

⅔ cup superfine sugar

⅔ cup cornstarch

FOR THE ICING

⅔ cup confectioners' sugar

1 tablespoon water

1 teaspoon freeze-dried
instant coffee

1 Preheat the oven to 350°F and liberally grease some small cake pans. Set aside about 3 tablespoons of the walnuts for the decoration and coarsely chop the remainder in a food processor.

2 Separate the egg whites from the egg yolks. Use an electric mixer to beat together the egg yolks and sugar until the mixture is pale. Add the cornstarch and chopped walnuts and mix well with a wooden spoon.

3 Whip the egg whites into stiff peaks. Mix 2 tablespoons of the egg whites briefly into the walnut batter to lighten it. Fold in the remaining egg whites carefully to avoid deflating them.

4 Pour the batter into the pans. Bake in the middle of the oven for 10 minutes, then reduce the temperature to 300°F. Continue to bake for another 10–12 minutes. Make sure the cakes are cooked by piercing one with a sharp knife; the blade should come out dry. Let the cakes rest for 5 minutes before removing them from their pans. Let them cool on a wire rack.

5 Prepare the icing: Mix the confectioners' sugar with the measured water, add the instant coffee, and mix well until you get a thick but runny paste. Spread it over the cakes with a rubber spatula. Decorate the tops with the whole walnuts.

ALMOND
tuiles

Makes 25 tuiles | **Preparation time: 20 minutes** | **Cooking time: 4 minutes per batch**

INGREDIENTS

5 tablespoons unsalted butter

½ cup superfine sugar

½ teaspoon vanilla sugar (*see* page 13)

⅔ cup all-purpose flour

2 eggs

A pinch of salt

¾ cup slivered almonds

1 Preheat the oven to 400°F. Line a baking sheet with nonstick parchment paper. Melt the butter.

2 In a large bowl, combine the sugars and sift in the flour. Add the eggs, one at a time, and salt, and mix with a wooden spoon. Incorporate the melted butter and slivered almonds (mix them in gently to avoid breaking them).

3 Use a little spoon to scoop small dollops of batter onto the parchment paper, leaving plenty of space between them. Spread each dollop lightly with the back of a wet fork, dipping it in cold water between each one. Bake for about 4 minutes.

4 Remove the baking sheet from the oven and, using a spatula, quickly lift the cookies from the baking sheet while they're still soft. Place 3 or 4 of them at a time on a rolling pin (or empty bottle). When they are hard, remove them from the rolling pin and place in a sealable container.

TIP

Bake these cookies in small batches to facilitate the molding on the rolling pin, because they are fragile.

HOT SNACKTIME
beverages

No snack worth its salt would be complete without a hot beverage. Some like to opt for an old-fashioned hot chocolate that harks back to their childhood, while others prefer tea or coffee.

Old-fashioned hot chocolate

> **Makes 4 cups • Preparation time: 5 minutes**
> **Cooking time: 5 minutes**

2½ cups milk • ¼ cup superfine sugar
4 oz bittersweet chocolate (70 percent cocoa solids), broken into pieces • ¼ cup unsweetened cocoa powder

Bring the milk and sugar to a boil. Add the chocolate and cocoa powder to the boiling milk, whisking vigorously. Remove from the heat and blend for 3 minutes with a handheld blender. Serve immediately.

A little something extra: Sprinkle some ground cinnamon on top for a hint of spice.

Nougat Ricoré coffee

> **Makes 1 cup • Preparation time: 5 minutes**
> **Cooking time: 5 minutes**

1 piece of nougat, finely diced • 1 cup milk
2 tablespoons Ricoré instant drink or other instant chicory coffee mix

In a small saucepan, heat the nougat and milk over low heat. Use a handheld blender to blend the mixture until it becomes frothy. Add the Ricoré instant drink to a cup, then pour the hot milk and nougat on top. Mix well and serve.

Matcha tea
with soy milk

Makes 1 cup • Preparation time: 5 minutes
Cooking time: 5 minutes

1 cup soy milk • 2 tablespoons matcha tea, plus extra for dusting
1 tablespoon agave syrup
⅓ cup cold heavy cream

Heat the soy milk in a saucepan, then add the matcha and agave syrup. Blend with a handheld blender until the mixture becomes frothy. Whip the cream into stiff peaks. Pour the hot tea into a cup, top with a dollop of whipped cream, and dust with tea powder.

Affogato

Makes 1 cup • Preparation time: 2 minutes
Cooking time: 5 minutes

1 scoop of vanilla ice cream
¾ cup hot, strong espresso

Scoop the ice cream into the bottom of a cup. Prepare the coffee, then pour it on top of the ice cream. Serve immediately.

IN DEFENSE OF *herbal infusions*

We know them as detox teas or hydrating teas, but they can be delicious in their own right. Here are some combinations to try for your next cup:

• 2 tablespoons white tea + 1 tablespoon coconut shavings + 2 tablespoons coconut sugar

• 1 teaspoon fennel seeds + 1 teaspoon turmeric + 2 cardamom seeds

• 1 tablespoon hibiscus flowers + 2 cloves + 2 teaspoons coconut sugar

• 1 clove + a little lemon juice + 1 teaspoon honey + a pinch of ground cinnamon

CIGARETTE
cookies

Makes 25–30 cookies

Preparation time: 30 minutes

Cooking time: 8–10 minutes
per batch

INGREDIENTS

7 tablespoons unsalted butter

¾ cup all-purpose flour

¾ cup + 1½ tablespoons
superfine sugar

1½ teaspoons vanilla
sugar (*see* page 13)

4 egg whites

1 Preheat the oven to 350° F. Line a baking sheet with nonstick parchment paper.

2 Melt the butter over a bain-marie (*see* page 494). In a large bowl, combine the flour, sugars, egg whites, and melted butter.

3 Using a pastry bag or a spoon, spoon the batter onto the parchment paper in 3¼-inch disks. Bake for 8–10 minutes. When the cookies begin to brown around the edges, remove them from the oven and use a spatula to remove the disks from the baking sheet quickly while they're still soft. Immediately roll them up tightly or over a wooden stick. Let them cool completely and store in a sealed container.

SHORTBREAD
cookies

Makes 25 cookies

Preparation time: 30 minutes

Cooking time: 30 minutes

INGREDIENTS

2 cups all-purpose flour

½ teaspoon salt

2 sticks (8 oz) unsalted butter, at room temperature, cut into pieces

¼ cup superfine sugar

1 Preheat the oven to 300°F. Line a baking sheet with nonstick parchment paper. Sift the flour onto a work surface, then add the salt and butter. Knead until the dough is smooth and even.

2 Roll out the dough to a thickness of ½ inch and cut it into little disks with a pastry cutter. Place the disks on the baking sheet and dust the tops with sugar. Bake for 30 minutes. The shortbread should not brown. Store the cookies in a sealed container.

Serving
suggestion
———
These cookies are intentionally
low in sugar and are great
accompaniments for ice
cream, sorbet, and
fruit salads.

VARIATION
———
Add ⅓ cup chopped clementine peel to the dough and
replace the superfine sugar with brown sugar.

RUM AND CURRANT
cookies

Makes 25 cookies

Preparation time: 15 minutes

Macerating time: 1 hour

Cooking time: 10 minutes per batch

INGREDIENTS

½ cup dried currants

⅓ cup rum

1 stick (4 oz) unsalted butter, at room temperature

⅔ cup superfine sugar

2 eggs

1¼ cups all-purpose flour

A pinch of salt

1 Macerate the currants in the rum for 1 hour.

2 Preheat the oven to 400°F. Line a baking sheet with nonstick parchment paper. In a large bowl, whisk the butter with the superfine sugar. Add the eggs, one by one, and mix well. Pour in the flour and add the currants, rum, and salt, mixing well before adding each new ingredient.

3 Place small spoonfuls of dough onto the parchment paper, leaving plenty of space between them. Bake for 10 minutes. When the cookies have cooled, store them in a sealed container.

LEMON
cookies

Makes 40 cookies

Preparation time: 25 minutes

**Cooking time: 10 minutes
per batch**

INGREDIENTS

1¼ cups lemon curd
(*see* page 490)
Confectioners' sugar, for dusting

FOR THE DOUGH

1⅓ cups + 1 tablespoon
all-purpose flour
1 unwaxed lemon
5¾ tablespoons unsalted butter
¾ cup superfine sugar
1 egg

1 Preheat the oven to 350°F. Line a baking sheet with nonstick parchment paper.

2 Prepare the dough: Sift the flour. Grate the lemon zest. In a large bowl, mix together the butter and superfine sugar until creamy. Add the egg and the lemon zest. Gradually add the flour while stirring continuously, then finish by kneading the mixture by hand.

3 Roll out the dough to a thickness of ¼ inch. Using a pastry cutter, cut out hearts, disks, or diamond shapes. Place them on the baking sheet and bake for 10 minutes.

4 Remove the cookies from the baking sheet, place them on a wire rack, and let them cool.

5 Spread lemon curd on top of half the cookies. Top them with the remaining cookies and sprinkle them with confectioners' sugar. Spoon some more lemon curd on top of each cookie and serve immediately.

FRENCH BUTTER
cookies

Makes 50 cookies

**Preparation time:
20 minutes**

**Dough resting time:
30 minutes**

**Cooking time: 10–12 minutes
per batch**

INGREDIENTS

1¾ sticks (7 oz) unsalted butter,
plus extra for greasing
½ cup superfine sugar
4 egg yolks
2½ cups all-purpose flour
⅓ cup + 1½ tablespoons milk
A pinch of salt

1 In a large bowl, combine the butter, superfine sugar, 3 egg yolks, and salt. Mix until creamy. Gradually add the flour and half the milk until the dough is pliable but not soft. Roll it into a ball and let rest for 30 minutes in a cool place.

2 Preheat the oven to 410°F. Grease a baking sheet. Roll out the dough to a thickness of ⅛ inch. Use a heart-shaped pastry cutter to cut out the cookies. Place them on the baking sheet.

3 Whisk the final egg yolk with the remaining milk. Use a brush to coat the cookies with the egg wash. Bake for 10–12 minutes, until the cookies are lightly browned.

4 Remove the French butter cookies from the oven and let cool on a wire rack. Store in a sealed container.

CHOCOLATE
macarons

| Makes 20 macarons | Preparation time: 25 minutes | Refrigeration time: 12 hours | Cooking time: 20–25 minutes |

4 egg whites

1¾ cups confectioners' sugar

¼ cup superfine sugar

1¼ cups ground almonds

1¼ cups light cream

6 oz semisweet chocolate

⅓ cup unsweetened cocoa powder

INGREDIENTS

4 egg whites

1¾ cups confectioners' sugar

1¼ cups ground almonds

¼ cup superfine sugar

⅓ cup unsweetened
cocoa powder

FOR THE GANACHE

6 oz semisweet chocolate

1¼ cups light cream

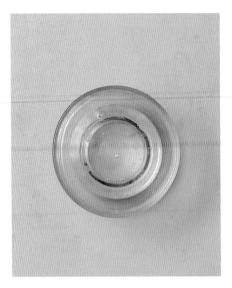

1 Refrigerate the egg whites the night before making the macarons.

2 Prepare the ganache: Melt the chocolate over a bain-marie (*see* page 494).

3 Add the light cream and mix the ganache with a spatula until smooth. Refrigerate the mixture.

4 The following day, preheat the oven to 325°F. Combine the confectioners' sugar and ground almonds. Spread the mixture onto a baking sheet. Bake for 5–10 minutes to dry it out.

5 Beat the chilled egg whites into stiff peaks in a large bowl, gradually adding the superfine sugar while continuing to beat.

6 Add the cocoa powder to the ground almond mixture.

7 Use a spatula to stir the cocoa powder mixture carefully into the egg white mixture.

8 Pour the mixture into a pastry bag fitted with a smooth tip.

9 Line a baking sheet with nonstick parchment paper. Pipe small, round disks of batter of the same size onto the baking sheet.

10 Let the macarons stand for 20 minutes, then bake for 12–15 minutes. Remove the macarons from the oven and let rest for a few minutes, then trickle a little water onto the nonstick parchment paper to detach them more easily.

11 Use a spatula to mix the chilled ganache, then pipe it onto half of the macarons. Cover with the remaining macaron disks. Keep refrigerated.

JAM-FILLED
sandwich cookies

Makes 20 cookies | **Preparation time: 15 minutes** | **Refrigeration time: 1 hour** | **Cooking time: 5–10 minutes per batch**

INGREDIENTS

1¼ sticks (5 oz) unsalted butter, at room temperature

⅓ cup + 1 tablespoon confectioners' sugar

1 cup + 2 tablespoons all-purpose flour

1 teaspoon baking powder

⅓ cup ground almonds

1 egg

1 tablespoon vanilla extract

3 tablespoons strawberry jam or preserves

3 tablespoons apricot jam or preserves

Confectioners' sugar, for dusting

1 Whip the butter and confectioners' sugar into a light cream. In a separate bowl, sift in the flour and baking powder with the ground almonds, then fold in the butter mixture with a spatula. Add the egg and vanilla extract and beat until the mixture is evenly combined. Knead the dough into a ball. Wrap it in plastic wrap and refrigerate for 1 hour.

2 Preheat the oven to 350°F. Line a baking sheet with nonstick parchment paper. Roll out the dough to a thickness of about ¼ inch and use a pastry cutter of your choice to cut out the cookies. Use a smaller pastry cutter to cut the center out of half the cookies.

3 Arrange all the cookies on the baking sheet and bake for 5–10 minutes, depending on how thick the cookies are. Let them cool on a wire rack.

4 Spread the jams or preserves over the whole cookies, alternating between strawberry and apricot, leaving a margin around the edges. Dust confectioners' sugar over the cookies with holes in them and place them on top of the jam-covered ones to make sandwich cookies.

BRETON
cookies

Makes 30 cookies | Preparation time: 10 minutes | Refrigeration time: 1 hour | Cooking time: 15 minutes per batch

INGREDIENTS

2 egg yolks

⅓ cup superfine sugar

5¾ tablespoons salted butter, at room temperature

1 cup all-purpose flour

1 teaspoon baking powder

1 Beat the egg yolks with the sugar until the mixture is pale. Add the butter and mix well. Finally, sift in the flour and baking powder and mix well until combined.

2 Roll the dough into a ball using your hands and wrap it in plastic wrap. Refrigerate it for at least 1 hour.

3 Preheat the oven to 350°F. Line a baking sheet with nonstick parchment paper. Roll the dough out to a thickness of ½ inch on a sheet of nonstick parchment paper. Cut out the cookies with a round pastry cutter.

4 Arrange the cookies on the baking sheet and bake for 15 minutes. Let them cool on a wire rack.

CHOCOLATE CHIP
cookies

 Makes 20 cookies

 Preparation time: 10 minutes

 Freezing time: 1 hour

 Cooking time: 8–10 minutes per batch

INGREDIENTS

1½ cups + 1½ tablespoons
all-purpose flour

1 teaspoon baking powder

½ teaspoon salt

1¼ sticks (5 oz) unsalted
butter, at room temperature

½ cup superfine sugar

⅓ cup packed light brown sugar

1 egg

3½ oz semisweet chocolate or
milk chocolate (or a combination),
chopped into small pieces,
or ½ cup chocolate chips

1 Sift the flour with the baking powder and salt. In a large bowl, combine the butter and sugars and whisk until the mixture is pale. Add the egg and whisk again. Incorporate the flour, then add the chocolate with a spatula and mix well.

2 Place the dough on a large rectangle of plastic wrap and shape it into a 2-inch-wide cylinder. Freeze for at least 1 hour.

3 Preheat the oven to 400°F. Line a baking sheet with parchment paper. Unwrap the dough and slice it into ¼-inch-thick disks. Place them on the baking sheet. Bake for 8–10 minutes, no longer. Remove the cookies from the oven when they start to look done around the edges but remain soft in the middle. They'll harden as they cool.

TIP

You can double or triple this recipe, keep the dough in the freezer, and cook the cookies whenever they're needed.

VARIATION

Sift in 1 tablespoon unsweetened cocoa powder or instant coffee along with the flour. Replace all or some of the chocolate chips with walnuts, hazelnuts, or pecans.

VITAMIN juices AND SMOOTHIES

There's nothing better than a smoothie or juice to recharge at snacktime. Whether they're 100 percent fruit or spruced up with herbs or vegetables, the combinations are endless.

know the golden rules
BEFORE STARTING

WHICH tool?

For smoothies, arm yourselves with a blender, or if you don't have one, use a handheld immersion blender. More powerful blenders will yield more finely blended ingredients. Choose your blender based on the texture you want. Whatever the case, always start by blending the softer or more watery ingredients; harder pieces of fruit or vegetables are at risk of getting stuck between the blades.

For juice, you'll need a juicer or centrifuge. The benefit of the first is that it can cold press fruits and vegetables, thanks to a slow rotational system, which lets you preserve nutrients that are vulnerable to heat.

- Always choose **high-quality ingredients.** They must be fresh, in season, and ripe (and therefore sweeter).

- Opt for **organic** ingredients, if you can, so you can use the skin—the part that is most packed with fiber and vitamins.

- Consider using **frozen fruits;** they will let you vary your recipes throughout the year and, when making smoothies, they will give you a creamy texture.

- For the best results, prepare your juice or smoothie and **drink it immediately!**

Spring
summer

Makes 2 glasses

Smoothie

5 cups green melon • 1⅓ cups red currants
10 lemon verbena leaves • ¼ cup lemon juice

Smoothie

2 apples • 2 cups grapes
1 cup pitted mirabelle plums • 3–4 ice cubes

Juice

1 pineapple • 2 cups strawberries
1⅔ cups raspberries

Juice

1 mango • 4 peaches • 2 apricots

fall
winter

Makes 2 glasses

Smoothie

2 fennel bulbs • 3 juicy apples • 3 kiwifruit

Smoothie

1 mango • 1 passion fruit • 2 small bananas
¼ pineapple • 3–4 ice cubes

Juice

2 papayas • 4 carrots • 2 oranges

Juice

4 cups fresh cranberries • 4 apples
¾-inch fresh ginger root, peeled

PALMIERS

Makes 30 palmiers | **Preparation time: 40 minutes** | **Dough resting time: 1 hour** | **Cooking time: 15–20 minutes**

INGREDIENTS

1 lb all-butter puff pastry
1¼ cups confectioners' sugar

1 Roll out the puff pastry into a rectangle that is 3 times longer than it is wide. Dust the top with confectioners' sugar. Fold it in 3 and let it rest for 30 minutes in the refrigerator. Repeat the process.

2 Preheat the oven to 410°F. Line a baking sheet with nonstick parchment paper. Roll out the dough into a ½-inch-thick rectangle. Dust the top with confectioners' sugar. Refold each side toward the center lengthwise, then fold again until you have the shape of a cylinder.

3 Cut the cylinder into ¼-inch-thick slices. Place these on the baking sheet, leaving plenty of space between them so they don't stick to one another (the dough will expand during cooking).

4 Bake for 15–20 minutes, turning the palmiers halfway through so that both sides can caramelize.

5 Let them cool and store them in a sealed container so that they don't soften.

TIP

Why not try preparing your own puff pastry (*see* page 472)?

ALMOND
gazelle horns

Makes 15

Preparation time: 45 minutes

Dough resting time: 1 hour

Cooking time: 10–15 minutes

INGREDIENTS

FOR THE DOUGH
2 cups all-purpose flour,
plus extra for dusting
A pinch of salt
2 tablespoons melted butter
1 tablespoon honey

FOR THE FILLING
2½ cups ground almonds
½ cup superfine sugar
A pinch of salt
2 tablespoons melted butter
2 tablespoons orange
blossom water

FOR THE DECORATION
1 egg yolk
Slivered almonds

1 Prepare the dough: In a large bowl, combine the flour and salt, then make a well in the center. Pour in the butter, honey, and 1 tablespoon water. Mix while bringing the flour in from the edges as you work. Knead thoroughly, adding a little more water as needed. Let the dough rest for 1 hour at room temperature.

2 Preheat the oven to 300°F. Line a baking sheet with nonstick parchment paper. Prepare the filling: Combine the ground almonds with the sugar and salt. Add the butter and orange blossom water. Mix until soft. Shape the filling into 15 finger-size cylinders.

3 Divide the dough into 2 or 3 portions. Roll out on a lightly floured surface to a thickness of about 1/16 inch. Place a filling piece 2 inches from the edge and fold the dough over it. Press down on the sides to seal the dough edges together, then cut off any excess dough with a pizza cutter or sharp knife. Curve the resulting turnover into a crescent shape. Repeat until all the filling pieces have been wrapped in dough.

4 Brush the gazelle horns with the egg yolk mixed with 1 tablespoon water, then sprinkle the slivered almonds on a plate and press the horns into them. Place the horns on the baking sheet and pierce them all the way through in 3 places. Bake for 10–15 minutes.

APPLE
turnovers

Makes 10–12 turnovers | **Preparation time: 30 minutes** | **Cooking time: 35–40 minutes**

INGREDIENTS

5 apples, preferably Reinette, peeled, cored, and diced

2 tablespoons lemon juice

¾ cup superfine sugar

1–2 tablespoons heavy cream

1 lb all-butter puff pastry (or 2 sheets of ready-to-use flaky pastry dough)

1 egg

2 tablespoons unsalted butter, cut into small pieces

1 Preheat the oven to 485°F. Line a baking sheet with nonstick parchment paper. As soon as they are diced, mix the apples with the lemon juice to prevent them from browning. Drain and mix them with the superfine sugar and heavy cream in a large bowl.

2 Roll out the puff pastry and cut out ten to twelve 4¾-inch disks. Beat the egg and brush some of it along the edges of the dough disks.

3 Arrange pieces of apple and butter on one half of each disk. Fold the other side over the filling to create turnovers. Seal the edges by pressing down with your fingers. Brush the top of the pastry with the rest of the egg. Let the egg wash dry, then use the tip of a knife to make an X pattern on the top of the turnovers, being careful to avoid piercing through the dough.

4 Bake for 10 minutes. Reduce the temperature to 400°F and continue to bake for another 25–30 minutes. Serve warm.

TIP

To make your turnovers shine like the pros do, dissolve 2 tablespoons confectioners' sugar in 2 tablespoons water and brush this mixture on top of the turnovers as soon as they come out of the oven.

VARIATION

Replace 1 apple with 1 cup pitted and diced, soaked prunes (dried plums).

RAISIN
rolls

| Makes 12 rolls | Preparation time: 30 minutes | Dough resting time: 2 hours | Cooking time: 20 minutes |

INGREDIENTS

1 small (⅔-oz) cake fresh yeast or 3½ teaspoons active dry yeast

⅓ cup + 1½ tablespoons milk

4¼ cups all-purpose flour

⅔ cup dried currants

2½ tablespoons superfine sugar

4 eggs

6 pinches of salt

1¼ sticks (5 oz) unsalted butter, at room temperature

Pearl sugar, to decorate

1 Prepare the leavening: Dissolve the yeast in ¼ cup of the milk and add ¼ cup of the flour. Mix well. Sprinkle another 2½ tablespoons of flour on top and let the mixture rise for 30 minutes in a warm place.

2 Soak the dried currants in a bowl of warm water, letting them swell.

3 Sift the remaining flour into a large bowl. Add the leavening, sugar, 3 eggs, and salt. Knead for 5 minutes, hitting the dough on the table to make it more elastic.

4 Add the remaining milk and mix well. Add the softened butter to the dough, then the drained currants. Knead for a little longer and let the dough rest for 1 hour in a warm place.

5 Preheat the oven to 410°F. Line a baking sheet with nonstick parchment paper. Divide the dough into 12 pieces, shape them into cylinders, roll them into spirals, and let them rise for 30 minutes on the baking sheet.

6 Beat the remaining egg with a fork. Brush the rolls with the egg, sprinkle them with pearl sugar, and bake for 20 minutes. Serve warm or cold.

SWEET
rolls

| Makes about 10 rolls | Preparation time: 30 minutes | Dough resting time: 3 hours | Cooking time: 20 minutes |

INGREDIENTS

FOR THE DOUGH

¾ cup + 1½ tablespoons milk

¾ small (⅔-oz) cake fresh yeast
or 2 teaspoons active dry yeast

3⅔ cups all-purpose flour,
plus extra for dusting

1 egg

1 teaspoon salt

⅓ cup superfine sugar

5½ tablespoons unsalted
butter, at room temperature,
plus extra for greasing

FOR THE TOPPING

2 tablespoons milk

2 tablespoons confectioners' sugar

1 Warm the milk and dissolve the yeast in it. Let it rest for 10 minutes.

2 Pour the flour onto a work surface and make a well in the center. Fill it with the dissolved yeast, egg, salt, superfine sugar, and butter. Knead everything for at least 10 minutes, until the dough is smooth and elastic (you can do this by hand, with a food processor equipped with a dough hook, or with a bread machine).

3 Place the dough in a large bowl, cover it with a dish towel, and let it rise for about 1½ hours in a hot place (close to a radiator, if it's winter) until it doubles in volume.

4 Punch down the dough and knead it lightly. Grease a gratin dish. Cover your hands with flour and shape the dough into mandarin-size balls. Place them in the dish, spacing them out a little. Let them rise again for 1½ hours.

5 Preheat the oven to 400° F. Prepare the topping: Mix the milk with the confectioners' sugar and brush the mixture over the rolls. Use a pair of scissors to score each bun with an X and bake for 20 minutes. Serve the rolls warm to your taste.

KNOW YOUR SPICES, *herbs, and flowers*

Herbs, flowers, and spices are your allies when it comes to flavoring your desserts. They bring added flavor and a touch of originality.

spices

Ginger: This is a key ingredient in gingerbread. In ground form, it can be sprinkled over preserves and tarts. When fresh, it pairs well with rhubarb (compote or preserves).

Cardamom: Crush the seeds from 1–2 pods and add them to rice pudding or semolina.

Pepper: It is great for bringing out the flavor in fruit; for example, you can grind some pepper over strawberries or drop a few peppercorns into a poached pear syrup.

Chili pepper: Mix a little fresh red chili pepper with sugar to flavor mango or pineapple slices like they do in Mexico. Espelette chili pepper also goes well with chocolate. Add a small pinch of it the next time you make a mousse.

herbs

Most of the time, these are steeped, or infused, in hot liquid:

A sugar syrup infused with a handful of basil, lemon verbena, or the leaves of 3–4 sprigs of mint for 30 minutes will make a base for a delicious sorbet.

An infusion with milk will make a great addition to a crème anglaise for an ice cream or ice cream float.

Steam some herbs by adding them to the water in which you're cooking fruit; for example, lemon verbena pairs well with figs.

Herbs also go well with fruit:

Rosemary: Slip about 20 leaves of rosemary into a tarte Tatin or a traditional apple tart, but not more than that, because rosemary has a strong flavor.

Thyme: It is delicious with apples, apricots, or peaches.

Lemon verbena: Add it to a summer peach soup.

As for preserves: The leaves of 1–2 sprigs of rosemary or thyme are enough for one pot of preserves. For less flavorful herbs, such as lemon verbena, lime, or mint, use about 30 leaves.

TIP

Any edible flowers can be used to decorate desserts, as long as they've been harvested for consumption. Avoid using any from a florist.

flowers

Blossom waters: Orange blossom or rose waters add delicate flavors to creams and crêpe batters—use a ratio of 1 tablespoon per 2 cups liquid.

Lavender: It goes well with peaches and apricots. Add flavor to ice cream by mixing 2 cups crème anglaise with 1 tablespoon dried flowers, or to sorbet by adding 2 cups syrup.

Hibiscus: It gives crème anglaise a nice pink or red color, depending on the amount used. Soak the dried leaves in milk before preparing the crème anglaise.

Acacia or wisteria: For a dessert with a subtle flavor, dip these flowers in a light doughnut batter and fry them.

SOFT
brioche rolls

Makes 6 rolls | **Preparation time: 30 minutes** | **Dough resting time: 1 hour** | **Cooking time: 20 minutes**

INGREDIENTS

⅓ cup + 1½ tablespoons milk

1 small (⅔-oz) cake fresh yeast or 3½ teaspoons active dry yeast

2⅓ cups + 1 tablespoon all-purpose flour

4 eggs

A pinch of salt

1½ tablespoons superfine sugar

2½ sticks + 1 tablespoon (10½ oz) unsalted butter, at room temperature, cut into small pieces, plus extra for greasing

1 Warm the milk and dissolve the yeast in it. Sift the flour over a large bowl and make a well in the center. Fill it with the eggs, salt, and superfine sugar and mix together well. Add the butter and dissolved yeast, then vigorously knead the dough.

2 Generously grease 6 small brioche molds and divide the dough among them. Let them rise for 1 hour in a warm place.

3 Preheat the oven to 350°F. Bake the rolls for 20 minutes. Let them cool a little, then serve warm.

Serving suggestion

Serve these rolls with
chocolate mousse or
a fruit compote.

BUTTERMILK
scones

Serves 6

Preparation time: 25 minutes

Cooking time: 20 minutes

INGREDIENTS

2 tablespoons unsalted
butter, cut into small pieces,
plus extra for greasing

2 cups all-purpose flour,
plus extra for dusting

A pinch of salt

A pinch of baking soda

1½ tablespoons superfine sugar

⅓ cup + 1½ tablespoons
buttermilk

1 Preheat the oven to 425°F. Grease a baking sheet. Put the flour and salt into a large bowl. Add the butter and rub in with your fingertips.

2 Combine the baking soda with the superfine sugar and add it to the flour-and-butter mixture. Mix well. Pour in the buttermilk and continue to mix until the dough is nice and thick. Transfer the dough to a lightly floured work surface and knead until it becomes pliable.

3 Roll out the dough to a thickness of ¾ inch. Divide the dough into 8 parts, then cut each section into triangles.

4 Arrange the triangles on the baking sheet and bake for about 20 minutes, until the scones have lightly browned. Remove them from the oven and place them on a serving dish. Serve warm.

TIP

If you can't find buttermilk, set ⅓ cup + 1½ tablespoons pasteurized milk in a warm place for 48 hours, until it turns.

SEMISWEET CHOCOLATE
truffles

Makes 20 truffles	Preparation time: 30 minutes	Refrigeration time: 2 hours	Cooking time: 3 minutes

7 tablespoons
unsalted butter

1 tablespoon
milk

2 egg yolks

1 cup confectioners'
sugar

10½ oz semisweet
chocolate

3 cups unsweetened
cocoa powder

¼ cup heavy cream

1 Place a small bowl over a bain-marie (*see* page 494) and add the chocolate.

2 Pour in the milk and stir until the chocolate is completely melted and smooth.

3 Gradually add the butter pieces.

4 Add the egg yolks, one at a time.

5 Add the heavy cream and the confectioners' sugar.

448

6 You have the option to add flavoring: rum, cognac, or another liqueur of your choice. Beat the mixture for 5 minutes.

7 Spread the mixture on a baking sheet lined with nonstick parchment paper to a thickness of about ¾ inch. Refrigerate for 2 hours.

8 Dust the cocoa powder onto a large plate or baking sheet.

9 Cut the refrigerated chocolate into small squares.

10 Dip your hands into the cocoa powder, pick up a chocolate square, quickly roll it into a ball, and immediately roll it in the cocoa powder. Work swiftly to prevent the truffles from softening.

11 When all the truffles are made, remove them from the cocoa powder and place them in a cup. Keep them in a cool place (but not in the refrigerator) until serving.

CHOCOLATE
caramels

Makes 50–60 caramels | **Preparation time: 10 minutes** | **Cooking time: 10–12 minutes**

INGREDIENTS

1 tablespoon sunflower oil,
for greasing

1¼ cups superfine sugar

⅓ cup + 1½ tablespoons
heavy cream

2½ tablespoons honey

½ cup + 1 tablespoons
unsweetened cocoa powder

1 Line a baking sheet with nonstick parchment paper. Put a rectangular cake ring (or an 8¾-inch round cake ring) onto the baking sheet. Lightly grease it using a brush.

2 In a saucepan, combine the superfine sugar, heavy cream, honey, and cocoa powder. Heat while stirring with a wooden spoon until the caramel turns dark amber. Pour the caramel into the cake ring and let it cool. Remove the ring and cut the caramel into squares.

VARIATION

Prepare soft coffee caramels: Follow the same recipe and use
1¼ cups superfine sugar, ⅓ cup + 1½ tablespoons heavy cream,
2 tablespoons coffee extract, and 12 drops lemon juice.

FRENCH
toast

Serves 4

Preparation time: 10 minutes

Cooking time: 5 minutes

INGREDIENTS

2 eggs

1¾ cups milk

1 teaspoon vanilla extract

¼ cup superfine sugar

8 slices of stale bread (or brioche)

1¼ tablespoons unsalted butter

1 Beat the eggs with the milk, vanilla extract, and half the sugar.

2 Dip the bread in this mixture.

3 Melt the butter in a skillet with the remaining sugar. Lightly brown the soaked bread slices on each side and serve immediately.

Serving suggestion

Serve for brunch with some fresh fruit, chocolate sauce, (*see* page 488) or dulce de leche.

VARIATION

Use rye or multigrain bread.

FLUFFY
pancakes

Makes 8–12 pancakes

Preparation time: 15 minutes

Cooking time: 4 minutes
per batch

INGREDIENTS

2 tablespoons unsalted butter

1 cup all-purpose flour

1 tablespoon baking powder

2½ tablespoons superfine sugar

1 egg

¾ cup + 1½ tablespoons milk

3 tablespoons sunflower oil

1 Melt the butter in a saucepan or in the microwave. In a large bowl, combine the flour, baking powder, and superfine sugar. Mix well. Add the egg and milk and mix again. Add the melted butter.

2 Grease a hot skillet with the oil using a piece of paper towel. Pour in large spoonfuls of batter, leaving plenty of space between them. Cook over medium heat until the tops of the pancakes have set and flip them with a spatula until lightly browned on the other side (about 2 minutes per side). Remove the pancakes from the pan as soon as they're cooked.

3 Keep the pancakes warm and repeat the process until all the batter is gone, greasing the pan in between each batch.

Serving suggestion

Serve these pancakes warm with butter, preserves, or maple syrup.

THE TOP 8 *light* RECIPES

page 250

WATERMELON AND BASIL SOUP
(111 calories per serving)

1

2

3

PAGE 20

SPONGE CAKE
(135 calories per serving)

COCONUT AND RED BERRY PANNA COTTA
(96 calories per serving)

PAGE 174

ROASTED SPICED BANANAS
(39 calories per serving)

PAGE 226

FIADONE
(195 calories per serving)

PAGE 62

MANGO SORBET
(141 calories per serving)

PAGE 290

**CHOCOLATE
SOUFFLÉS**
(224 calories per serving)

PAGE 364

RASPBERRY PAVLOVA
(181 calories per serving)

PAGE 356

CINNAMON AND APPLE
fritters

Makes 20 fritters

**Preparation time:
30 minutes**

**Dough resting time:
1 hour**

**Cooking time: 4 minutes
per batch**

INGREDIENTS

4 apples (preferably Belle de Boskoop, King of the Pippins, or Pink Lady), peeled, cored, and thickly sliced

Sunflower oil for frying

FOR THE FRITTER BATTER

1 cup all-purpose flour

½ teaspoon salt

1 egg

1 tablespoon peanut oil

⅔ cup beer

FOR THE CINNAMON SUGAR

¼ cup superfine sugar

1 teaspoon ground cinnamon

1 Prepare the fritter batter: In a large bowl, combine the flour and salt. Make a well in the center and crack the egg into it, then add the oil. Mix well using a whisk, gradually adding the beer as you stir. Let the batter rest for at least 1 hour in the refrigerator.

2 Prepare the cinnamon sugar: Combine the superfine sugar with the cinnamon on a flat plate. Dip each apple slice into the cinnamon sugar, making sure the sugar sticks well.

3 Heat the cooking oil to 350°F. Use a long fork to lift each apple slice and dip it in the fritter batter, then plunge it into the hot oil. Cook the fritters for about 4 minutes, turning them over with a slotted spoon halfway through the cooking time. When they're lightly browned, remove them from the oil and place on paper towels to soak up excess oil. Place them on a serving dish and serve immediately.

TIP

Never beat fritter batter or it won't stick to the apples. Instead, stir it with a spatula.

VARIATION

Fritters lend themselves well to various interpretations; use the
same fritter batter with bananas, brioche, cherries, and so on.

NUNS'
puffs

Makes 30 puffs | **Preparation time: 30 minutes** | **Cooking time: 25–30 minutes**

INGREDIENTS

Sunflower oil, for frying
Confectioners' sugar, for dusting

FOR THE CHOUX PASTE

3½ tablespoons water
¼ cup whole milk
½ teaspoon salt
½ teaspoon superfine sugar
3 tablespoons unsalted butter
½ cup all-purpose flour
2 eggs

1 Prepare the choux paste: Add the measured water, milk, salt, superfine sugar, and butter to a heavy saucepan and bring to a boil. Immediately add all of the flour and mix vigorously with a wooden spoon until the batter is smooth and even. When it begins to come away from the sides, reduce the heat and continue to stir for 2–3 minutes to "cook it down." Remove from the heat and let the dough cool a little. Add the eggs, one at a time, while continuing to stir until smooth.

2 Heat the cooking oil to 340–350°F. Use 2 small teaspoons to scoop out and shape about 10 walnut-size balls of dough, then drop them in the oil. Cook for 2–3 minutes, turning them over with a slotted spoon halfway through the cooking time. When they're lightly browned, remove them with the slotted spoon and place on paper towels to soak up excess oil. Repeat the process until the dough has been used up.

3 Place the nuns' puffs on a serving dish and dust them with confectioners' sugar. Serve immediately or they'll deflate—and they can't be reheated.

VARIATION

Use this recipe to make almond fritters: add ½ cup slivered almonds to the choux paste and prepare the recipe in the same way. Serve the choux warm with a fruit coulis of your choice.

CHURROS

Makes 45 churros

Preparation time:
10 minutes

Dough resting time:
1 hour

Cooking time:
10 minutes

INGREDIENTS

1 cup water

4 tablespoons unsalted butter

A pinch of salt

⅓ cup superfine sugar

1¾ cups + 1 tablespoon
all-purpose flour

2 eggs

Sunflower oil (or grapeseed
oil), for frying

1 Bring the measured water to a boil with the butter, salt, and 2 pinches of the superfine sugar. Immediately add all of the flour and mix well with a wooden spoon until the mixture is thick and smooth.

2 Remove from the heat. Beat the eggs, add them to the batter, and mix well. Let the batter rest for 1 hour in a cool place.

3 Heat the oil to 350° F. Place the batter in a churro maker or in a pastry bag fitted with a fluted tip. Drop 4-inch-long strips of batter into the oil, cutting the dough with scissors as it comes out of the tip. Do this in multiple batches so that the churros don't stick to each other.

4 Cook the churros for 3–4 minutes, until golden brown, turning them over halfway through the cooking time, using a slotted spoon. Remove them from the oil and place on paper towels to soak up excess oil. Dust the top with the remaining superfine sugar and serve warm.

TIP

You can find special churro makers online.

WAFFLES
with confectioners' sugar

Makes 5–10 waffles | **Preparation time: 15 minutes** | **Dough resting time: 1 hour** | **Cooking time: 4 minutes per batch**

INGREDIENTS

Oil for greasing
Confectioners' sugar

FOR THE WAFFLE BATTER

¼ cup light cream
¾ cup + 1½ tablespoons whole milk
½ teaspoon salt
⅔ cup all-purpose flour
2 tablespoons unsalted butter
3 eggs
1 teaspoon orange blossom water

1 Prepare the waffle batter: Bring the cream and half the milk to a boil in a saucepan. Let it cool. In a separate saucepan, bring the remaining milk to a boil with the salt. Add the flour and butter. Cook the mixture down for 2–3 minutes while stirring with a spatula, as you would for a choux paste. Pour this mixture into a large bowl, add the eggs, one by one, then the boiled milk and cream, and finally the orange blossom water. Mix well and let it cool completely. Let the waffle batter rest for at least 1 hour.

2 Use a brush dipped in oil to grease a stove-top waffle iron, then preheat it. Pour a dollop of batter into one half of the open waffle iron, enough to fill it but not to make it overflow.

3 Close the waffle iron, then flip it upside down so that the batter can spread evenly across both sides. Cook on each side for 2 minutes. Remove the waffle from the iron and top it with confectioners' sugar.

BUGNES

Makes 50 bugnes

Preparation time:
45 minutes

Dough resting time:
12 hours

Cooking time: 2–3 minutes
per batch

INGREDIENTS

2 cups all-purpose flour,
plus extra for dusting

2 eggs

3½ tablespoons superfine sugar

1 teaspoon salt

2 tablespoons sunflower oil

5¾ tablespoons unsalted
butter, at room temperature

Zest of ½ unwaxed lemon,
finely grated

3½ tablespoons dark rum

Sunflower oil, for frying

Confectioners' sugar, for
dusting (optional)

Apricot preserves or jam,
to serve (optional)

1 The day before, sift the flour onto a work surface and make a well in the center. Crack the eggs into the well and add the superfine sugar, salt, oil, and butter. Mix by hand, gradually incorporating the flour from the edges. Knead thoroughly, until the dough is smooth and no longer sticks to your fingers. Add the lemon zest and rum and knead for another few minutes. Place the dough in a large bowl and let it rest in a cool place until the following day.

2 The following day, heat the oil to 350°F. Roll out the dough as thinly as possible on a lightly floured work surface. Cut through it with a serrated pizza wheel or with a sharp knife. Cut it in any shape you want.

3 Drop the pieces of dough into the hot oil, one by one. Avoid squeezing them so that they can puff out properly. Let them lightly brown, turning them once.

4 Drain the bugnes on paper towels to soak up excess oil and dust them with confectioners' sugar, if using. Serve hot or warm, accompanied by apricot preserves or jam, if you like.

TIP

Be sure to remove all traces of flour from the bugnes with a large dry brush before cooking them, because flour will burn and darken the oil.

Baking
workshop

Makes 1 lb dough (1 double-crust
pie/2 single-crust tarts)
Preparation time: 10 minutes
Refrigeration time: 30 minutes

FLAKY PASTRY DOUGH

INGREDIENTS

2 cups all-purpose flour
1 stick + 1 tablespoon (4½ oz) cold
lightly salted butter, cut into pieces
⅓ cup + 1½ tablespoons cold water

1 Put the flour onto a work surface and make a well in the center. Add the butter.

2 Combine the butter and flour by rubbing them together with your fingertips until the mixture resembles fine bread crumbs.

3 Add the water in 2 or 3 stages, mixing the dough as little as possible.

4 Quickly roll the dough into a ball. Small pieces of butter should still be visible. Wrap the dough in plastic wrap and let it rest in the refrigerator for 30 minutes.

1

2

3

4

Makes 1 lb pie dough (1 double-
crust pie/2 single-crust tarts)
Preparation time: 10 minutes
Refrigeration time: 1½ hours

SWEET FLAKY PASTRY DOUGH

INGREDIENTS

1 stick (4 oz) unsalted butter,
at room temperature

⅓ cup superfine sugar

1 egg

2 pinches of salt

1¾ cups all-purpose flour,
plus extra for dusting

1 Whisk together the butter, sugar, egg, and salt—you're not trying to obtain a smooth texture.

2 Add the flour and quickly finish mixing the dough by hand. Wrap it in plastic wrap and let rest in the refrigerator for at least 1 hour, ideally overnight.

3 Roll out the dough on a floured work surface, wrap it around the rolling pin, and place it in the baking pan. Trim off the excess dough by passing the rolling pin over the edge of the pan. Refrigerate for 30 minutes.

4 Cover the pastry dough with nonstick parchment paper, weigh it down with pie weights (or dried beans), and bake blind (*see* page 475) for the time that is indicated in the recipe.

1

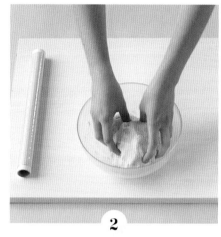

2

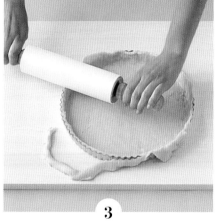

3

4

Makes 1¾ lb dough
Preparation time: 30 minutes
Refrigeration time: 6 hours

PUFF PASTRY DOUGH

INGREDIENTS

2¾ cups + 1 tablespoon all-purpose flour, plus extra for dusting

2½ tablespoons unsalted butter, at room temperature, plus 1¾ sticks + 2 tablespoons (8¾ oz) cold unsalted butter

1½ teaspoons salt

½ cup + 1 tablespoon water

1 Put the flour, softened butter, and salt onto a work surface and add the measured water. Quickly mix together until the mixture is smooth and even.

2 Roll the dough into a ball, wrap it in plastic wrap, and refrigerate it for 2 hours.

3 Place the cold butter between 2 sheets of nonstick parchment paper and roll it out into a square of about 8 inches.

4 Flour a work surface and roll out the dough into a rectangle measuring about 8¼ × 16½ inches, then place the butter at the top of the rectangle.

5 Fold the dough over the butter and pinch the edges closed.

6 Turn the dough one-quarter of the way to the right and roll it out so that it's 3 times longer than it is wide.

7 Fold the dough in 3 into the shape of an envelope.

8 Press down on the dough with your thumb to mark the completion of round one. Wrap the dough in plastic wrap and refrigerate for 2 hours.

9 Repeat steps 6 and 7 and refrigerate the dough for 2 hours. Make two marks with your thumb to indicate completion of round two.

10 Repeat steps 6 and 7. The dough is now ready for use. Refrigerate it until you're ready to use it.

1

2

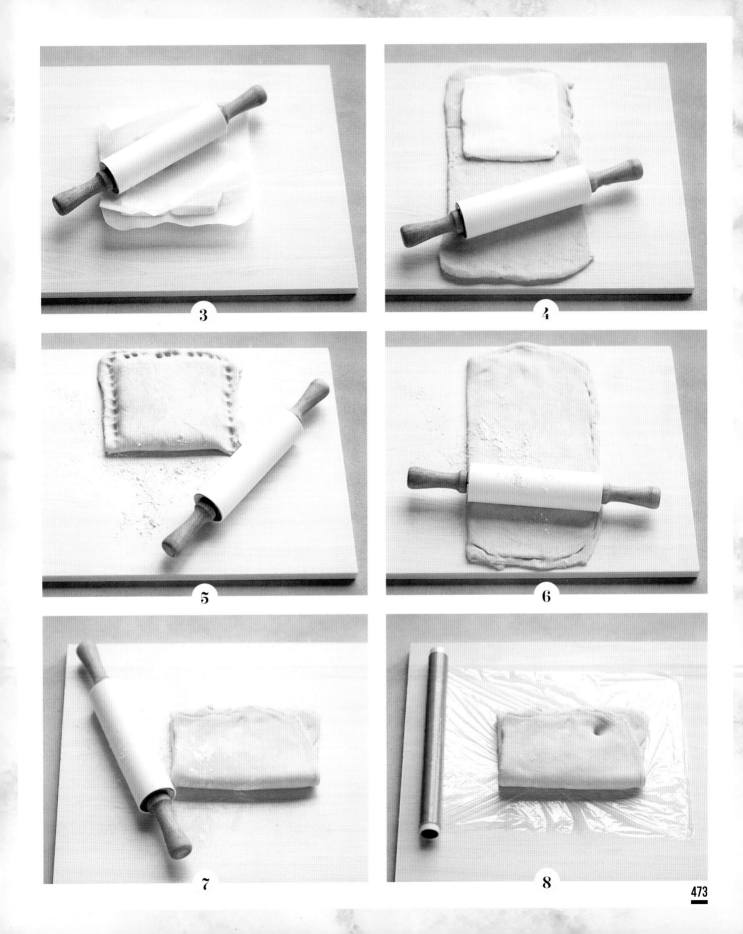

Makes 8¾ oz dough
Preparation time: 10 minutes
Resting time: at least 30 minutes

SWEET DOUGH

INGREDIENTS

1 egg

⅓ cup confectioners' sugar

2 tablespoons ground almonds

A pinch of salt

¾ cup + 2 tablespoons all-purpose flour, plus extra for dusting

4 tablespoons unsalted butter, at room temperature, cut into small pieces

1 In a large bowl, beat the egg with the confectioners' sugar, ground almonds, and salt. Stir vigorously with a wooden spatula until the mixture is frothy and pale

2 Immediately sift in all of the flour and mix rapidly with the spatula.

3 Flatten small pieces of the dough between your fingers. They shouldn't stick together but should crumble into small pieces like bread crumbs.

4 Turn out the dough onto a lightly floured surface. Sprinkle the butter pieces on top of the dough, then knead it in by hand to incorporate it. Shape the dough into a ball. Wrap it in plastic wrap and let it rest in the refrigerator for at least 30 minutes.

HOW TO LINE TART PANS AND HOW TO BLIND BAKE

1 Roll out the dough onto a floured work surface. Wrap it around a rolling pin, then carefully unroll it over the pan. You can adjust the dough when in the pan by lifting it from the edges.

2 Roll the rolling pin over the edge of the pan to trim off any excess dough. Follow these same steps for mini tart pans; line them up in a row with a little space between them before rolling out the dough.

3 Pierce the bottom of the dough with a fork.

4 Cover the bottom of the dough with nonstick parchment paper and top it with ceramic pie weights (or dried beans). Bake for the time indicated in the recipe, then remove the weights and paper.

Makes 1 lb paste
Preparation time: 15 minutes

CHOUX PASTE

INGREDIENTS

⅔ cup milk

⅓ cup + 1½ tablespoons water

1 teaspoon salt

1 tablespoon superfine sugar

7 tablespoons unsalted butter

1 cup + 4 teaspoons all-purpose flour

4 eggs

1 In a heavy saucepan, combine the milk, measured water, salt, sugar, and butter.

2 Bring to a boil, then immediately sift in all of the flour while mixing vigorously with a wooden spoon. Mix until the dough is smooth and even.

3 Over low heat, cook down the mixture, stirring continuously, until it starts to come away from the sides of the saucepan.

1

2

3

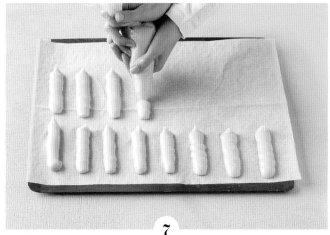

4 Remove the saucepan from the heat, let it cool slightly, then add 1 egg, incorporating it using the wooden spoon.

5 Add the remaining eggs, one by one, stirring vigorously and making sure each egg is mixed in completely before adding the next. Lift the mixture once in a while; when it drops off the spoon in a ribbon, it's ready.

6 Put the batter in a pastry bag fitted with a smooth tip.

7 To make éclairs, pipe the batter onto a lined baking sheet in 6-inch-long strips.

8 To make choux pastries or religieuses, pipe 2½-inch dollops onto the baking sheet. To make the small choux that go on top of the religieuses, or for chouquettes, pipe 1¼-inch dollops.

TIP

Use a ¾-inch tip to make éclairs, religieuses, or choux pastries. Use a ½-inch tip for mini éclairs or chouquettes.

Makes 1 (1-lb 2-oz) cake
Preparation time: 20 minutes
Cooking time: 40–45 minutes

GENOISE SPONGE CAKE

INGREDIENTS

4 eggs

⅔ cup + 2 teaspoons superfine sugar

2¾ tablespoons unsalted butter,
plus extra for greasing

1 cup + 2 tablespoons all-purpose
flour, plus extra for dusting

1 Preheat the oven to 350°F. Grease and flour an 8¾-inch round springform pan. In a large bowl, combine the eggs and sugar. Place the bowl over a simmering bain-marie (*see* page 494).

2 Whisk until the mixture triples in volume and reaches 130–140°F, a temperature that is still tolerable to the touch. Remove the bowl from the bain-marie and whip the mixture with an electric mixer until it has completely cooled.

3 Melt the butter and let it cool. Put 2 tablespoons of the previous mixture in a small bowl and incorporate the melted butter. Sift the flour into the large bowl, fold it into the egg–sugar mixture with a spatula, then carefully mix in the contents of the small bowl.

4 Pour the batter into the pan and bake for 35–40 minutes. Let the cake cool before removing it from the pan.

1

2

3

4

ALMOND DACQUOISE

INGREDIENTS

1 cup + 3 tablespoons confectioners' sugar

1⅓ cups + 1½ tablespoons ground almonds

5 egg whites

¼ cup superfine sugar

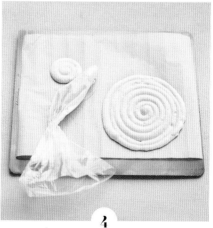

1 Line a baking sheet with nonstick baking paper. Combine the confectioners' sugar and ground almonds and sift them onto a sheet of nonstick parchment paper.

2 In a large bowl, beat the egg whites with an electric mixer. Add the superfine sugar in 3 stages to avoid deflating the beaten eggs. Continue to beat until the mixture becomes a pliable meringue.

3 Pour in the ground almond mixture and carefully fold it in with a spatula.

4 Draw 2 circles on the parchment paper. Put the batter into a pastry bag fitted with a smooth ½-inch tip and pipe the batter onto the parchment paper in a spiral, starting from the center, to make 2 disks.

TIP

Dacquoises are best eaten 24 hours after their preparation. They're often paired with mousses or ganaches.

Makes 1 cake
Preparation time: 20 minutes

CHOCOLATE SPONGE CAKE

INGREDIENTS

1½ cups all-purpose flour,
plus extra for dusting

⅓ cup unsweetened cocoa powder

2½ teaspoons baking powder

6 eggs

7 tablespoons unsalted butter, at room
temperature, plus extra for greasing

½ cup superfine sugar

1½ teaspoons vanilla
sugar (*see* page 13)

1 Sift the flour into a bowl with the cocoa powder and baking powder. Separate the egg whites from the yolks. In a large bowl, beat the butter with the egg yolks and sugars until creamy.

2 Add the sifted mixture and stir until the batter is smooth.

3 Whip the egg whites into stiff peaks and carefully fold them into the mixture with a spatula.

4 Grease and flour a springform pan and pour in the batter.

VARIATIONS

You can personalize this basic recipe. For example, substitute the cocoa powder with the same amount of ground hazelnuts or poppy seeds. Depending on the topping, the batter can also be flavored with a small amount of liqueur, such as rum or Grand Marnier.®

Serves 8
Preparation time: 10 minutes
Refrigeration time: 3 hours

HOW TO MAKE A JELLY ROLL

INGREDIENTS

1 Genoise sponge cake (*see* page 478),
cooked in a rectangular pan
Confectioners' sugar, for dusting
Creamy filling of your choice
about 1½ cups mixed berries (optional)

1 When the Genoise has cooled, dust a clean dish towel with confectioners' sugar and place the sponge on top with the longer side perpendicular to you. Carefully peel away the parchment paper.

2 Spread your filling over the Genoise leaving a 1½-inch margin, then top with the mixed berries, if you want.

3 Carefully roll the cake while holding it firmly and tucking it in neatly with the dish towel to avoid breaking it.

4 Refrigerate for 3 hours, keeping the roulade tightly wrapped until the time comes to decorate and serve it.

1

2

3

4

Makes 1¼ cups cream
Preparation time: 10 minutes
Cooking time: 10 minutes

CRÈME PÂTISSIÈRE

INGREDIENTS

3 egg yolks

¼ cup superfine sugar

2 tablespoons + 2 teaspoons
all-purpose flour

1 cup whole milk

1 In a large bowl, whisk the egg yolks with the sugar until the mixture is pale, then quickly mix in the flour.

2 Bring the milk to a boil in a heavy saucepan.

3 Dilute the contents of the large bowl with a little of the boiling milk, then pour everything back into the saucepan while mixing continuously.

4 Cook over heat, whisking continuously, until the cream thickens. Remove the saucepan from the heat and pour the cream into a bowl.

1

2

3

4

TIP

To keep a skin from forming during the cooling period, stick a fork into a piece of butter and rub it on the surface of the hot cream without pressing down. Another method is to place plastic wrap directly on the surface of the cream.

Makes 2½ cups cream
Preparation time: 25 minutes
Cooking time: 10–15 minutes

CHANTILLY CREAM

INGREDIENTS

2 cups cold heavy cream
¼ cup confectioners' sugar
1½ teaspoons vanilla sugar (*see* page 13)

1 To make sure the cream is cold enough, pour it into a large bowl at least 1 hour before preparing the Chantilly cream and place it in the coldest part of the refrigerator. Remove it from the refrigerator just before using.

2 Lightly whip the cream by hand or with an electric mixer for 1 minute. Speed up the movement of the whisk or mixer as the volume of the cream increases.

3 Add the sugars and continue to beat. Stop beating when the cream is double in volume and begins to stick to the whisk. Refrigerate until serving.

CRÈME ANGLAISE

INGREDIENTS

½ vanilla bean
2 cups milk
6 egg yolks
⅓ cup superfine sugar

1 Split the half vanilla bean lengthwise. In a heavy saucepan, bring the milk and vanilla bean to a boil, then remove it from the heat and let the vanilla steep in the milk for about 20 minutes.

2 In a large bowl, beat the egg yolks and sugar vigorously until the mixture is frothy and pale.

3 Remove the vanilla bean from the milk and scrape out the seeds into the milk. Bring the milk to a boil again. Carefully whisk the boiling milk into the egg mixture.

4 Return the mixture to the saucepan and heat it over low heat, without bringing it to a boil, while stirring continuously until thickened. When you run your finger over the spatula and leave a trace, you'll know you've reached the right consistency. Pour the crème anglaise into a large bowl or place the saucepan in a container filled with iced water to stop the cooking. Let it cool.

Makes 1 lb 2 oz meringue
Preparation time: 5 minutes

Makes enough for 1 tart
or 6 mini tarts
Preparation time: 20 minutes

FRENCH MERINGUE

ITALIAN MERINGUE

INGREDIENTS

5 egg whites
1½ cups superfine sugar
1 teaspoon vanilla extract (optional)

INGREDIENTS

⅓ cup + 1 tablespoon superfine sugar
2 tablespoons water
2 egg whites

1 In a large bowl, whip the egg whites into soft peaks with an electric mixer and gradually add half the sugar.

2 When the egg whites double in volume, add half the remaining sugar and the vanilla extract (if using). Continue to beat until the egg whites become stiff, smooth, and shiny. Add the remaining sugar and mix well to incorporate. The mixture should be firm and stick to the beaters.

1 Bring the sugar and measured water to a boil in a small saucepan. Heat until the mixture reaches 248°F (a rolling boil; a little of the syrup dropped into cold water should form a very soft bead).

2 Meanwhile, begin to whip the egg whites. Halfway through, gradually pour in the boiling syrup while continuing to whisk until the mixture is velvety.

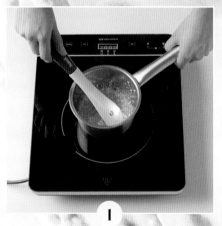

1

2

GOOD *to know!*

- French meringue is a great base for vacherins or dry pastry shells that are flavored and colored. It's also used to make tarts, baked Alaskas, and ice cream floats.

- Italian meringue is used to decorate the top of tarts that are then lightly browned in the oven or with a chef's torch. It can also be used to prepare mousses, sorbets, or frozen soufflés.

- Meringues can be flavored with coffee extract, orange blossom water, or lemon zest. Use food coloring to add all kinds of colors to a meringue.

- Baking process: Bake your meringues in the oven with the door ajar. Bake small meringues, created with a pastry bag, for about 40 minutes and larger meringue disks for about 1½ hours.

How to top a tart with meringue

1 Prepare the meringue and spread it onto the top of the tart. You can also pipe it on in small rosettes.

2 Lightly brown the meringue using a chef's torch or put it under the broiler for 2–3 minutes.

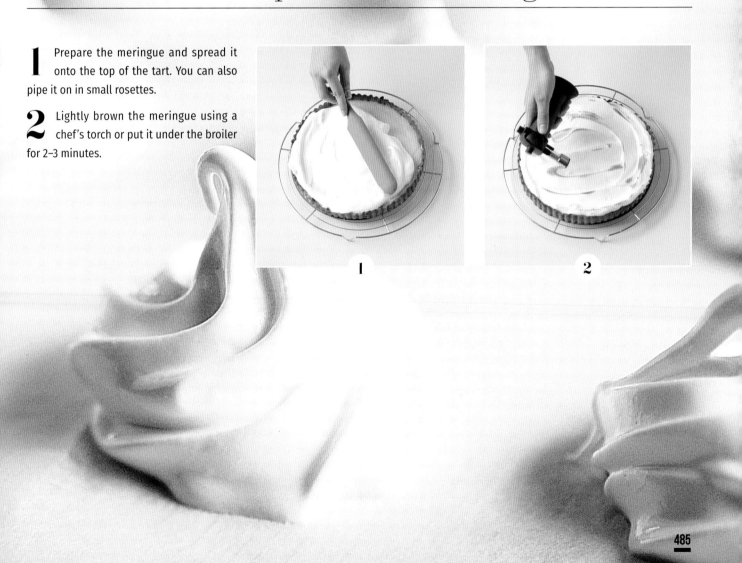

1

2

Makes enough for 1 large cake
Preparation time: 10 minutes
Cooking time: 5 minutes

CHOCOLATE GLAZE

INGREDIENTS

4 oz bittersweet chocolate (at least 70 percent cocoa solids), broken into pieces

⅔ cup confectioners' sugar

4 tablespoons unsalted butter, at room temperature

5 tablespoons cold water

1 Melt the chocolate over a barely simmering bain-marie (*see* page 494), stirring with a wooden spoon.

2 Add the confectioners' sugar, then the butter. Continue to stir until the mixture is smooth. Gradually stir in the measured water. Let it cool.

3 Place your cake on a wire rack over a large plate. When the icing has mostly cooled, pour it on top of the cake.

4 Smooth out the top and sides of the cake with a metal spatula.

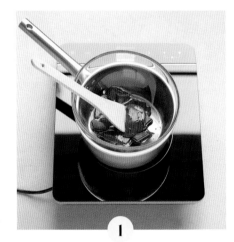

1

2

3

4

TIP

For best results, avoid leaving the chocolate over the bain-marie for too long.

Makes 10½ oz chocolate
Preparation time: 15 minutes
Cooking time: 5 minutes

TEMPERED CHOCOLATE

INGREDIENTS

10½ oz chocolate of your choice

1 If you are using a chocolate bar instead of using wafers (sometimes labeled as "callets") or other chocolate pieces, chop up the chocolate with a knife.

2 Melt half the chocolate over a bain-marie (*see* page 494), without letting the water boil. If using white chocolate, remove the chocolate from the bain-marie as soon as the water starts to simmer.

3 Remove from the heat and add the remaining chocolate.

4 Whisk well. The added chocolate will reduce the temperature of the mixture, making it nice and shiny.

1

2

3

4

TIP

Use professional couverture chocolate pieces to coat cakes and sweet baked goods. It makes a real difference: It's easier to work with and comes out shinier.

Makes 2 cups coulis (sauce)
Preparation time: 10 minutes

Makes 2 cups sauce
Preparation time: 5 minutes
Cooking time: 10 minutes

MIXED BERRY COULIS

INGREDIENTS

6 cups (about 1½ lb) mixed berries (raspberries, red currants, strawberries, blackberries)
⅓ cup + 1 tablespoon superfine sugar
3½ tablespoons lemon juice
⅓ cup + 1½ tablespoons water

1 Put the fruit into a large bowl with the sugar and lemon juice. Crush it in a blender, first pulsing, then continuously for 2–3 minutes, until pureed and smooth.

2 Strain the puree while pressing down with a spatula to collect as much juice as possible. Gradually add the measured water, stirring, until the coulis reaches the desired consistency.

CHOCOLATE SAUCE

INGREDIENTS

7 oz semisweet chocolate (at least 70 percent cocoa solids), broken into pieces
2 tablespoons unsalted butter, cut into small pieces
¾ cup + 1½ tablespoons milk
2 tablespoons heavy cream
2½ tablespoons superfine sugar

1 Put the chocolate into a large bowl over a saucepan filled with hot water. Gently melt the chocolate over the bain-marie (*see* page 494) while stirring with a wooden spoon. Add the butter to the chocolate and stir gently until the mixture is smooth and creamy.

2 Bring the milk to a boil in a small saucepan. Remove it from the heat and add the cream and sugar. Mix well with a whisk and bring it to a boil again.

3 Pour the contents of this saucepan over the chocolate mixture while whisking continuously until the mixture is smooth and even. Pour into a bowl or pitcher. Serve warm over ice cream or profiteroles, or let it cool and enjoy it with cake.

TIP

Use a semisweet chocolate with a high percentage of cocoa butter and as little sugar as possible.

Makes ½ cup caramel
Preparation time: 2 minutes
Cooking time: 8–12 minutes

Makes 1⅓ cups caramel
Preparation time: 5 minutes
Cooking time: 10 minutes

CARAMEL

INGREDIENTS

½ cup superfine sugar
3 tablespoons water

1 Bring the sugar and measured water to a boil over high heat in a heavy saucepan.

2 When the caramel begins to color around the edges, swirl the saucepan carefully and regularly in a circular movement to stir its contents.

SALTED CARAMEL

INGREDIENTS

½ superfine sugar
3 tablespoons water
⅔ cup light cream
2 tablespoons lightly salted butter, cut into pieces

1 Prepare a light brown caramel (*see* Caramel recipe, left). Remove the caramel from the heat and add the cream and butter (watching out for splattering).

2 Return the saucepan to the heat and cook over high heat for 1 minute while whisking well.

TIP

You can stop the cooking process at different stages, depending on how you use the caramel. Light brown is good for toppings; brown or dark brown is good for flavoring or decorations. If you need liquid caramel, add a little hot water before removing it from the heat, being careful to avoid letting it splatter.

TIP

When making a lemon or orange tart, you can spread the caramel over a store-bought flaky pastry or sweet flaky pastry bottom before adding some lemon curd or marmalade. Alternately, spread the caramel over a pear, apple, or pineapple tart, or use it as the base for a chocolate ganache.

Makes about 1¼ cups curd
Preparation time: 15 minutes
Cooking time: 10 minutes

Makes 2 cups slices
Preparation time: 20 minutes
Cooking time: 1½ hours
Macerating time: 12 hours
Drying time: 24 hours

LEMON CURD

CANDIED ORANGE PEEL

INGREDIENTS

2 unwaxed lemons
2 eggs
½ cup superfine sugar
3½ tablespoons unsalted butter, at room
temperature, cut into small pieces
1 teaspoon cornstarch

INGREDIENTS

6 unwaxed oranges with a thick rind
2 cups water
2½ cups superfine sugar
⅓ cup + 1½ tablespoons orange juice

1 Use a zester to zest the lemon into a bowl. Juice the lemons. Pour the juice and zest into a saucepan.

2 Beat the eggs in a large bowl. Add the sugar and butter while whisking. Dilute the cornstarch in a tablespoon of this mixture and pour everything into the saucepan.

3 Cook over low heat while whisking continuously until the mixture thickens. When the mixture is creamy, filter it through a fine strainer and pour it immediately into a sterilized glass jar. Let it cool before sealing the jar. The lemon curd will keep for 15 days in the refrigerator.

1 Bring a saucepan full of water to a boil. Cut off both ends of the oranges. Score the orange rind 4 times from one end to the other with a small knife and peel away 4 equal quarters. Boil them for 1 minute. Drain them in a strainer, then rinse them in cold water.

2 In a large saucepan, bring the measured water to a boil with the superfine sugar and orange juice. Add the orange peels, cover, and cook over low heat for 1½ hours. Let the peels cool in the syrup overnight, then drain them on a wire rack. Let them dry out for 24 hours before storing them in a sealed container.

TIP

Spread this over the base of a fruit tart, brioche, toasted bread or a Genoise sponge.

TIP

These candied (or crystallized) orange peels can be used in a number of desserts and cakes. To make them into sweets, slice them into strips and roll them in granulated sugar. You can also dip them in chocolate (*see* opposite).

HOW TO COAT ORANGE SLICES OR CANDIES

INGREDIENTS

Candied orange peel (*see* page 490), sliced into strips
Candies of your choice
10½ oz tempered chocolate

1

2

1 Temper the chocolate by following the steps on page 487. Dunk three-quarters of each orange peel slice in the chocolate, then let them drip dry.

2 Place the slices on a sheet of nonstick parchment paper or silicone sheet.

3 Soak your chosen candies (ganaches or pralines that have been prefrozen in small molds) in the chocolate with a dipping fork, let them drip dry and place them on the nonstick parchment paper.

4 Use a spiral chocolate fork to draw patterns on your candies.

3

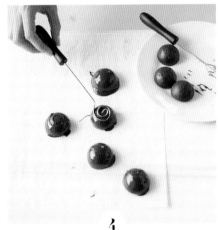

4

HOW TO COLOR AND ROLL OUT FONDANT

White ready-to-use fondant
Food coloring gel or powder
Confectioners' sugar, for dusting

1 Coarsely roll out the fondant, then dust the top with food coloring (or lightly spread out the gel with the tip of a knife).

2 Fold the fondant over onto itself.

3 Knead the fondant as if it were Play-Doh until you obtain an even color (or keep a marbled look).

4 To use it for coating, using a rolling pin, spread out the fondant over a work surface dusted with confectioners' sugar.

1

2

3

4

HOW TO TOP A CAKE WITH FONDANT

INGREDIENTS

1 cake, already covered with frosting
or marzipan, according to the recipe
Ready-to-use fondant
Confectioners' sugar, for dusting

1 Place the cake on a revolving plate (or on a serving plate). Knead the fondant to soften it and roll it out as thinly as possible on a work surface dusted with confectioners' sugar (*see* facing page), then lay it on top of the cake.

2 Carefully smooth out the top by hand to make it nice and flat, then press the fondant down along the edges of the cake, carefully stretching it, if necessary.

3 Cut off the excess fondant carefully using a sharp knife.

4 Smooth out the sides of the cake with a plastic dough scraper.

1

2

3

4

A glossary
of French terms

A–B

ABAISSE (BLOCK or ROLL): A block of dough rolled out to the required shape and thickness on a work surface dusted with flour and using a rolling pin.

ABAISSER (ROLL): The action of using a rolling pin to spread out and flatten dough in an even layer. Also known as *étaler* (to spread out).

APPAREIL: The various ingredients required in the preparation of a dessert before it is cooked or chilled in the refrigerator.

AROMATIZE (FLAVOR): To flavor a mixture by adding an aromatic or fragrant ingredient (for example, a liqueur, coffee, rose water or orange blossom water).

BAIN-MARIE: A water bath; a culinary procedure designed to keep a mixture warm, to melt ingredients (such as chocolate, gelatin, or butter) without the risk of them overheating or burning, or to cook dishes gently using the heat from hot water. The mixture or preparation is put into a hot water bath or double boiler, or alternatively in a heatproof bowl set over a saucepan of hot water, without the bottom of the bowl touching the water. The water must not come into contact with the contents of the dish.

BATTRE (BEAT): To briskly beat an ingredient or mixture to change its consistency, appearance, or color. To beat egg whites to soft or firm peaks, placing the whites in a large mixing bowl and using an electric or handheld mixer.

BEURRER (BUTTER): To incorporate butter into a mixture, or to use a brush to coat the inside of a mold, cake pan, or baking sheet with a layer of melted or softened butter to prevent a dish from sticking during cooking and make it easier to turn out. Other ingredients that are an integral part of a dish can also be used in the same way (for example, a mold could be spread with a layer of ice cream when preparing a *bombe glacée*). Molds are also sometimes lined with parchment paper to facilitate turning out.

C

CHIQUETER (CRIMP): To make light, regular cuts at an angle with the point of a knife around the edge of rolled-out puff pastry; for example, on a pie top or *galette des rois* (kings' cake) to help the pastry puff up during baking and to enhance the appearance of the baked dish.

CLARIFIER (CLARIFY): To clarify a syrup or gelatin by filtering or letting it settle so it becomes clear. For clarified butter, melt the

494

butter in a bain-marie, without stirring, so the whey separates out and forms a white deposit at the bottom. Carefully pour off the clear fat on top into a bowl or pitcher.

COUCHER (PIPE): To pipe choux paste onto a baking sheet using a pastry bag fitted with a piping tip.

CUIRE À BLANC (BAKE BLIND): To prebake a pastry shell before any filling is added and known as "baking blind" in English. This is done when the filling requires only a short baking time, when the filling is already cooked, or when it does not need to be cooked completely (for example, as with soft fruits). Baking blind is also necessary when a filling is wet or runny and could soak into the pastry crust, making it soggy. To avoid this happening, the inside of the unfilled pastry shell is often brushed with beaten egg and baked for an extra 3–5 minutes.

D

DÉCANTER (DECANT): To give a cloudy liquid time to settle so the impurities it contains are deposited at the bottom before the liquid is poured into another container, leaving the residue behind. To remove aromatic ingredients that are added to a liquid to infuse it with their flavor but are not served.

DÉMOULER (TURN OUT): To turn out a baked or set dish from its pan or mold.

DÉNOYAUTER (PIT): To remove the pit from certain fruits (for example, cherries or olives, using a pitter.

DESSÉCHER (DRY OUT): To evaporate water from a mixture by placing the saucepan containing it over the heat. Used specifically for the initial cooking of choux paste when the mixture of water, butter, flour, salt, and sugar is beaten over high heat with a wooden spoon or spatula until it forms a smooth ball that comes away from the sides of the pan, letting excess water evaporate before the eggs are incorporated.

DÉTAILLER (CUT INTO PIECES): To cut out defined shapes (such as rounds or slices of identical size) from a rolled-out sheet of dough using a cutter or sharp knife.

DÉTENDRE (SOFTEN): To soften a dough, paste, or mixture by adding a liquid or other wet ingredient (for example, milk or beaten eggs).

DÉTREMPE (MOIST DOUGH): A paste made from flour and water mixed in varying proportions; this is the first stage in preparing a dough before other ingredients (for example, butter, eggs, or milk) are added. The French word *détremper* means to "water down" and this happens when the flour absorbs enough water to become a dough as you knead it with your fingertips.

DÉVELOPPER (DEVELOP): Used to describe a mixture (for example, a dough, cream, or cake) "developing" as it increases in volume, either through baking, whipping, or fermentation.

DORER (EGG WASH): To brush beaten egg over pastry or bread dough, perhaps diluting the egg first with a little water or milk. This "gilds" the dough so it develops a shiny, golden crust when baked.

DRESSER (DRESS or ARRANGE): To arrange the individual elements of a savory or sweet dish on a serving plate so they are presented harmoniously and to best advantage. Also to pipe choux paste (*see* COUCHER).

E

ÉCUMER (SKIM): To skim off the froth that collects on the surface of a liquid or mixture while it is cooking (for example, syrup being brought to a boil or preserves boiled to setting point). This can be done with a skimmer tool, a small ladle, or spoon.

EFFILER (CUT, TRIM, or TAPER): To cut (for example, almonds) lengthwise into fine slivers or flakes.

ÉGOUTTER (DRAIN): To drain or remove excess liquid from a mixture (or an ingredient) by placing it in a colander, strainer, fine-mesh sieve, or on a wire rack.

ÉMINCER (SLICE THINLY or CUT): To cut fruit into slices, strips, or rounds into fairly thin slices of equal thickness.

ÉMULSIONNER (BLEND or MAKE AN EMULSION): To combine one liquid with another liquid (or mixture) in such a way as to create a smooth emulsion without the two separating. An example of such an emulsion is mixing egg yolks into melted butter.

ENROBER (ENROBE or COAT): To coat or cover food completely with a layer of another ingredient, such as coating petits fours or candies in melted chocolate, fondant, or boiled sugar.

ÉVIDER (HOLLOW OUT): To carefully hollow out the center of a fruit without damaging the surrounding flesh and peel, such as removing the middle of an apple (the core and seeds) with an apple corer.

EXPRIMER (PRESS): To remove juice, water in vegetables, or excess liquid from other foods by pressing them. A citrus press or lemon squeezer is used to extract the juice from citrus fruits.

F

FAÇONNER (SHAPE): To form pastry, dough, or other preparation into a desired shape.

FARINER (FLOUR): To coat a food in flour or dust flour over a baking pan, mold, or work surface. A marble slab or pastry board can also be dusted with flour before rolling out dough or kneading bread dough on it.

FILTRER (FILTER): To pass a more or less liquid mixture (syrup, etc.) through a fine-mesh conical sieve (chinois) or strainer to remove any impurities or deposits.

FLAMBER ("FLAME"): To baste a hot dessert with a liqueur or liquor that has previously been warmed and then set alight.

FONCER (LINE): To line the bottom and sides of a large tart pan or individual tart pans with rolled-out pastry dough. To make sure the dough fits the shape and size of the pan or pans exactly, either roll a rolling pin firmly over the top of a tart pan so the excess dough falls away or, if using individual pans, use a pastry cutter to stamp out shapes of the correct size before lining them into the pans.

FONDRE (HEAT & MELT): To heat an ingredient, such as chocolate or a block of solid fat, until it melts and liquifies. This is often done in a bain-marie to prevent it from burning or overheating.

FONTAINE (FOUNTAIN): A mound or "fountain" of flour piled on a marble slab or board with a dip or "well" hollowed out in the center into which various ingredients needed to make dough are added.

FOUETTER (WHISK): To beat vigorously using a manual or electric mixer to achieve an homogeneous mixture (for example, egg whites until they stand in peaks or cream until it is light and thick). *See also* BATTRE.

FOURRER (STUFF): To fill certain sweet preparations, such as cakes or cookies, with cream, fondant, or buttercream.

FRAISER (GENTLY KNEAD): To coarsely mix the ingredients for rich flaky pastry dough and then work them together by pushing the dough away from you with the palm of your hand on the work surface so everything is evenly combined and the finished dough is smooth but not elastic.

FRAPPER (COOL or CHILL): To rapidly cool and then chill a cream, liqueur, fruit, or mixture.

FRÉMIR (SIMMER): To simmer, the term applied to a liquid when the surface of it begins to tremble just before boiling.

FRIRE (FRY): To fry food, or finish cooking it by deep-frying, immersing the food in a large pan of fat that has been heated to a high temperature. Prior to frying, the food is often coated in flour, batter, pancake batter, or choux paste, which results in a beautifully crisp, golden brown crust.

G

GLACER (COAT or CHILL): To coat hot or cold entremets (layered desserts and cakes) with a thin layer of fruit or chocolate to make them shine and look more attractive. To cover the top of a gâteau with, for example, a layer of fondant, confectioners' sugar, or syrup. To dust confectioners' sugar over a cake, soufflé, or other dessert when it comes out of the oven so the top caramelizes and develops a sheen. Finally, to chill a prepared dish to be eaten cold by sitting it in crushed ice.

GRAISSER (GREASE): To grease a baking sheet or the inside of a baking ring or pan to prevent mixtures from sticking during baking and make turning them out easier.

GRATINER ("MAKE A GOLDEN CRUST"): To cook or finish cooking a dish in the oven so it has a thin golden crust on top.

GRILLER (TOAST): To toast nuts (for example, slivered almonds, hazelnuts, or pistachios) by spreading them out on a baking sheet, placing them in a hot oven, and turning them regularly so they color lightly and evenly.

H–I

HACHER (CHOP): To chop ingredients (for example, almonds, hazelnuts, pistachios, fresh herbs, citrus zest) finely, using a sharp knife or chopper.

HUILER (OIL): To brush a fine film of oil over the inside of a mold or a baking sheet to prevent food from sticking. The term can also be applied to almond paste/marzipan or praline, both of which have an "oily" sheen.

IMBIBER (MOISTEN): To moisten certain types of cake (for example, babas or sponges) with a syrup, liquor, or liqueur to soften, sweeten, and flavor them. *See also* SIROPER (to soak in syrup).

INCISER (INCISE): To make cuts of varying depths using a sharp knife. Dough is "incised" to enhance its appearance, and fruit to make peeling or cutting it easier.

INCORPORER (INCORPORATE): To add ingredients to a mixture and incorporate them thoroughly (for example, flour and butter); to mix, introduce, or blend.

INFUSER (INFUSE/STEEP): To pour a boiling liquid over an aromatic ingredient and let it stand and steep in it so that the liquid absorbs its flavor and fragrance. Vanilla beans can infuse milk or cinnamon sticks red wine.

L

LEVAIN (STARTER): A sour dough starter made from a mixture of flour, organic yeast, and water that is left to double in size before the rest of the dough is incorporated.

LEVER: To leave yeasted doughs to rise in a warm place as the result of fermentation.

LIER (THICKEN or BIND): To thicken (for example, a liquid or cream) to a desired consistency by adding flour, egg yolks, or crème fraîche/heavy cream.

LUSTRER (GLOSS): To make a dish shine by coating it with an ingredient that enhances its appearance. For hot dishes, this "glossing" is done by brushing clarified butter over the dish. For cold dishes, gelatin on the point of setting is used. Some layered desserts and pastries are given a glossy sheen by being brushed with fruit gelatin or a neutral glaze called nappage (coating). *See also* NAPPAGE.

M–N

MACÉRER (MACERATE): To soak, for varying lengths of time, fresh, candied (crystallized), or dried fruit in a liquid (for example, a liquor, liqueur, syrup, wine, or tea), so the fruit is infused with the fragrance of the liquid.

MALAXER (KNEAD): To work or knead an ingredient (for example, fat or dough) by hand to soften or stretch it. The ingredients used to make some doughs require lengthy kneading to produce a smooth, not sticky dough.

MASQUER (COAT): To completely cover a layered dessert or cake with an ingredient that coats it smoothly and evenly (for example, cream, almond paste/marzipan, or preserves).

MERINGUER: To cover or top a pastry or cake with meringue. Also, to add sugar to egg whites while they are being whisked to soft or firm peaks. In France the part of the cake or dessert consisting of the cooked meringue mixture is called the *meringage*).

MONDER (SKIN): To remove the skin from a nut or fruit (for example, an almond, peach, or pistachio) that has first been plunged into boiling water for a few seconds and then drained. The skin is carefully split with the tip of a sharp knife and then peeled away, without the flesh of the nut or fruit being pierced by the knife.

MONTER (WHISK or BEAT): To use a manual or electric mixer to beat egg whites, crème fraîche/heavy cream, or a sweet mixture to trap as much air as possible in them. This increases their volume and gives them a specific consistency and color.

MOUILLER (MOISTEN): To add a liquid to a preparation, either prior to cooking or to make a sauce. The liquid, called *mouillement* (a moistening agent), can be water, milk, or wine.

MOULER (PUT INTO A MOLD): To put a liquid or a firm mixture, such as a dough, into a mold so it takes the shape of the mold when changing its consistency either during cooking, chilling, or freezing.

NAPPAGE (COATING): An unset jelly made from a fruit jam (for example, apricot, strawberry, or raspberry) that is heated, strained, and then often has a setting agent, such as gelatin, added to it. This *nappage* (coating) is brushed over fruit tarts, babas, savarins, and various layered desserts to give them a beautifully shiny finish.

NAPPER (COAT FOOD EVENLY): To pour a coulis or liquid cream, for example, over a dish to cover it as fully and uniformly as possible. When making a custard, to heat the mixture to 181°F so it thickens and *nappe* (coats) the back of a spoon.

P

PANACHER ("JUDICIOUSLY MIX"): To mix together two or more ingredients of contrasting colors, flavors, and shapes.

PARFUMER (PERFUME/FLAVOR): To add an additional flavor in the form of a spice, herb, wine, or liquor to enhance the natural aroma and taste of an ingredient or dish.

PASSER (STRAIN): To pass a thin cream, syrup, jelly, or coulis through a fine mesh conical strainer to make it smooth.

PÂTON: The name given to a block (or package) of puff pastry that has been given the required number of folds and turns. In the broader sense, it can refer to any type of pastry dough before it is baked.

PÉTRIR (KNEAD): To thoroughly knead flour with one or more additional ingredients, either by hand or in a stand mixer (fitted with a dough hook), to obtain a smooth, even-textured dough.

PILER (GRIND): To crush or grind certain ingredients to a powder or paste (for example, almonds or hazelnuts).

PIQUER (PRICK): To use a fork to prick small, even holes over the surface of a sheet of rolled-out pastry dough to stop it from puffing up in the oven.

POCHER (POACH): To cook fruit in a gently simmering poaching liquid (for example, water or syrup) that covers the fruit.

POINTER (PROVE): To leave a yeast dough to ferment after kneading until it doubles in volume, before punching it down with your fist.

POMMADE: To work butter until it has the consistency of a "pomade" (a creamy ointment for the hair or skin). The butter needs to be at room temperature so it can be beaten with a wooden spoon or spatula until soft, smooth, and creamy.

POUSSER: The term that is used to describe a dough rising and increasing in volume due to the action of yeast producing bubbles of carbon dioxide that become trapped inside the dough, making it expand.

R

RAFFERMIR (FIRM UP): To firm up pastry or a dough or to thicken or set a mixture by chilling it in the refrigerator for as long as necessary.

RAFRAÎCHIR (CHILL or REFRESH): To put a cake, layered dessert, fresh fruit salad, or cream to be served chilled in the refrigerator.

RÉDUIRE (REDUCE): To reduce the volume of a liquid by evaporation, keeping the temperature of the liquid at boiling point. This concentrates and increases the liquid's flavor, making it richer as well as thicker.

REPÈRE: Marks made on a cake to make decorating or assembling it easier. *Repère* (edible glue) also refers to a mixture of flour and egg white used to affix edible decorations to a plain dessert or cake or around the edge of a dish.

RÉSERVER (RESERVE): To set aside ingredients, mixtures, or preparations for later use, keeping them chilled or hot. To prevent them from spoiling, they are often wrapped in parchment paper, aluminum foil, plastic wrap, or even a clean dish towel.

ROMPRE (PUNCH DOWN or KNOCK BACK): To momentarily stop the fermentation (or "growth") of a yeast dough by flattening and folding it over on itself several times. This is repeated twice during the preparation of the dough to help strengthen and develop it fully.

RUBAN (RIBBON): Egg yolks and confectioners' sugar whisked together, either at room temperature or in a large bowl over a saucepan of hot water, until the mixture is thick and smooth enough that it doesn not slip straight back into the bowl when the beaters of the mixer are lifted (for example, genoise sponge cake batter falling off the beaters in a thick "ribbon").

S–T

SABLER ("CREATE A SANDY TEXTURE"): To rub the ingredients together when making flaky or sweet flaky pastry dough until they resemble coarse sand or bread crumbs (the term comes from *sable*, the French word for "sand").

SIROPER (SOAK IN SYRUP): To soak a sweet yeast cake (for example, a baba or a savarin) in a syrup, liquor, or liqueur or baste it several times with the soaking liquid until it is completely saturated.

STRIER (MAKE A PATTERN): To mark a pattern of lines or grooves across the top of iced or frosted cakes using the tines of a fork, an icing comb, or brush.

TAMISER (SIFT/STRAIN): To sift flour, a leavening agent, or sugar through a sifter or sieve to get rid of any lumps. Certain liquids of varying degrees of viscosity are also strained through a colander, strainer, or sieve.

TAMPONNER: To carefully place a small piece of butter on top of a still-warm custard or cream sauce so that the butter melts and spreads out to cover the sauce with a thin film of fat, thus preventing a skin from forming.

TOURER: To give the dough the required number of single or double *tours* (turns) when making puff pastry.

TRAVAILLER: To beat or mix together, as vigorously as necessary, the various elements of a dough or liquid mixture, either to incorporate different ingredients, make it homogeneous or smooth, give it body, or make it creamy. Depending on the type of mixture, this can be done on the heat, off the heat, by using a wooden spoon or spatula, a manual or electric mixer, a stand mixer, a liquidizer or blender, or even by hand.

V–Z

VANNER: To stir a creamy sauce (or similar mixture) regularly with a wooden spoon or mixer as it cools to keep it smooth but mainly to prevent a skin forming on its surface. Regular stirring also speeds up the cooling process.

ZESTER (ZEST): To remove just the colored, aromatic, outermost part of the rind of a citrus fruit (the "zest") using a paring knife or zester tool.

Index
of ingredients

Index
of recipes

Credits for recipes and text

Bérengère Abraham: p. 40, 180, 184, 236, 274, 346, 379 (l); Séverine Augé: p. 54; Blandine Boyer: p. 72, 208, 238; Valéry Drouet: p. 86, 216, 360; Sophie Dupuis-Gaulier: p. 240, 406 (l); Coralie Ferreira: p. 452; Isabelle Guerre: p. 18, 28–29, 46, 50–53, 70, 84–85, 88, 110–111, 196–197, 220–223, 244–245, 276–279, 300, 302, 328, 344, 398, 440–441; Béatrice Lagandré: p. 228; Juliette Lalbaltry: p. 326, 327; Delphine Lebrun: p. 112, 378, 406 (r), 407; Anne Loiseau: p. 214, 314, 379 (l), 402; Mélanie Martin: p. 248; Caroline Pessin: p. 340, 341; Aude Royer: p. 152, 382, 422, 424; Julie Soucail: p. 429 (tr, bl, br); Noémie Strouk: p.1 88, 218, 246, 252; © Larousse, p. 6, 8, 10, 12, 16, 20, 22, 24, 26, 30, 32–35, 36,38, 42, 44, 48, 56, 58, 60, 62, 64, 66, 68, 74, 76, 78, 80, 82, 90, 92, 94, 98, 100, 102, 104, 106, 108, 114, 116, 118, 120, 122, 124, 126, 128, 130, 132, 134, 136, 138, 140, 142, 144, 146, 148, 150, 156, 158, 160, 162, 164, 166, 168, 170, 172, 174, 176, 178, 186, 190, 192, 194, 198, 200, 202, 204, 206, 210, 212, 224, 226, 230, 232, 234, 242, 250, 254, 258, 260, 262, 264, 266, 268, 270, 272, 280, 282, 284, 286, 288, 290, 292, 294, 296, 306, 308, 310, 312, 316, 318, 320, 322, 324, 326, 330, 332, 334, 336, 338, 342, 348, 350, 352, 354, 356, 358, 362, 364, 366, 370, 372, 374, 376, 380, 384, 386, 388, 390, 392, 394, 396, 400, 404, 408, 410, 412, 414, 416, 418, 420, 426, 428, 430, 432, 434, 436, 438, 442, 444, 446, 448, 450, 454, 458, 460, 462, 464, 466, 470, 472, 474, 476, 478, 480, 482, 484, 486, 488, 490, 492.

Photography credits

Stéphane Bahic (styl. Sophie Dupuis-Gaulier): p. 406 (l); Martin Balme (styl. Lucie Dauchy): p. 393; Fabrice Besse (styl. Bérengère Abraham): p. 181, 185, 237, 275, 347, 397; Fabrice Besse (styl. Aude Royer): p. 153, 425; Fabrice Besse (styl. Sabine Paris): p. 69, 199; Fabrice Besse: p. 40; David Bonnier (styl. Noémie Strouk): p. 189; Charlotte Brunet (styl. Caroline Pessin): p. 340, 341; Nathalie Carnet (styl. Camille Antoine): p. 371; Aimery Chemin (styl. Coralie Ferreira): p. 453; Emanuela Cino: p. 214, 379 (l); Emanuela Cino (styl. Mélanie Martin): p. 249; Delphine Amar-Constantini (styl. Juliette Lalbaltry): p. 326, 327; Delphine Amar-Constantini: p. 4; Guillaume Czerw (styl. Sophie Dupuis-Gaulier): p. 241; Guillaume Czerw (styl. Alexia Janny): p. 375; Charly Deslandes: p. 55, 429 (bl, br); Sophie Dumont (styl. Delphine Lebrun): p. 113, 378, 407; Amandine Honegger (styl. Sylvie Rost): p. 229, 429 (tr, tl), 443, 445; Olivier Ploton: p. 39, 136, 209, 219, 239, 247, 253, 433, 463; Aline Princet: p. 19, 47, 49, 71, 89; Aline Princet (styl. Isabelle Guerre): p. 6–7, 10, 14–15, 50–51, 59, 84–85, 96–97, 99, 110–111, 154–155, 210–211, 220–223, 256–257, 276–277, 298–299, 301, 303, 329, 345, 368–369, 399, 440–441, 468–469; Amélie Roche (styl. Aude Royer): p. 435; Pierre-Louis Viel (styl. Valérie Drouet): p. 87, 217, 332–337, 361; © Larousse, Olivier Ploton (styl. Blandine Boyer): p. 17, 21, 32–35, 73, 74–77, 78, 81, 83, 104–107, 128–131, 144–147, 232–235, 264–265, 269, 285, 286–289, 309, 310–313, 321, 323, 339, 348–351, 353, 364–367, 373, 386–389, 401, 427, 437, 439, 446–449, 470–493; Olivier Ploton (styl. Noëmie André): p. 23, 25, 63, 115, 121, 127, 149, 157, 159, 163, 168–169, 171, 173, 175, 187, 195, 203, 205, 213, 259, 319, 357, 359, 363, 377, 381, 385, 391, 405, 411, 413, 415, 417, 418–421, 431, 455, 459, 461, 465, 467; Olivier Ploton (styl. Bérengère Abraham): p. 27, 37, 43, 57, 61, 67, 93, 95, 103, 109, 117, 119, 123, 125, 133, 135, 139, 141, 143, 151, 161, 165, 177, 179, 191, 193, 201, 207, 225, 227, 231, 243, 251, 255, 261, 263, 271, 273, 281, 283, 291, 293, 295, 317, 331, 355, 395, 409, 451; Olivier Ploton (styl. Anne Loiseau): p. 32–33, 45, 65, 91, 101, 166–167, 297, 307, 315, 325, 343, 403; Olivier Ploton (styl. Aude Royer): p. 383, 423.

Measurement conversion charts

Weight conversions

U.S. Standard	Metric	U.S. Standard	Metric	U.S. Standard	Metric	U.S. Standard	Metric
⅛ oz	5 g	4 oz	115 g	13 oz	375 g	2 lb 2 oz	950 g
¼ oz	10 g	4½ oz	125 g	14 oz	400 g	2¼ lb	1 kg
½ oz	15 g	5 oz	140 g	15 oz	425 g	2¾ lb	1.25 kg
1 oz	25/30 g	5½ oz	150 g	1 lb	450 g	3 lb	1.3 kg
1¼ oz	35 g	6 oz	175 g	1 lb 2 oz	500 g	3 lb 5 oz	1.5 kg
1½ oz	40 g	7 oz	200 g	1¼ lb	550 g	3½ lb	1.6 kg
1¾ oz	50 g	8 oz	225 g	1 lb 5 oz	600 g	4 lb	1.8 kg
2 oz	55 g	9 oz	250 g	1 lb 7 oz	650 g	4½ lb	2 kg
2¼ oz	60 g	9¾ oz	275 g	1 lb 9 oz	700 g	5 lb	2.25 kg
2½ oz	70 g	10 oz	280 g	1 lb 10 oz	750 g	5½ lb	2.5 kg
3 oz	85 g	10½ oz	300 g	1¾ lb	800 g	6 lb	2.7 kg
3¼ oz	90 g	11½ oz	325 g	1 lb 14 oz	850 g	6½ lb	3 kg
3½ oz	100 g	12 oz	350 g	2 lb	900 g		

Volume conversions

U.S. Standard	Metric	U.S. Standard	Metric	U.S. Standard	Metric	U.S. Standard	Metric
¼ tsp	1.25 ml	5 tbsp	75 ml	1¼ cups	300 ml	4¼ cups	1 liter
½ tsp	2.5 ml	⅓ cup	80 ml	1½ cups	350 ml	5 cups	1.2 liters
1 tsp	5 ml	⅓ cup + 1½ tbsp	100 ml	1¾ cups	400 ml	6 cups	1.4 liters
2 tsp	10 ml	½ cup	125 ml	2 cups/1 pint	475 ml	7¼ cups	1.7 liters
1 tbsp/3 tsp/½ fl oz	15 ml	⅔ cup	150 ml	2 cups + 2 tbsp	500 ml	8½ cups	2 liters
2 tbsp/1 fl oz	30 ml	¾ cup	175 ml	2½ cups	600 ml	10½ cups	2.5 liters
3 tbsp	45 ml	¾ cup +1½ tbsp	200 ml	3 cups	700 ml	12 cups	2.8 liters
3½ tbsp	50 ml	1 cup	240 ml	3½ cups	850 ml	12¾ cups	3 liters
4 tbsp/¼ cup	60 ml	1 cup + 1 tbsp	250 ml	4 cups/1 quart	950 ml		

An Hachette UK Company
www.hachette.co.uk

Originally published in France by Éditions Larousse in 2019.

First published in Great Britain in 2019 by Hamlyn,
an imprint of Octopus Publishing Group Ltd
Carmelite House
50 Victoria Embankment
London EC4Y 0DZ
www.octopusbooks.co.uk
www.octopusbooksusa.com

Distributed in the US by
Hachette Book Group
1290 Avenue of the Americas
4th and 5th Floors
New York, NY 10104

Distributed in Canada by
Canadian Manda Group
664 Annette St.
Toronto, Ontario, Canada M6S 2C8

ISBN 978-0-600-63687-8

Printed and bound in China.

10 8 6 4 2 3 5 7 9

English edition 2020
Group Publishing Director: Denise Bates
Translation: Elettra Pauletto (main) and JMS Translation & Editorial (glossary)
Senior Editors: Leanne Bryan, Louise McKeever, and Sarah Reece
Art Director: Jaz Bahra
Designer: Geoff Fennell
Production Controller: Emily Noto

French edition 2019
Publishers: Isabelle Jeuge-Maynart and Ghislaine Stora
Editorial Director: Émilie Franc
Editorial Team: Ewa Lochet and Maud Rogers assisted by Claire Royo
Graphic design: Aurora Elijah
Layout design: Émilie Laudrin and J2Graph
Production: Émilie Latour